CAUGHT IN TRAFFICK

FREYA BARRINGTON

First published in 2016 by
FARAXA
www.faraxapublishing.com
Email: info@faraxapublishing.com

Caught in Traffick

Book cover from an original idea by Freya Barrington, beautifully designed and brought into reality by Samuel Hurt; Misty Fell Productions.

ISBN 978-99957-48-48-7
Printed in the USA

Dedication

For all the lost children; lest we forget

Acknowledgements

I would like to express my heartfelt thanks for all the encouragement and support I have received while writing this book.

My first thank you goes as ever, to my husband Steve; for all the carefully measured words of wisdom, his patience when I wanted to give up, and his never ending faith in me.

Thanks also to all those who gave me advice on the distressing world of child trafficking and who work so tirelessly in their efforts to eradicate it.

Thank you as always to Faraxa Publishing, and the efforts of Joanne Micallef and her editor.

And to all of you who have urged me on in writing this book, thank you. Here it is at long last.

Foreword

The trafficking of human beings is not a new problem. It dates back many millennia and continues to grow at an alarming level. Trafficking takes many forms; adults are trafficked for many reasons, including; the sex trade, forced labour, illegal organ donation, forced marriage, debt bondage, and domestic servitude. In regard to children, they are trafficked for the child sex trade, forced labour and illegal adoptions. They are also recruited and forced to serve in lesser known schemes, such as children's armies or illicit sports activities for the purpose of gambling.

Conservative estimates put the figure of adults and children currently enslaved by human trafficking at an astonishing 29 million; 27% of this number are children. Human trafficking has now surpassed the sale of illegal arms in terms of criminal activity, and is a growing international problem surpassed only by the drug trade. It is big business for those involved, generating over *$10 billion in illegal revenue. The laws currently in place to protect victims are numerous and complex. Statistic vary, but it is agreed that few perpetrators are brought to justice.

* Statistics from Wikipedia and correct at time of writing.

A 2007 US State Department report put the figure at approximately 1 in 800 people.

The ways in which children are "recruited" are as varied as can be imagined. With the explosion of the Internet, many older children and teenagers succumb to online **grooming. A seemingly innocent chat page turns out to be the hiding place of a paedophile, who lures the unsuspecting child into their world of depravity.

Some children, especially those in third world countries, are sold into slavery by their impoverished parents; many of whom, naively but genuinely, believe that their child is going to a better life, an education, or even a job. This is almost never the case. It is an unsavoury fact that some children are sold by parents who know *exactly* what awaits their son or daughter, but their own needs outweigh the needs of their children's safety.

Kidnap and abduction are perhaps the most shocking methods employed to bring children into the trafficking industry. High risk and high profile, the abduction of a child will grab the headlines in a way that grooming and quiet disappearance may not. However, traffickers are desperate, ruthless people, driven by the increasingly depraved requirements of their "clients". It is a world of supply and demand, and high risk acquisitions bring high priced returns.

While some victims are forced to work in sweat shops, commercial industry or private homes, a distressingly high number of children are taken for one purpose only; the sex industry. With no regard for age, children are forced into the sordid and dangerous world of prostitution; few escape.

** Grooming refers to the seemingly innocent befriending of a child by an adult in order to gain their trust, with an intent to harm. The adult will establish an emotional connection with the child, and maybe buy them gifts, use flattery or even bribery to pave the way for sexual abuse.

Caught in Traffick is the sequel to my bestselling debut book, *Known to Social Services*. It offers a fictional snapshot into the world of child trafficking, in which I have endeavoured to highlight the issue in its most heinous form, that of sexual exploitation.

My choice of Thailand as a setting was deliberate. Rated as one of the worst countries in the world for human trafficking; it has gained notoriety as a place where one can live, free of the most basic moral codes of decency. With high profile cases involving the victimisation and exploitation of children dating back many decades, it is hardly surprising that Thailand has earned a reputation as a sink hole of depravity.

Given the subject matter, this was a difficult novel to write. While creating a fictional world of heroes and villains, it is impossible to forget that the tragedies, which I have portrayed, happen worldwide, every day of the week. Even the most cursory glance at the web page of any of the agencies who are dedicated to fighting this evil in our midst will leave you cold. The blank faces of missing children stare back at you in silent appeal. Some web pages can only feature a missing child for one month, before they make way for more pitiful faces; such are their numbers.

My primary motivation in writing this novel, is not only to bring this subject to the fore, but also to highlight some of the divergent faces of child trafficking. I have endeavoured to draw a contrast between the inequalities of the often high profile response to the abduction of western children, with the almost unspoken acceptance of the enslavement of local and third world children – by their own Governments.

In its simplest form, this is a book of good and evil; of those who perpetuate the atrocities, and those who are committed to fighting it. The corruption, bribery and sheer complexity of the hierarchy of organised crime syndicates who undoubtedly run the operations, are evident throughout. On balance, there are the agencies and individuals, who quite literally put their lives at risk in combatting the scandalous violation of our children.

While the characters within these pages are imaginary, I am acutely aware that the problems are not. This book may be fictitious, but the underlying story is all too sickeningly real.

Disclaimer; Please be aware that some of the narrative accounts in this book are of a disturbing nature. This may be especially true if you have been a victim of abuse. Please protect yourself, and if you do read it, make sure you have appropriate support.

Chapter 1

The beach at Jomtien, was crowded with tourists doing what tourists do. They sunbathed, swam, drank cocktails, and played with their children on the fine white sands. Screams and shouts of laughter emanated from the banana boats out on the Gulf of Thailand, filled with willing passengers who had paid for the dubious pleasure of being flung off into the warm blue ocean. A string of ponies, sweated in the hot February sun, carrying their cargo of small, equally hot children. No one paid any attention to the old man in the wheelchair, whose feeble demeanour was a signpost of his advanced years. He was simply an old man of no account who had been pushed into a shady spot by his nurse, to enjoy the warmth of the late morning sun. He wore a large straw hat, which obscured his face. Underneath the hat however, The Old Man's deep set eyes were keen and searching, and the unsuspecting people on the beach could not have guessed the sinister purpose of his presence. Their indifference would be costly, for The Old Man had played this game many times before and was as sharp as he was cunning.

The Old Man observed the tableau, which played out before him; with his shrewd eye for detail, he already knew where all the main players were situated. He knew the beach well, and had already committed many details of today's particular scenario to memory. It was with good reason that The Old Man was known to the people who sought him out, as "The Watcher".

He watched the fishing boats go by as they made their way back to the fishing ports. He watched the waiters making cocktails behind the gaily decorated bars, he watched two lovers kissing on the white sands, mistaken in the notion that they were hidden from view by the garish umbrellas. He watched the hippie types who still came to the area to smoke a little dope, get high and remember the good old days. He watched the parents; but most of all, as a hawk watches its prey, he watched the children. His seasoned eye was drawn to one family in particular. Two parents with two young children, a blonde haired girl wearing an eye catching pink and white polka dot swimsuit, and a younger boy. Their father was swimming in the sea, leaving mother tending to both children. The Old Man watched and waited, knowing that the opportunity would arise as it always did. It had been over six months since The Old Man had been out hunting like this, and he felt his pulse quicken in anticipation. He had travelled with special purpose from his home in Bangkok, with one thing in mind and now he had it in his sights.

A woman approached from his left hand side; she was a pretty young thing, dressed as a nurse; she attracted as little attention as The Old Man. She said nothing, but bent down to rearrange the blanket over his skinny legs. As she did so, she glanced up at him; "Soon" he whispered in an almost indiscernible voice, "it will be soon, stay close, and be ready." The woman melted back into the crowds, but her sad eyes stayed constantly on The Old Man. She waited, as he waited; the sweat ran down her back in rivulets betraying the anxiety she felt at her situation.

The minutes ticked by.

Somewhere on the beach, a child cried out in pain. The woman did not turn her head to look; her eyes were fastened on The Old Man, knowing that this could be the moment. The Old Man had heard it of course, but unlike the woman, he fixed his gaze on the unfolding drama on the beach like a hawk on a mouse. The boy had wandered off and fallen; the mother turned, spoke briefly to the girl, and ran to her son. People instinctively turned their heads in the direction of the crying boy, some continued to watch as his mother comforted him, some smiled in sympathy, *and no one, but no one had eyes on the girl*; no one that is apart from Ruang Sak Yunram. Dropping his hand to his side, he clicked his fingers, and as he did so, another man appeared from nowhere and began to push his wheelchair away; just an Old Man being taken back to the comfort of his home, perhaps by a loyal son. Over on the beach, the woman in the nurse's uniform moved in obedience to the click of his fingers. Her heart thumped in her chest, and her breathing was rapid. Ignoring the cries of the fallen boy, she moved directly to the girl, who sat building a sandcastle, waiting confidently for her mother to return. The woman leaned down and spoke quickly and quietly to the child, and just like that, it was done. Across the beach, the boy was comforted by his mother and the crying stopped. People went back about their business and the incident was forgotten. For Darcie Taylor and her family however, the nightmare was just beginning.

Chapter 2

Director of Social Services, Nicholas Bishop, sat in the monthly manager's meeting in the conference room of Cedar House just outside the Deacon Hill Estate in Millbrook. He glanced at the clock, and stifled a yawn. It was past four o'clock already and he knew that there would be at least another hour of discussion before the meeting concluded. He tried to maintain a serious and thoughtful expression, but the reality was that he had lost interest in the meeting a long time ago and could not wait for it to finish. He was only half listening when he realised that one of the Service Managers was speaking to him.

"Sorry Glenda," he said apologetically.

"What was that?" Glenda Rogers hid her annoyance behind a patient smile; she had known full well he was not listening to her and had deliberately directed her question to him to make the point.

"I was just asking Nicholas, what are the realistic possibilities of us getting some more agency social workers? I'm sure you're aware that many of the teams are reaching crisis point and the social workers have just about reached their limit. They simply cannot cope with the relentless volume of work, which continues to come their way, and I really do fear that something is going to be missed. I'm sure you'll agree that the last thing this Department needs is another Daniel Thompson," she said finally. Her comments were met with nods and uncomfortable murmurs of agreement from other managers around the table, and they all looked at Nicholas expectantly.

Nicholas knew that Glenda was right; three-month-old Daniel Thompson had been tragically killed by his mother's boyfriend Neil O' Grady six months ago. This was despite the best efforts of his over worked social worker Diane Foster, who was still off sick due to the emotional stress of the case and the ensuing criminal trial. Diane had been required to give evidence at the trial, which had lasted almost three weeks. It had been an extremely difficult experience for Diane, but she had stood up to it well. She had managed to remain strong throughout the gruelling cross examination, where the defending barrister had dragged not only her good reputation, but her personal and professional life through the dirt. Diane stood firm, telling her version of events with dignity and clarity, though the effort of reliving the nightmare had left her physically and mentally exhausted. Eventually a jury found Neil O' Grady guilty of the manslaughter of three-month-old Daniel.

O' Grady remembered little of the fateful night he had subjected the infant to the sickeningly brutal attack. He had spent the evening drinking in a local bar, returning drunk and angry after being rejected by a woman he had propositioned there. He had then attacked Daniel who had been crying in his room. O' Grady had shown no remorse whatsoever, and had smirked when the spokesperson had read out the guilty verdict. He had however ceased to smirk when a stony faced Judge sentenced him to ten years in prison. Daniel's mother Kirsty Thompson had also received a custodial sentence for her part in neglecting Daniel and failing to protect him from O' Grady. She had screamed abuse at the same Judge on receiving her two-year sentence. The story had hit the headlines in spectacular fashion and had done the Local Authority no favours at all. As usual, the media had blundered in without any real knowledge of the truth or complexity of the case and had blamed the social worker. Had they known the efforts Diane had gone to in her attempts to keep Daniel safe, they might have written quite a different story. Sadly, in cases such as Daniel's, it was almost inevitable that the media would whip up an emotional storm, generate a witch-hunt, and lay the blame directly at the door of an individual social worker. The headlines had been accusing and unforgiving;

Tragic Baby Daniel was Known to Social Services

Came the message screaming from the tabloids; and in their insatiable hunger for a scapegoat, Diane had been hounded to the point of despair.

Nicholas held up his hands, "I completely understand Glenda," he agreed, "and I can assure you I am doing everything in my power to secure funding for six more agency social workers who will be spread across three teams. However, you are aware of the high cost of employing agency staff and the negotiations are ongoing."

Glenda rolled her eyes; she knew that it could take weeks before a decision was reached on this subject, and even if she was given the go ahead, it would take many more weeks to identify, interview and get new staff in place. Meanwhile, her team of social workers were about on their knees with the impossible workloads they were expected to manage. With Diane still off sick, and two others on maternity leave, Glenda was fighting a losing battle with a reduced team of less experienced staff. She knew that they were all doing their utmost to maintain the pace, but it was a frustrating and demoralising time for them all. Any time that there was a child death within a team, everyone suffered, and they were all still coming to terms with the tragedy of Daniel. They were also dealing with the fact that following his death, and overwhelmed with misplaced guilt, Diane had tried to take her own life. Thankfully, she had failed, but it had hit everyone hard, and seriously lowered team morale. Glenda nodded, "I appreciate your efforts on our behalf," she said to her Director, trying to keep the sarcasm out of her voice.

Nicholas Bishop had been wrong; it was almost two hours later before the meeting concluded and he could leave the office. He climbed into his black BMW X5 sports vehicle, turned his radio on and headed for home. Nicholas had an exclusive address in one of the most sought after neighbourhoods in the area, almost an hour's drive from his Office. He and his wife occupied a large, detached four bedroomed house in one of the quiet, well maintained cul-de-sacs, where equally well to do people mowed their lawns, played golf at the weekends and generally enjoyed their retirement. At 58 years of age, Nicholas Bishop was looking forward to his own retirement later that year, and the thought of it made him smile. No more meetings, deadlines and endless worries and frustrations regarding budgets, staff or office politics. No, he could leave it all behind and concentrate on his golf game and other more diverting activities, which he preferred to keep to himself.

After an uneventful drive home through the usual Friday night traffic, he pulled into the driveway of his house where the automatic garage door opened accommodatingly. Having parked the car, he went into the kitchen where his wife of five years awaited him.

"Hello dear," he said as he greeted her with an obligatory kiss.

Melanie Bishop lifted her cheek to receive her husband's cool affection, "Tea won't be long," she smiled back at him, "I'm making a special pasta dish for you."

Nicholas nodded, "I'm sure it will be lovely," he said as he poured a generous three fingers of 25-year-old Laphroaig whisky onto a single ice cube, "But you'll have to hold off for a while. I'm going into my study for an hour and I'm not to be disturbed."

"Nicholas," said Melanie reasonably, "it will be ready in half that time."

Nicholas stopped in his tracks and turned back to face her. "Melanie," he began in a voice usually reserved for young children, "I said I do not want to be disturbed for an hour, now which bit of that did you not understand?" With that, he went into his study and locked the door leaving his frustrated wife staring after him shaking her head.

Melanie had met Nicholas six years ago at a social function at the golf club, where they were both members. She had been introduced to him via her mother's friend Dorothy who had assured her that he was quite a catch. Nicholas could not have been described as a good-looking man; at five feet ten inches tall, with a shambling gait; he had a slightly disorganised, helpless air about him, which belied his brilliant mind. He had a head of shaggy brown hair and a beard to match. However, what Nicholas lacked in looks and sex appeal, he made up for with his unarguable charisma, his enigmatic personality and his undeniable power; all of which worked as powerful aphrodisiacs where women were concerned and Melanie had not been immune.

Nicholas Bishop was however somewhat of an enigma. He never spoke of his past, and would brush off any questions in this regard with an impatient shrug. Nicholas was careful and highly selective in regard to what information he shared about his past. People were aware that he had graduated from University with a first class honours degree in Business Studies, and that he had spent some time in the Far East. What they were NOT aware of was, that on leaving University, Nicholas had initially acquiesced to his father's wishes and followed him into the highly lucrative family clothing and textile business. With two factories in Thailand, trips to South East Asia were the norm. Nicholas learned to speak the language, and his father became more and more reliant on him; trusting him to go to Thailand alone and represent the business and family interests with great results.

Nicholas' affinity with the area grew, and in time, he developed a second life in Thailand, one that his parents knew nothing about. It was a life, which brought only heartbreak and chaos into his world; one which had shaped his future and determined the path he now walked. His parents had been shocked to the core when after barely three years of success overseas, Nicholas terminated his involvement with the family business, saying he no longer had the heart for it. However, their shock at this announcement, paled into insignificance, when he revealed his future plans to go into the world of social work.

Despite their insistence, Nicholas would not be drawn into explaining to his stunned parents, the reasons for this dramatic change in his life. He had worked extremely hard since then to maintain a veil of secrecy in regard to anything which pre-dated his social work career. Suffice to say Nicholas Bishop had a plan, and that plan was to work his way up through the ranks of his chosen profession until he was top dog. It had not taken very long for those in authority to realise that they were dealing with an unusual and particularly gifted young man. He moved quickly up through the ranks and was managing his own team within five years. His ambitions knew no bounds and he moved on to become Area Manager of the whole County before he was forty. His Directorship was almost a foregone conclusion, and he had held this rank now for ten years. People who knew Nicholas Bishop, including Melanie, were still blissfully unaware that he had ever held a position other than one relating to social work.

While he could be charming and socially adept, Nicholas had a reputation at work for being dogmatic, determined, and stubborn to the point of belligerence. He cared little for the opinions of people, telling them he was not here to be popular, but to get results. Despite his slightly eccentric characteristics, he succeeded in instilling respect into all who worked with him. While he could undoubtedly have earned a great deal more money, had he worked in finance or similar, Nicholas Bishop's plan had worked well for him so far. Not that people were ever aware of his plans, and that was how he intended to keep it.

Nicholas' particular area of expertise was in regard to the trafficking and exploitation of children at home and overseas. He had written many papers on the subject and was in demand as a key note speaker both in the UK and abroad. Nicholas had made several trips to Thailand in this regard. As a country with a massive problem regarding human trafficking and the exploitation of children in the sex trade, Nicholas' presence there, was always welcomed and his knowledge of the language had been an undeniable asset.

Melanie had found Nicholas intriguing; however, she was twenty years his junior and she expressed her reservations in this regard. Dorothy brushed her objections aside, "Nonsense Melanie darling," she argued, gin and tonic in hand and slightly owl eyed, "he's perfect for you, and believe me, if I were younger, I'd be setting my cap for him myself," she had added with a girlish wink.

Melanie laughed and eventually agreed to go to dinner with him. Dorothy had been right; he was quite a catch. He told her that he had never been married, and explained over a perfectly cooked lobster dinner that he had been waiting for the right woman to come along. He had been charming and polite, opening doors for her and treating her with old-fashioned courtesy. Their courtship had been brief, and they married after only seven months; holding their champagne reception at the same golf club where they had met. Now, five years later, Melanie knew full well that she was little more than a trophy wife. She was a strikingly beautiful woman with long chestnut hair, hazel eyes and a slim athletic figure, thanks to the years of tennis she had played in her youth. She maintained her enviable figure now with golf, yoga and regular sessions in the golf club's private gym and sauna. Up until meeting Nicholas, Melanie had taught music in a private girl's school, but he had insisted she give this up to be his full time wife. Melanie missed her work and wished with all her heart that she had never agreed to give it up. She was bored with her life, which apart from her gym and sports, consisted of little more than shopping, cooking elegant meals and attending charity functions. Nicholas was always busy with work, and when he wasn't working, he was off playing golf or locking himself in his study for hours on end. What he did in there was a total mystery to Melanie; he would not discuss it with her and she was forbidden from entering this seemingly hallowed sanctuary. She sighed and turned her attention to trying to salvage the pasta she had been so carefully preparing, but which she now knew was a lost cause.

Chapter 3

Diane Foster sat on the edge of the dive boat with her feet dangling into the warm waters of the Gulf of Thailand. It was a perfect day; from an eggshell blue sky, the sun scattered a million shards of sparkly diamond chips generously over the water like ice shattering on a marble floor. Across the deck, Ethan Montana busied himself making the final checks on their scuba gear prior to their planned dive. Diane studied his impossibly handsome, and now beautifully tanned face, and reflected for the hundredth time on his unexpected return to her life. She and Ethan had been together for five years before her job as a social worker had driven a wedge between them and Ethan had gone on the road with his band, touring Germany. Diane's life spiralled out of control as she struggled to come to terms with their relationship breakdown as well as juggling her impossible workload. Things had come to a head when three-month-old Daniel Thompson had been killed at the hands of his mother's boyfriend. Hounded and vilified by the press and consumed with guilt, Diane had attempted to take her own life, an action which she was now thoroughly ashamed of. Diane's best friend Maxine Montgomery and her husband John had thankfully realised that something was wrong and had arrived at her flat in time to alert the emergency services. That night, unbeknown to Diane, Maxine had contacted Ethan, who had immediately flown back from Germany, and had never left her side since that day.

Ethan had stood by her when she endured the criminal trial for Neil O' Grady and Kirsty Thompson, which only concluded a month ago. He attended every single day on which she had given evidence, and had been an absolute tower of strength for her. Following the trial, Diane had been totally wrung out, emotionally and physically, and it was Ethan who had already set the wheels in motion for them both to go to Thailand on a working holiday. More accurately, the plan was for Ethan to work, and for Diane to recover and heal. As well as being a musician, Ethan was a dive instructor and through a friend of a friend had invested in the rental of a small but functional day boat for the season. At just under 60 feet in length, the wooden boat, which was named, *The Lady Elizabeth*, was perfect for taking clients to the many dive sites around the Gulf. Well equipped with its own galley, toilet, shower and small lounge, the boat was able to cater to 12 people in comfort, and up to 20 at a pinch. The sun deck allowed clients to sunbathe as well as dive, and Ethan already had several bookings, through the goodwill of his friend's friend. Ethan had managed to get the rental for a fairly decent price, though it could not be considered cheap. He would have to work hard all season in order to make it pay but he was confident that he could do just that. While the boat was not considered a "live-aboard," it did have two small cabins making it ideal for him and Diane to stay over in a location if there was demand in the area.

There was only one snag; *The Lady Elizabeth* had her mooring in a marina close to Pattaya, and Diane had her heart set on staying close to Bangkok, which was an area she had always wanted to visit. Unfortunately, Bangkok was a 2-hour drive from Pattaya *and* from *The Lady Elizabeth*. In the end, Ethan had agreed that he could pick up tourists in Bangkok as well as Pattaya, and maybe have the best of both worlds. They had taken a small one-bedroom apartment on the outskirts of Bangkok, which was only a short walk from the hustle and bustle of the centre of the city. Ethan had got a good deal on an old Mitsubishi 4x4, which was perfect for transporting his clients and their dive gear, to and from *The Lady Elizabeth*, though it only just squeezed under the height bar of their underground car park. After a few days of making the 2-hour trip back and forth to Pattaya, Diane had conceded that it added too much time and cost to the day, so they had ended up spending most of their time living on the boat. They returned to their flat in Bangkok a couple of times a week to get clean clothes, take a long hot shower and make a decent meal. They had let the apartment for the season, so were stuck with it, and Diane had argued they might as well use it. Besides, she had made it abundantly clear to Ethan that she was not prepared to turn into a savage and live full time on a dive boat.

Diane was a proficient diver and they had taken many trips in the past indulging in their shared hobby. Ethan had brought her out here hoping that the laid back lifestyle on the island would be therapeutic for her. He also hoped she would be able to assist in running the business, and get her mind off the many burdens she carried. Diane was gradually beginning to relax, but her wounds were deep, and it was a slow process.

There were a few rare occasions, when Ethan went to the boat alone, such as when he only had a couple of clients for a few days. Diane did not mind, and indulged herself in visiting the many tourist attractions she had wanted to see for so long, such as the sacred and revered Grand Palace. Built in 1782 and housing the old King of Thailand for 150 years, Diane had been almost speechless at the beauty and peace of the place. She had also been to Wat Arun, the Temple of Dawn and been equally impressed.

"You should have been with me," she chided Ethen when he had arrived back late the same night, "you don't know what you missed."

Ethan's eyebrow had gone north as he replied, "All well and good darlin, but some of us got to work."

After that, Diane had usually gone with him, unless she was having a particularly bad day, and then, all she wanted to do was stay in the apartment, eat chocolate and watch old movies on TV – alone.

Diane could not believe that Ethan had returned to her and she lived in constant fear of him leaving again. She could not help but think that he had only come back out of pity, and that he would go again when she was stronger. Ethan had worked hard to dispel her anxieties in this regard, assuring her that he regretted their break up as much as she had. He told her that he had missed her every day, but that his pride had prevented him from contacting her sooner. However, his words fell on deaf ears. Diane's self-esteem and confidence had taken an almost fatal blow and she was plagued with doubts and worries about the future. She knew that though she missed her job, she was not ready to attempt to return to work. Daniel's death hit her extremely hard and she still wept for him.

Ethan's voice snapped her out of her reverie as he called to her in his cowboy drawl, "You ready darlin?"

Shaking off the dark clouds of depression, which threatened to overwhelm her even in this tropical paradise, Diane rallied as best she could. "Ready," she agreed as brightly as she could and went over to gear up for the dive.

Chapter 4

Back in England, Melanie Bishop sat picking idly at her chicken salad. She was out to lunch at the exclusive *Chez Maison* restaurant in town, with her best friend Olivia De Santiago. Olivia had been Melanie's best friend since Prep School and the two were as close as sisters and trusted each other implicitly. Olivia was Spanish, with dark eyes and the luxuriant long black hair of a Senorita, and a fiery temperament to match. Olivia had married into the wealthy, De Santiago family at the young age of nineteen and enjoyed a life of privilege and comfort in a large villa in Spain. She was over on one of her frequent visits to her daughter Isabella who was at University in England, and always made time to see Melanie. She ate her grilled tuna with relish as she listened intently to her friend lament about her marriage.

"I don't know what to say Livvy," said Melanie using her friend's pet name and pushing her salad disinterestedly around her plate as she confided in her. "I mean, he's just so distracted these days; I know he's really busy, but it's like he's not interested in me anymore."

Olivia stabbed at a cherry tomato with her fork, "What can I say carino?" she said using the Spanish endearment, "He is a man."

Melanie looked up and rolled her eyes, "Well, gee thanks for that Livvy, I hadn't noticed. Oh you're no help; seriously Livvy, I don't know what to do. He spends hours in that study of his and keeps saying it's for work, but I'm beginning to have my doubts. What if he's having an affair? I mean, what with the Internet and social dating and everything, he could be secretly chatting to other women in there and I'd never know."

Olivia put down her fork and clapped her hand to her forehead in dramatic continental style, "Dios mio," she exclaimed theatrically, "I had not thought of that. You must find out my friend and the sooner the better."

Melanie looked disheartened, "That's okay for you to say Livvy, but how am I supposed to find out? I mean it's always locked, even when he's inside, he locks himself in; I can't just go in on some pretence. It's hopeless."

Olivia looked unimpressed, "What kind of a woman are you?" she asked with an edge of contempt in her voice. "You need to get into that study and see what is going on; what is so important that it requires him to lock the door on you?" She lowered her voice to a conspiratorial whisper, "You must do it carino, you owe it to yourself, and don't forget to let me know," she laughed as she resumed her lunch. "You know how I live for gossip. Now, let's finish this and go shopping."

Melanie smiled, "You always cheer me up Livvy, I'll think of a way to get into that study if it's the last thing I do." Melanie Bishop could not have known how life changing a decision she had just made.

Chapter 5

Five-year-old Angelique Berlioz bounced up and down on the pink lacy coverlet of her bed in huge excitement. The coverlet in the bedroom of her home in Paris, was not alone in being pink; it was like everything else in Angelique's room, which had been designed with taste befitting a special and much loved little princess. The name Angelique means Angel, which, with her silver blonde hair and large blue eyes, is precisely how Angelique Berlioz looked. As she bounced, her almost perfectly round blue eyes widened, and a cloud of silver white blonde hair rose and fell with her.

"Maman," she demanded of her mother, "When are we going? I cannot wait."

Robyn Berlioz smiled indulgently at her youngest child, "Not until Wednesday Cherie," she answered, laughing at her daughter's antics and excitement. "Papa will be back from Rome on Tuesday and then we will all be going off on our holidays the very next day; that's only four more sleeps and then it will be time."

Angelique bounced herself right off the bed at this point and landed in an undignified heap on the fluffy pink rug. She quickly got up and ran to her mother, hugging her legs, "But I cannot wait so long," she wailed with all the drama of her tender years and her half French genes, "Why can Papa not come home today and then we can go on holiday tomorrow?" she asked hopefully.

Robyn shook her head of dark curls, which were in stark contrast to Angelique's startlingly blonde locks. "Papa has important business Cherie, he will come home as quickly as he can; do not fret, it will soon be here. Now, be a good girl and go and ask your brother to come and wash his hands for dinner, it will be ready in ten minutes."

Angelique adopted a downcast look, stuck her bottom lip out and shouted at the top of her voice, which was quite considerable given her age, "Fabien; Fabien, Maman wants you."

Robyn spoke quickly in exasperation, "Angelique, manners, please; I could have shouted for Fabien like that myself. Please, go and find him and ask him properly and no shouting thank you." Angelique slunk off to do her mother's bidding, leaving Robyn to straighten the coverlet before going back downstairs to finish preparing the children's dinner.

As she stirred the pot of homemade soup, which would be today's dinner, along with her famous homemade bread, Robyn looked at the photograph of her husband Claude. The picture was on the kitchen wall, where she could always see it. It was one she had taken of him on holiday in the Rocky Mountains several years ago. He was smiling directly at her and her heart warmed on seeing his familiar, but slightly crooked smile. His springy black hair was hidden and kept under control by a ski hat, and his lovely blue eyes, which he had passed onto both children, were obscured by his ray ban sunglasses. However, there was no hiding the large Berlioz nose; for which he blamed his grandfather, and which he was eternally thankful neither of their offspring had inherited.

Robyn's mind wandered back to the day she had met Claude. She had been a gauche young woman of 18, on her first lone visit to Paris. While she had visited France many times during her lifetime, her parents insisted she go to Paris for a year, to work, and to polish her French to perfection. Robyn's parents were both University language professors and Robyn had inherited their brilliance and aptitude for languages. By the time she was 12, and having been coached by her parents, she spoke fluent French, German, Spanish, and Italian, and now at 36 years, she counted Russian, Swedish, Portuguese and a fairly decent bit of Thai in her repertoire. It was in the café Renoir where she had secured her summer job, that she first met the suave and debonair Claude Berlioz. The café was his regular haunt, and he had come in for his usual morning café au lait and croissant, and, on seeing a new, young and pretty waitress had behaved in a mock theatrical manner. He placed his hand upon his heart, bowed low, taken her hand and kissed it gently, declaring, “Enchante Mademoiselle, vous êtes très belle.”

The advantage had been Robyn’s however, and without missing a beat, she had answered him in perfect French, declaring, “Et vous monsieur, est très audacieux’, which had the effect of making Claude Berlioz laugh out loud. No one had ever called him bold before and he rather liked it. From that moment on, Claude Berlioz was smitten and he pursued Robyn with unashamed adoration.

Like many of his Gallic counter parts, Claude Berlioz was a romantic; he showered Robyn with flowers, candle lit dinners and small, but thoughtful gifts. Despite herself, Robyn found herself falling for the charms of the elegant Frenchman with the big nose. At 25 years, Claude had been 7 years her senior, which had not mattered in the slightest. He was Robyn’s first serious love affair, and it was a love, which had endured. Over the course of that year in Paris, she and Claude became inseparable and when the time came for her to leave, he had pleaded with her to stay. Robyn knew that her parents fully expected her to return to England and begin her studies in earnest at the University, where they were both professors. However, Robyn’s parents had not reckoned with the Frenchman’s persistence. Desperate to demonstrate his serious intentions, he had taken Robyn to La Café Rouge, which was one of the finest French restaurants in Paris. He had then ordered champagne, and when Robyn had excused herself to go to the ladies; he had slipped an engagement ring into her glass. She discovered the ring on her return, and was eternally grateful she had not swallowed it. She had no hesitation in accepting Claude's proposal of marriage and had eventually managed to convince her distraught parents that she could just as easily remain in Paris and complete her studies there as Claude's wife. Her parents had flown out to Paris to meet Claude, and he had won them over as easily as he had won Robyn's hand in marriage.

Eighteen blissful years later, they still lived in Paris, though Claude had to travel extensively in his role as a financial advisor. Robyn had fulfilled her parent's desires in following a successful career as an interpreter, working for a private agency, who specialised in providing interpreters for a wide variety of clients. Robyn's work was often mundane; more often than not, she would work late into the night translating some wordy, legal document for one of the many law firms in the city. At other times, her work took her overseas; she was in great demand for her unobtrusive but highly skilled talents within diplomatic circles. Though lucrative, Robyn tried to avoid these assignments as they took her away from her beloved home and family.

The entrance of twelve-year-old Fabien, along with Angelique bounding noisily into the room, brought Robyn out of her reverie. She smiled at them and wondered for the millionth time at the enormity of her love for them.

"There you both are," she smiled fondly; "well done Angelique, I see you found Fabien." Her son returned her smile and sat down at the dinner table. Well, more like he folded himself up and squeezed his long legs under, while his arms seemed to take on a life of their own as they sprawled onto the table knocking over the salt.

"Sorry Maman," he apologised immediately.

Robyn shook her head, "Don't apologise son, it was an accident, here, have some soup and bread."

Fabien Berlioz was at that awkward in-between stage of life where he was not quite a child, yet nowhere near grown up. He had recently had a growth spurt and seemed to be having difficulty in getting used to his new gangly extremities. He now stood five feet ten inches tall, and towered over his mother's petite five feet two inch frame. Robyn knew that he would no doubt overtake his father's six feet one inch frame before he was out of his teens. As Fabien had taken his father's height, Angelique had inherited Robyn's tiny neat frame. She smiled indulgently at them both and counted her blessings as they all sat down to eat their dinner, chatting about their impending holiday as they shared their food.

"Maman," said Angelique through a mouthful of bread, "tell me again where we are going on holiday?"

Robyn frowned sternly as she replied, "I shall tell you all about it, only if you promise me not to speak with food in your mouth young lady."

Angelique's eyes sparkled back at her mother as she recognised Robyn's "not really cross" face; she hurried to swallow the hunk of bread coughing as she did so in her haste to hear about their holiday.

Fabien and Angelique's eyes narrowed in unison as they listened to their mother explain where they were bound.

"What's Thailand?" demanded Angelique after Robyn had disclosed this as their destination, "Do they all wear ties?" she added thoughtfully.

Robyn laughed at her daughter's comment, "No Cherie," she replied smiling, Thailand is a country, and it is where we are going to have a lovely holiday. We are going to a lovely place with a pretty beach. We can go out in the boats, play in the water, and enjoy the sunshine." Fabien and Angelique both let out shouts of delight, with Angelique being the louder of the two.

"Can I have a bucket and spade please maman?" she asked hopefully. "Of course you can Cherie, we will all have a wonderful time, and Fabien can learn to dive if he so wishes."

Fabien looked as if he might cry, but his newly acquired grown up persona saved him from this embarrassment. Instead, he took a deep breath and answered gravely, “I should be delighted to finally learn to dive maman,” and it was true. Fabien had pestered his parents to allow him the opportunity to learn to scuba dive, and now it appeared his dream was to come true. His bedroom wall was festooned with photographs and posters of sharks, whales, dolphins and all things aquatic. Fabien had always loved the water and dreamed of visiting exotic locations, where he might actually explore the world beneath the waves. He sank back in his chair and closed his eyes as he tried to imagine himself finally getting the opportunity to go diving.

Robyn noticed his daydreams and smiled again at her children, “It will be the best holiday ever,” she said firmly, little realising her statement could not have been further from the truth.

Chapter 6

Nicholas sat hunched in his study at home, his face scowling in concentration as he stared at the screen of his laptop. "Damned idiots," he complained to himself, "Can't you get anything right?" He sat back in his chair yawning and rubbed his eyes. A glance at the clock told him it was 4:30 a.m., but Nicholas Bishop had been in his study for many hours already. He had a full day of work ahead of him at the office, but other pressing matters demanded his attention; matters to which other people, including his wife, were not privy. He reached for his coffee cup, and sighed when he realised it was empty. Leaving the sanctity of his study, he headed to the kitchen in search of more coffee. He needed to be alert for the day ahead, and despite the fact that he could function on very little sleep; he knew he was sleep deprived. However, a good strong shot of caffeine would offer a temporary solution. As he stepped into the kitchen, he stopped in surprise at the sight of his wife standing next to the Aga sipping what he knew would be herbal tea. Melanie did not share his addiction to caffeine.

"Darling?" he said by way of an enquiry. Melanie smiled wearily and came to him, kissing him softly on the cheek.

"Nicholas, what on earth are you doing?" she began, "I know you've been up half the night and you have to go to work in less than two hours. You're going to wear yourself out."

Nicholas responded by ruffling her hair and kissing the top of her head. "Don't you worry," he said soothingly, "I'm just fine; well I will be when I've had another shot of coffee," he smiled.

Melanie bit her lower lip as she always did when she was anxious, "Nicholas, what is so important that you have to spend all night in your study?" she asked bluntly.

Nicholas looked at her sharply, "What's this now? You know full well that I can't discuss my work with you Melanie, and I'm disappointed that you feel the need to question me like this. My work is of a confidential nature as well you know. I have always been in the habit of working into the night; what has changed to make you question me now?"

Nicholas' tone was reproachful and Melanie flushed at his rebuke. He had a knack of making her feel like a naughty schoolgirl caught in some childish misdemeanour. She felt tongue tied and foolish and wished she had never asked the question. Stumbling over her words, she tried to make amends, "I'm sorry Nicholas, I suppose I'm just feeling a little bit neglected," she offered.

Nicholas' face softened, and he put his hand under her chin and lifted her head, "Silly girl," he said, "jealous of a work schedule. Go back to bed now and we'll talk about this later tonight when I'm home; go on, off with you."

Melanie knew the conversation was over and any talking that might be done later, would consist of Nicholas giving her another lecture as to how foolish she was and how she should count herself lucky he wasn't the sort of husband who went out drinking every night. She had heard it all before and was swiftly coming to the conclusion more direct action would have to be taken, but when, and more importantly - how?

***

Diane sat on the deck of *The Lady Elizabeth*, and closed her eyes, luxuriating in the warmth of the sun. She and Ethan had just completed a morning's dive with six new clients, and it had gone extremely well. They had rebooked for the following week, and had promised to tell their friends about Ethan's business as well. As she relaxed, the sound of him pottering around on the boat comforted her. Just knowing he was there made her feel safe and secure. She felt a million miles away from her home town of Millbrook, and wondered, not for the first time, if she would ever be ready to face social work again. Her manager and trusted friend, Glenda Rogers was in regular touch with her through e-mails and though Glenda never burdened Diane with news of work, Diane knew how stretched her old team was. Diane's mind wandered as she began to think about her colleagues and the struggles, they were experiencing back home. Abruptly, she sat up and reached for a towel, her good mood suddenly washed away in a flood of guilt and remorse. *Here I am lazing about in the sun*, she thought to herself, *while my friends do battle on the front lines.*

Ethan looked up from his task of repacking the diving gear, "You okay darlin?" he asked, concerned on seeing Diane's expression.

"I have to go back Ethan," Diane said flatly, "I can't be here floating around on a boat while there is so much to do back home."

Ethan nodded in silent understanding and came over to her and held her hands in his; he looked into her eyes, which he noticed were filling with unbidden tears. "Listen to me Diane," he said gravely, "you are in no fit state to go back just yet, and you know it. You would be doing no one a service; you would only make yourself ill again. Now, I want you to promise me, that you'll get off this guilt trip and concentrate on getting well again." That was all that was required for Diane's tears to flow freely; she surrendered to her emotions as Ethan's arms surrounded her and she sobbed.

When she was done, he held one arm around her shoulder and stroked her hair with his other hand. "I've got some new clients tomorrow," he said softly, hoping to change the subject and draw Diane out of the depression, which threatened to overwhelm her. "Some local guys and I think a couple of Brits too," he continued, "they want to go down to Koh Samet and dive there; I could do with you with me to help, if you feel able," he said hopefully.

Diane sat very still enjoying the love and warmth of his touch and breathing in the scent of him. She knew exactly what he was doing; he was trying to save her sanity and bring her back to where they'd been before. However, Diane feared that she had gone too far down the road to find her way back. The pain she still felt about baby Daniel was all-consuming and she knew that she had to deal with it, or risk losing Ethan for ever. His had sustained her thus far, but Diane was fearfully aware that even Ethan would eventually run out of patience, and that was something she did not want to dwell on.

She forced a smile onto her face as she looked up at him; "Of course I'll help you, but let me guess; I get to stay in the galley and do all the cooking," she said with more humour than she felt.

Ethan grinned at her, grateful for the respite in her mood. "It'll be great Di, and it could lead to more work."

Diane nodded her agreement, "Okay my love, then I guess we'd better get back to dry land and get prepared, otherwise these new clients of yours aren't going to be too impressed."

They spent the rest of the day sorting out new gear, checking the tanks for oxygen and making sure all the supplies were on board the boat.

They finally fell exhausted, into their tiny cabin bed at around 2am. As Ethan closed his eyes, he felt Diane reach out and entwine her fingers though his own; the last thought he had was that sea otters hold hands to stop themselves drifting apart at sea. He fell asleep smiling.

Chapter 7

Verity Taylor hugged her young son until his indignant crying gave way to muted sobs. "You're okay," she soothed as she rubbed his bumped knee, "all better now; come on, let's go and find Darcie and tell her what a brave boy you've been." Verity took Jack by the hand and walked back to where she had left Darcie building sand castles only a minute or two ago; it was a walk of less than 100 yards. She stopped at the spot and stared blankly at the sand castles, which stood unattended. She looked quickly around, her mind unable to accept the fact that Darcie was no longer there. She stifled the panic, which gripped her, "Darcie" she called urgently, "Darcie, where are you baby?" Scooping Jack up into her arms, Verity extended the parameters of her search and began to walk in wider circles working outwards from the sand castles. As she walked, she called repeatedly to her daughter, fighting the urge to scream, and refusing to allow herself to give in to the possibilities of what might have happened. Her throat was tightening as she called Darcie's name, but she forced herself to recall the time she had lost Darcie in the local supermarket. She had felt the same panic on that occasion, but Darcie had been found in the very next aisle. This was no different, she reasoned with herself; Darcie would be close by, Verity would find her any minute, and they would all go and get an ice cream and laugh when they told daddy how worried she had been. However, a minute passed with no sign of Darcie; it felt like an hour. Verity wanted to go and get her husband, but dare not leave the immediate area where she had last seen Darcie in case she missed her.

Another woman noticed her distress and came over, "What's the matter?" she asked in concern, "Are you alright?"

Verity grabbed her arm, her composure evaporating by the second, "I've lost my daughter," she said in a voice, which did not sound like her own, "She was here a minute ago, but now she's gone, please, help me."

The woman put a sympathetic arm around her, "Don't worry, she can't have gone far, she's probably wandered off to play or something, you know how kids are." Verity pushed the hair back from her face, Jack suddenly felt too heavy. She could hear her own heart beating in her ears; it sounded very loud. She scanned the beach, desperately searching for the pink swimsuit with white polka dots, which Darcie had been wearing. Her world shrunk; all that existed were the white sands around her, which suddenly seemed to be swarming with people … too many people. It was too hot, too loud and altogether too crowded. All Verity could see were deck chairs, umbrellas, and people, but not Darcie.

"Darcie," shouted Verity as loudly as she could, "Darcie, where are you?" Her shouts drew the attention of other people, and word that a child had gone missing spread hastily round the crowded beach. Within minutes, almost everyone had joined in the search and were calling Darcie's name. A man, dripping with seawater appeared at Verity's side,

"What's happened?" he demanded of his wife, "Verity, what's happened?" At the sight of her husband, any confidence Verity Taylor had been feeling, dissolved.

She collapsed into his arms sobbing, "She's gone David, I'm so sorry, oh God help us, Darcie's gone."

The following hours passed in a blur. Someone called the local police, and David, Verity, and two-year-old Jack had gone to the police station where to Verity's horror, Jack had been taken from her care and given to a children's social worker in an adjoining room. Her protests were ignored, and it had been David in the end, who calmed her enough to allow her to accept that this was a formality. Verity and David had been separated and had to answer what felt like an endless round of questions. However, it hadn't taken long for the police to accept Verity's version of events and Jack had been returned to her care in less than two hours. What David and Verity were not aware of however was that Verity's account of what had occurred was almost identical to one told six months ago by another distraught mother, whose five-year-old daughter had disappeared from the very same beach. The child had not been seen or heard of since. The Thai authorities had been keen to keep a low profile on the matter, which was potentially so damaging to the local tourist economy. The child had been from a village close by, rather than a holidaymaker and her parents had been locked in a bitter custody dispute leading the police to conclude that the father had taken the child to his home in another province. However, despite the fact that they had failed to track down the child's father; their interest in the case had waned and in the absence of any incriminating evidence, and in the face of more pressing cases, they had closed it.

One officer however recalled that the child's mother had insisted a stranger had abducted her child. She had resolutely maintained her story, even stating that another person at the time told her a nurse had been seen leading her daughter away from the beach. At the time, the police believed that even if there had been a third party, she was undoubtedly acting on behalf of the father and dismissed the mother's claims as hysteria. They gave assurances to David and Verity that they would do everything in their power to locate Darcie and told them not to leave the country.

David and Verity returned to their hotel exhausted with grief and made several highly emotional phone calls to their family back in the UK. In less than 24 hours, Darcie Taylor's face was on the front page of every tabloid newspaper at home, in Thailand and around the world. Her long blonde hair and blue eyes, the epitome of helplessness as the headlines screamed the message ... MISSING.

Chapter 8

Sunan Simsek sat hunched in the corner of one of Bangkok's many seedy bars, his thin sallow face obscured in shadow as he downed another Lao Khao, whisky. He had been mixing this with the strong local chang beer, and the effect of both beverages was beginning to have a distinctly detrimental effect on his wiry frame. Sunan was 25 years of age and, like his father and grandfather before him, he was a fisherman. However, an unfortunate obsession with gambling, led to debts, which had forced him into accepting employment of an unsavoury and questionable nature. The enormity of his actions drove Sunan into the bars on a regular basis in a futile attempt to assuage his guilt, though he knew that his situation was entirely self-inflicted. Desperation over his increasing debts had led Sunan to almost suicidal despair, when he had been approached by a bald-headed, well-built, softly spoken man, who said he understood how difficult things were for him and offered him a lifeline. How the man knew about his problems, Sunan did not know, neither did he ask. He was only too happy to accept the work without question, and in a very short space of time, he had been able to clear his considerable debts. However, the attraction of such easy money, combined with his ongoing gambling addiction meant that Sunan was now reliant on the work from the man he knew only as "The Mover". He was, in effect, trapped.

Sunan's first instruction had been to bring his small fishing boat to a pre-arranged meeting place in one of the quieter spots along the mighty Chao Phraya River, which ran like a living artery through Bangkok. He did so without question under the cover of a moonless night. Once in place, he had waited for over an hour, and had almost given up and gone home when The Mover had appeared like a silent ghost. With him was a small boy, who Sunan guessed was around five years of age. The boy was clearly afraid; his wide eyes showing white in the darkness. The boy was Thai; Sunan guessed he was from one of the local villages. The Mover spoke quietly to Sunan, telling him where to take the terrified boy and had pressed a large number of baht into his hand – more than he could earn in 6 months. Sunan was wise enough to realise that the money was not only for services rendered, it was for his silence. As Sunan cast off, The Mover leaned in and whispered softly in his ear as to what he might expect should he ever be foolish enough to speak about what was going on. The threat had been effective and Sunan had not told a single soul. There had been many children since then, and the knowledge of his deeds weighed heavily on his conscience. Sometimes, he took the children up river, sometimes, he even went to where the river joined the sea and moved them many miles away to the distant shores of Pattaya and beyond. He now drank heavily, and regularly, in a futile effort to block out the horror of what he had become involved in. Tonight was no different and he knocked back one more beer. He had another "job" tomorrow and had been given a time and place, where he knew there would be some other terror-stricken child going into the unknown. What kept Sunan drinking was, that unlike the children he moved, he did know; he knew only too well what awaited them, and the knowledge of it was crushing him.

Though a simple man from a poor background, Sunan had a conscience, and the guilt and shame of his situation, coupled with the alcohol, which now confused his troubled mind were contributory factors in his next ill-judged actions. Sunan stumbled out of the bar, tears of remorse coursing down his leathery cheeks. He could not do this anymore; he would not do this anymore; if there were to be more children taken down the river, they would not be taken in his boat. Sunan's path led him into another bar, one frequented by a more respectable clientele than the one Sunan usually drank in. He stood in the doorway, his mind distracted and bewildered. Across the smoky interior, Sunan spied his cousin Prasert, the local police officer. Sunan faltered as he approached; compared to Sunan, Prasert was a man of some consequence in the community and one who was to be treated with appropriate respect. However, Sunan was past the point of common courtesy; he threw himself at his cousin's feet and attached himself to his legs weeping like a child. Prasert's initial response was one of embarrassment at the highly irregular interruption to his evenings socialising. However, when he realised that the person clinging to his limbs was none other than his lowly cousin Sunan, who was clearly drunk, his chagrin turned to fury. Prasert shook Sunan off his legs like a dog might shake off a fly. Reaching down, he pulled Sunan roughly to his feet and hissed at him, "What are you doing man? Have you no pride? What is the meaning of this?" Sunan kept his head down, still weeping; the alcohol slowed his tongue and his struggled to find the words. Exasperated, Prasert bundled him out of the bar, ignoring the amused stares of his friends and colleagues.

Once outside, Prasert shook Sunan and delivered an open handed slap to his face. "Sober up," he demanded, "explain yourself."

The slap brought Sunan to his senses; he looked Prasert in the eye, "Cousin," he began in a sombre tone, "there are things I must share with you, things so terrible, I am ashamed even to speak them aloud."

Prasert rolled his eyes, "You try my patience cousin, out with it man." Sunan took a deep breath and began to unburden himself to his cousin, not knowing that he was sealing his own fate as he did so.

Chapter 9

Ruby Wong heard the child stirring before she made any real noise and she rose quickly to go to her. Though only 18 years of age, it was Ruby's job to hear things and to prevent any unnecessary attention being drawn to the safe house, which was situated in one of the quieter areas of Pattaya. She knew from bitter experience that there would be a high price to pay if the child managed to shout or scream, though given the large doses of cough syrup Ruby had administered to her today, this was highly unlikely. She unlocked the door to the tiny bedroom, and went briskly inside, "I told you to be quiet," she hissed unkindly, "have you already forgotten what I said would happen if you made a noise?" Darcie froze immediately as the woman approached her with menace in her eyes.

Ruby grabbed Darcie's arm and gave it a savage twist, "Now shut up."

Darcie stifled a sob as Ruby pushed her back onto the stained mattress. "Please," she whispered, "I want my mummy."

Ruby let out a hollow laugh, "Yes and I want a diamond necklace, so I guess we'll both be disappointed; now do as I say and shut up. If I have to come back in here again today, you'll wish I hadn't, you little brat"; and with that, Ruby was gone.

Alone again in the darkness, four-year-old Darcie was struggling to breathe. She felt as if she was suffocating, and drew her breaths in short ragged gasps. She had no idea where she was and the fear was paralysing her. She had been on the beach building sand castles with her mummy, when her 2-year old brother Jack had fallen. When her mother heard him cry, she immediately went to find him, calling over her shoulder to Darcie, “Stay there darling, mummy won’t be long,” but everything had gone wrong. Mummy seemed to have been gone for ages; though in reality it was less than two minutes. Darcie knew vaguely that her father was swimming in the sea, and in the absence of her mother, another woman had appeared and reassured her that her brother was okay but had gone to hospital. The woman was a nurse, and had told Darcie that her mother had sent for her. Darcie had no reason to disbelieve the woman, and with all the trust of a four-year-old, had taken the woman’s hand and allowed herself to be led away.

The nurse-woman had pulled her quickly towards a white van, bundled her into the back, and got in beside her. The van’s side windows were covered in what looked like white paint, so Darcie could not see out. She twisted around to see if she could see out of the back window, but that was tinted black and afforded her no view at all. The nurse-woman had held her tightly by the arm, and when Darcie said that she was hurting her, the nurse-woman had only laughed. Darcie was confused; why would someone laugh if you’d hurt yourself?

“Where’s my mummy?” she had asked nervously.

“I’m taking you to her now,” the nurse-woman had replied, the lie tripping easily off her tongue, as the van had sped off. After a little while, the van stopped; the nurse-woman had grabbed Darcie without any warning and held something over her face. It made her eyes sting and she felt funny, sick, and dizzy.

When she woke up, Darcie found herself in the small bedroom, where she had remained ever since. Darcie did not know how long she had been here, having lost track of time almost immediately. She felt fuzzy and tired all the time and she was frightened, very frightened. Then another woman, different to the nurse-woman in the van, had come into the room and told her that she was going to cut her hair. Darcie told the woman that she didn't want a haircut, and had wriggled out of her grasp and tried to take refuge on the solitary bed. Darcie had cowered as far back in the corner as she could, like a dog recoiling from a beating. Her insolence had been met with a stinging slap to the face and her protests had proved futile. Her long blonde hair had been crudely hacked off and dyed, leaving her with a ragged dark brown bob and a fringe. She had been ordered to remove her polka dot swimming costume and given different clothes to wear, which smelled funny and didn't fit properly. When Darcie had cried, and said that she wanted her mummy and her own clothes, the woman, had smacked her again and told her to shut up. Darcie bit her fingernails down to the quick and had wet her pants more than once as no one had let her go to the toilet. When she had asked to go, the woman had pointed to a bucket in the corner of the room and said, "Go there," but she hadn't been able to. The only thing in the room apart from the bucket was the bed where Darcie now sat. There was a thin cover, which was dirty and smelly; there was no pillow. Every now and again, the woman would come in and make her take two spoons of medicine, which tasted of strawberries. After the medicine, she always felt sleepy and dozed off, waking up only when she was too hungry to sleep any more. So far, all she had to eat was a bowl of plain rice, with water to drink. Her tummy hurt and her throat and eyes were sore with crying. She was hungry, thirsty, cold and so afraid. She wondered if her brother was okay and when her daddy and mummy would come for her.

In the adjoining room, Ruby Wong complained loudly to her friend Suzy Meesang. "She is a difficult one," she opined sourly, "wilful."

Suzy shrugged, “It is not my concern,” she began, “my job was to get her off the beach and bring her here; a role I have carried out precisely. You however Ruby Wong will doubtless incur the wrath of The Organisation as you have acted according to your own inclinations.”

Ruby looked perturbed, “Why do you say such things?” she asked crossly, “I am doing the best I can.”

Suzy regarded the younger woman with disdain, knowing that she occupied a lower rank in the pecking order. “You cut her hair,” she observed drily, “and dyed it; this was a stupid action, and one, which will be costly.”

Following delivery of her opinion, Suzy stood up, “It is time I must go,” she said, “you will be visited soon, make sure the child is cared for, she is of great value, which means that her whereabouts must remain the most highly guarded secret. She is sought by many; do not make any more mistakes.” Without another word, Suzy left an apprehensive Ruby Wong to consider her own fate in this twisted tangled web of deceit.

Once away from the safe house, Suzy Meesang made a phone call using a cheap phone, which she would discard after today. “The child is safely in hiding,” she said when the call connected. “However, the senseless whore in charge has acted ill advisedly. The child’s hair has been cut and dyed. Her value is markedly decreased by such a thoughtless and stupid action.” Suzy listened gleefully as the Man at the other end made his opinions on this known. Hanging up, she smiled spitefully to herself. Having spent most of her unhappy life on the receiving end of retribution, it felt good to deflect some of it towards someone else for a change.

Chapter 10

Melanie stared at the locked door of her husband's study and wondered again, what he was doing in there. Why she should be so concerned after all this time, she did not know. It had always been this way, and had never bothered her in the past. Melanie knew that she was feeling neglected and insecure and that her worries stemmed from the fear that Nicholas was having an affair. Nicholas had always been a bit of a dark horse, and Melanie suspected that there was much she did not know about this brilliant husband of hers. Nicholas never talked about his past, about ex-girlfriends or anything like that. She had never met his parents, as they had died several years before she had met him. He had no brothers or sisters, or at least, none she was aware of, and few, if any, close friends. Melanie often felt that for Nicholas, life had not existed before she came along. All he ever talked about was their life together, no reminiscing about the past, no discussion of memories, good or bad, from the years prior to their meeting. Melanie sighed, she knew Nicholas was somewhat eccentric, but lately, he seemed to be more distracted than ever.

As she stood contemplating a way into the forbidden study, she heard the door being unlocked, and Nicholas appeared from within. He stopped when he saw her; she immediately felt foolish, and as guilty as a child caught with their hand in the cookie jar.

"Hi darling," she said brightly trying to cover her embarrassment, which she felt must be obvious; "did you want a coffee?"

Nicholas frowned and looked suspiciously at his wife. "What were you doing lurking out here?" he asked. Melanie did not answer, and Nicholas clearly had other things on his mind as he continued without waiting for her to reply. "Listen," he said, "I have to go on a business trip at short notice. There's an international conference on child trafficking and I'm required to attend, I'll be leaving on Wednesday and I'll be gone a week, so it's not for too long." Melanie was used to him going on business trips and understood that his job was demanding and his presence required at high-level conferences. The news was unremarkable, even when Nicholas added, "Oh by the way, it's in Thailand."

***

To the uninitiated, Sampeng market in Bangkok is a confusion of noise, colour, smells and people; hundreds of people. Brightly coloured towels and other garish gifts hang from the many stalls, vying for the attention of tourists. People sit on red plastic chairs on the street, eating their meals, cooked in enormous cooking pots, which balance precariously on stoves seemingly too small for the task. Steam rises, smoke billows and the smells dissipate into the morning air, adding to the collision of scents. Dozens of different kinds of fish look out at you, their mouths agape in surprise. Sacks of rice, wheat and corn meal lie carelessly in shop doorways. Men rush by, bare footed on scooters, sometimes shared with a child or two or even a dog or a chicken. Above the street, for those who care to look up, are balconies, most of which are festooned with washing, Chinese lanterns and flags.

For The Man who pushed his way through the crowds on this particular Saturday morning however, it was a chance to blend in; unobserved, invisible, and silent, which served him better than camouflage. This was the way The Man liked it and exactly the way he had planned it. Planning was one of The Man's many specialities; he took pride in the minutia of any arrangements he made, which were meticulous, down to the most seemingly insignificant detail. For his expertise in this, and other areas, The Man was held in high esteem, and as a consequence, had amassed an abundance of wealth.

The Man lowered his head, and ducked inside the frontage of a shop, outside of which was selling chicken's feet and other local delicacies. The Thai woman, who was serving, considered him briefly with flat dead eyes and said nothing. Once inside, he made his way through the shop, which was piled from floor to ceiling with spices. Hundreds of bags of spices, wrapped in plastic and stacked in such a haphazard manner they threatened to topple over at any moment. The Man continued through a tattered curtain and into a room at the back of the shop. He waited a moment for his eyes to adjust to the gloom before easing himself into the only available seat in the room. He inclined his head in greeting to the wizened figure sitting across from him, and wondered to himself in amusement if The Old Man still lived. Ruang Sak Yunram's resemblance to a cadaver was legendary, though it would have been impolite to speak of it in his hearing. Ruang Sak was reported to have attained 80-years. His small frame had a desiccated shrunken appearance. His paper-thin skin was stretched tight over his bones, affording him a look of permanent discomfort. He stared back at The Man from sunken soulless eyes and grimaced, displaying a few remaining black teeth. Despite his startling presentation, The Man was acutely aware that Ruang Sak was a man of power; indeed, his name meant, "Mighty, and powerful" and The Man was eager to maintain the fragile working relationship they had shared these past few months.

Ruang Sak considered The Man before him, and noted with ill-concealed distaste how healthy and virile he looked in comparison to himself. Though The Man was the son of a worthless Bangkok whore, his father was of Turkish descent, and from him, The Man had inherited his powerfully built frame. Ruang Sak guessed his age, to be around 35 years, and though he was not a tall man, he was stocky and strong. His bald head was as smooth as a boiled egg and oiled to give it a sheen, which was noticeable even in the dim light of the room. He had dark brown eyes, which Ruang Sak had heard drove women to high passion, though he knew that The Man's predilections lay elsewhere. His most outstanding feature was the four-inch scar, which traversed his face from eyebrow to chin, a gift, or so he had heard, from a less than enthusiastic young man, who did not wish to share The Man's affections. Ruang Sak's eyes took in the younger Man's impressive muscular frame, wide shoulders, and barrel chest. He noted begrudgingly, that he dressed in an appropriately conservative manner, and today wore a simple grey suit in traditional Thai style. Despite The Man's elegant presentation and manners, Ruang Sak knew him to be a dangerous adversary, and one, which he would do well to keep close.

"So Charn Chai Boonjan, you have come to me again," stated Ruang Sak in a tremulous voice. "What favour do you seek from me this time?"

Charn Chai was momentarily taken aback at this blatant lack of etiquette. Ruang Sak had not only uttered his name aloud, but he had not offered him a glass of Cha Yen, and had failed to make any enquiries as to the wellbeing and health of his father.

Ignoring this contravention of good manners, Charn Chai smiled at the Old Man; "You honour me with an audience esteemed grandfather," he began, clasping his hands together at eye level. "However, may I respectfully remind you, that my name is known only to a few and to utter it is to invite misfortune."

Ruang Sak raised a sparse eyebrow and asked drily, "Misfortune for who Charn Chai, for me or for you?"

Charn Chai allowed himself the smallest of smiles, inclined his head, and moved on. "I seek your wisdom in a certain matter, which is, how shall I put it? Delicate, to say the least."

Ruang Sak leaned forward, the effort of which almost toppled him from his chair. "Speak," he commanded, "I will know about this delicate matter and give my judgement on it."

Charn Chai breathed an inward sigh of relief; The Old Man could just as easily have refused to hear him. However, Charn Chai's father had named him well, in that his name meant "Good in fighting." This was reflected not only in his physical prowess, but also in matters of mental fighting, and negotiation. Charn Chai was a master in his field. He had spoken truly though; his good name was known only to a select few. To those who sought his services, he was known only as "The Mover." He shifted his weight to get comfortable and explained his dilemma to The Old Man.

Ruang Sak listened intently as Charn Chai explained his predicament concerning the child. The Old Man made no effort to disguise his open contempt for the younger man's inept handling of the situation. Charn Chai however, was blaming the woman who had cared for the child. He had it on good authority, that Ruby Wong had cut and dyed the child's long blonde hair, which was as good as money in the bank in Ruang Sak's world. Ruang Sak closed his rheumy old eyes, sank back into his chair ignoring Charn Chai altogether as he applied his still alert mind to the problem.

Charn Chai coughed politely, which caused Ruang Sak to open his eyes and stare in disapproval at him. Charn Chai bowed his head slightly at the indiscretion, "If I may old grandfather?" he asked politely.

Ruang Sak sighed deeply, "Continue," he invited frostily.

Charn Chai took a deep breath; this would not be an easy discussion. "Revered Grandfather," he began, "it has come to my attention from one of my sources, that the one known as Sunan Simsek, has been seen speaking with an officer of the law. This is indeed disappointing, and naturally compromises our situation." Charn Chai waited for the information to sink in, and for the Old Man to process it.

Ruang Sak contemplated the intelligence for no more than 30 seconds, before asking, "The police officer? He is in our pay?"

Charn Chai nodded almost imperceptibly, "Of course," he replied calmly.

Ruang Sak gave a half smile, "And we have another in mind to take his place?" he asked sharply.

Charn Chai tried not to look smug, "Naturally," he murmured, "it is all in hand."

Ruang Sak adopted a look of satisfaction before declaring, "Then you know what to do; deal with it." He paused for a moment before adding, "And as for the child, move her immediately, and I trust you will deal most severely with Ruby Wong, I am most displeased with her."

Ruang Sak Yunram then closed his eyes once more to indicate that this time, the conversation was terminated. Charn Chai bowed politely, unseen, and slipped quietly into the busy market.

***

Diane frowned as she read the daily newspaper from home. "Hey, have you seen this?" she called to Ethan who was busy making coffee in the galley. "A little girl from England has disappeared from the beach we were on the other day. God, Ethan, she's only four-years-old, I dread to think what's happened to her."

Ethan appeared in the doorway looking serious, "I know, I saw it," he said sadly, "Like you say, it doesn't bear thinking about."

Diane shook her head sadly and tried to push all thoughts of the little girl out of her mind, but something about the child's wide eyes haunted her. "What time are we off?" she asked changing the subject.

Ethan glanced at his watch, "They should be here in about twenty minutes; we've just got time for coffee, then we'd better get going. Diane put the paper down and gulped her coffee, but the image of the child remained in her mind, her pitiful face staring out at her pleadingly. Shaking off dark thoughts about the inevitable horrors, which would befall the child, Diane joined Ethan in greeting their new clients. There were four men in total, two local men, and two from the UK.

Chapter 11

Darcie woke up feeling groggy, and for a moment thought she was back in her own bed, until she realised that things were still the same. There was no warm cover over her, no teddy beside her to cuddle, and no mummy to stroke her face and tell her she loved her. Darcie began to cry, but quietly, as she did not want the woman to come in and shout at her and smack her again. She sat up on the bed and began to suck her thumb, something she had not done since she was a baby. She stared at the wall and thought about her mummy and daddy and her little brother Jack. The sound of a door slamming made Darcie jump; the noise was followed by the sound of voices. She could hear the familiar voice of the woman who shouted and smacked, but Darcie could also hear an unfamiliar voice; that of a man who sounded very cross. Darcie pulled the thin stained cover over her head to hide from the noise. She heard footsteps, then her door unlocking and someone coming into her room. She hoped it wasn't the woman again; she did not like the woman at all. Darcie stayed hidden under her cover, shaking with fear.

However, it was a man's soft voice, which spoke to her, rather than the shouty woman. "Hey little one," he said, "how are you today?"

Darcie lowered the corner of the cover and regarded the man. He was a big man with no hair on his head. He had a scar on his face, which made him look scary, but he was smiling at her. Darcie was confused and said nothing. The man held out his hand, "Don't be afraid," he said kindly, "I've come to take you away from here."

Darcie's heart leapt, "Are you taking me to my mummy?" she asked pathetically.

The man frowned, "I'm afraid I can't do that; you see, mummy and daddy have had to go back home to England but they could not take you with them. They asked me to look after you and to make sure you were okay."

Darcie's head was spinning; she did not understand this at all. Why did mummy and daddy have to go home and why could she not go with them.

The Man seemed to read her mind, and he put his finger on her lips; it smelled of flowers. "Shh," he said, "everything will be explained to you, but now, let's get you to your new home where there's a new nanny and granddad to take care of you."

At this point, the woman who shouted, came into the room looking sulky. "I have taken good care of her," she said sullenly to The Man. Darcie sensed that the two grown-ups were cross with each other.

The Man turned, so Darcie could not see his face, nor hear his whispered exchange with the woman, "Oh I can see exactly how good your care of our valuable package has been Ruby Wong," he hissed. For his size, The Man moved remarkably quickly as he delivered a stinging back handed blow to her face before continuing his diatribe. "She stinks like an unwashed whore, and to my intense disapproval I note that with your usual vicious temper, you have marked her. However, what is worst of all, is that you have cut off her long blonde hair, which was of such high value and dyed the remainder of it. The Watcher is *most* displeased and I fear that this will not go well for you," he said bitterly.

The woman looked suddenly afraid, "She was difficult," she stammered, "she would not do as I bid and as for her hair, I thought it wise to change her appearance."

The Man regarded her with contempt, "I can only imagine how challenging it must have been to care for one four-year-old child," he said disdainfully. "And as for her appearance, you are not paid to think, Ruby Wong, you are paid to care and keep quiet. You have overstepped yourself and as a result have damaged an asset of significant value. You may expect consequences of a severe nature. Now get out of my way, we are leaving," and with that, The Man picked Darcie up as easily as if she had been a new born kitten, swept past the woman and out of the house.

Darcie was surprised to see that it was dark outside, though she had long ago lost all sense of day and night. The Man went quickly to a black car, unlocked the door, and put her gently on the back seat. He leaned over and fastened her seatbelt, smiling as he did so, "To keep you safe," he said by way of an explanation. Darcie could smell flowers again and decided that it was a nice smell. The Man got into the driver's seat and drove away. He did not speak to her again, and before long, the rhythm of the car and her own sheer exhaustion caused her to fall into a deep sleep.

***

Melanie sipped her berry spice tea as she confided in her friend; "He's going away," she said bluntly, to Olivia as they sat in the upmarket and decidedly overpriced cafe. "He's off to Thailand again, so he'll be away for a week."

Olivia De Santiago leaned back in her chair and smiled like a contented cat, "Then this is the opportunity you have waited for, no?" she declared. "It is past time, you got into that study to see for yourself what he does in there."

***

Darcie awoke to the sound of the man's voice, "Wake up little one, we are here," he said as he shook her gently. Darcie rubbed her eyes and yawned. It was still dark and as she got out of the car, the cool of the evening was not the only thing, which made her shiver. They were in the middle of nowhere, and the only sound Darcie could hear was her own fragmented breathing as she struggled to make sense of her new surroundings.

"Where am I?" she asked nervously. The Man pointed to a house about a hundred yards from where the car had stopped.

"Look," he said, "that's your new home; doesn't it look nice?" he asked, as he took her by the hand and began to lead her up the path towards the house. There was a dim light on the front porch and Darcie could just make out the shape of two people standing outside.

"I want to go home," she said in a small voice, which was barely a whisper. "I want my mummy."

The Man stopped, bent down to her level, and whispered, "But Darcie, you are home, and this is your new nanny and granddad." He waited a moment for that information to sink in, before adding in a sinister tone, "You do understand, don't you Darcie? Everything is different now. Everything; this is your home now and I know that you will love it. You will call these people nanny and granddad and they will call you Holly. Do you hear me? Your name is no longer Darcie, its Holly. Can you remember that? Your name is Holly Bailey."

The Man had been right; everything was different now. Darcie Taylor no longer existed; she had been replaced by Holly Bailey who lived with her nanny and granddad in a nice little house away from town. Holly had a sweet bedroom all of her own, with toys, books and games aplenty. She was not expected to go to school and she had no TV, as this was not a good influence for a growing girl. Holly Bailey's "grandparents," Rose and William Bailey fulfilled their role with unspoken resentment and great reluctance. For them, like the now replaced Darcie Taylor, everything was different. Their lives had changed forever when their only son Nathan, known to everyone as Nate, had moved to Thailand five years ago, and thrown himself with wholehearted enthusiasm into the most base elements of the Thai sex trade. After many years of easy living, Nate Bailey had finally been caught in a highly compromising position with four-year-old twin girls and was awaiting trial, after which he could confidently expect to be sentenced to a lengthy term in one of Bangkok's most notorious prisons.

Rose and William had naturally been distraught, and, up until this point, totally unaware that "this kind of thing" went on. A quietly spoken Scottish couple, the Bailey's had lived a life, which to many outsiders may have seemed dull and ordinary. William Bailey was an unassuming grocer, with a modest but busy store in a small and peaceful Scottish village; a man who could be easily overlooked despite his shock of white hair, beard and burly frame, which lent itself to him playing Father Christmas each year for the children of the community where they had lived all their lives. Popular with the locals, the store had provided them with a reasonable living up until their retirement two years ago. Rose was a small neat woman, with bright blue eyes and a ready smile, who always sported an equally neat and tidy bun; it was rumoured that no one ever recalled seeing Rose Bailey with her hair loose. Rose had many friends and interests and had always helped William in the shop, baking home-made cakes and scones, which were always sold out before lunchtime. Rose had always wanted a large family but had been cruelly denied, losing two babies to miscarriages and heartbreakingly, having endured the loss of a still born daughter at full term. They finally had to accept that they would never have children of their own, and so had looked into adoption. When they had received the phone call to say that a little boy had been born, who perfectly matched their profile, Rose had wept tears of joy. With Nate in their lives, Rose Bailey discovered a new purpose, and had poured her entire body and soul into raising her one and only son. To say she had doted on him was an understatement of some enormity. Rose acquiesced to Nate's every whim, firstly as a child, and then as an adult. In Rose's eyes, Nate could do no wrong. William had tried his best to intervene and introduce some boundaries and a stern hand with his increasingly unruly son, but this only served to distress Rose, and so, for a quiet life, William allowed her to indulge the boy, with little more than a weary shake of his head.

By the time Nate reached the age of 12, William knew that he was out of their control. Nate had grown into a startlingly handsome boy, and everyone who knew him drew comparisons between Nate and a young Elvis Presley. There were only slight differences; one being that Nate had kept his almost white blonde hair, whereas Elvis dyed his black. Nate had unusual ice blue eyes, which were piercing and almost hypnotic; unfortunately, he also had a petulant, sulky mouth, though he could turn on the full charm of a dazzling smile when it suited him. William struggled with feelings of resentment at this spoilt child who he now considered little more than a cuckoo in his nest. He looked to the day when Nate would leave their home and allow him to finally have his wife to himself again, instead of having to witness her be at Nate's beck and call with little or no time for her husband.

In light of the current situation in Thailand, William looked back with a deep sense of unease, on an incident, which occurred when Nate was 13-years-old. William had been pottering in his garden one evening, when he thought he heard a noise coming from his shed. He cocked his head on one side; yes, there it was again. William crossed the garden to investigate and on opening the shed door, he was met by the sight of Nate and his three-year-old cousin Rebecca. At first glance, William could not take in the scene before him. Nate had his back to him, and was unaware that William had entered the shed. Rebecca was crying, and the noise had obviously drowned out the sound of him opening the door. Rebecca was naked from the waist down and making pathetic attempts to cover herself with her tiny hands.

Nate's voice sounded flat and emotionless as he spoke. "Move your hands Becky," Nate ordered, "do it now."

William had hesitated only a second before intervening, "NATHAN BAILEY," he had shouted, using Nate's full name, usually reserved for when he misbehaved, "what in God's name do you think you are doing?" he demanded. On seeing her beloved Uncle, Rebecca had run to him and buried her face against his legs, sobbing. William took off his jacket to cover the child, while glaring at his son who stood considering his father with a look of such arrogance on his face that even William had been taken aback. "Well?" he roared at the boy, "what's your explanation?" Nate had shrugged his shoulders while attempting to walk past his father and out of the shed. However, William was in no mood for his insolence, and for the first time in his life, William had got hold of Nate and stopped him dead in his tracks. "Answer me boy, what were you doing to your cousin?"

Nate met his father's gaze and sneered in contempt. "The big baby had wet her pants," he began "I was only helping her to change."

William's eyes narrowed suspiciously, while his mind refused to believe the bald and unpalatable truth of what his son had really been doing to the child. "Really?" he said sarcastically, "So you thought you'd bring her into my shed to do this "helping" did you?"

Nate's expression changed; he suddenly acquired a look of total innocence and smiled with the full force of his undeniable good looks. "Why yes sir, I didn't want her to be in trouble, so I said she could get changed in here. Why? What did YOU think I was doing dad?" the question was a challenge, which William Bailey was not up to. He thought of Rose and the devastating impact an incident like this would have on her.

With a deep sigh, he let go of Nate, "You had better not let me catch you doing anything like this again boy," he had said by way of a warning.

Nate walked away with a smirk, which his father could not see and whispered to himself, "Oh don't worry dad, you won't ever catch me again," – and he hadn't. Nate had been far more careful from that day on.

When Nate had moved to Thailand, Rose had been distraught, but William's feelings were mixed. He had been secretly relieved that Nate was finally moving away. He was far too old to still be living at home with his parents, and it would be a luxury to have the house to themselves after so long. However, William had a sense of foreboding about his move overseas, and when the news of Nate's arrest came, he found he was almost expecting it.

Rose on the other hand had been completely convinced of Nate's innocence, and had insisted on standing by her son and so they had flown out to Thailand for his trail. The weeks that followed were disheartening. They could get no information about Nate, and their efforts to visit him had been frustrated at every turn. They had just about reached the end of their patience, not to mention their rapidly depleted financial reserves, when they had been approached by a bald headed Man who said he could help Nate in return for a small favour. The Man had said that he could make sure that Nate did not go to prison in Bangkok, but that he would, "get him off" with nothing more than probation as it was a first offence. Rose had jumped at the chance, though William had been more cautious. Rose's seriously misplaced belief in her son's innocence, was surpassed only by her naivety, and she had predictably agreed to do whatever she could to support their son. William had been no more than a passenger in the whole affair.

When the true enormity of their role had been explained to them however, they had been shocked and even Rose had expressed her resistance and said as much to The Man. Sadly, the terrible knowledge of exactly what they were getting themselves into had become horrifyingly apparent, when the Man had explained the potential consequences of non-compliance, not only for them, but also for their disgraced son.

They were now trapped in a never-ending nightmare from which they longed to wake up.

Darcie was only the second child they had cared for, the first being a little boy of six years. He had been with them only a week before being "moved," to where, they did not know. They had been told not to ask questions, but to care for the children and if anyone asked, to say they were their grandchildren visiting from Scotland. However, no one asked, as no one saw them. They were required to live as isolated a life as possible, and under no circumstance were they to speak of the labyrinth of deceit and corruption in which they were now embroiled. They had been promised that after one year of "service" Nate's debt would be considered paid, and they would be free to return home to Scotland and live out their days in peace. They were not permitted to see Nate, and were told that his fate lay in their hands, thus ensuring their continued co-operation and compliance. They were trapped, as neatly as flies in a spider's web.

Chapter 12

Wednesday arrived, and Melanie packed Nicholas' case with care. She knew that he was hopeless at taking care of himself, and liked to ensure that she had attended to every possible detail. She went through her mental checklist one more time; *ten clean shirts, one for every day and three to spare, trousers, pants, socks, handkerchiefs, belt, shoes, toiletries, ear plugs for on the plane.* She frowned as she tried to think if she had forgotten anything. She knew that Nicholas would pack his own briefcase with his IPad, wallet and other personal effects, but felt she was missing something.

Passports and tickets she realised with a start; *oh my goodness, how did I not have those out ready*? She went to the wall safe behind the original Degas painting, where such items were safely stored, punched in the digital code and took out the all-important documents. Glancing at the tickets, which had been booked through Nicholas' office, she noted that the flight time was 14:25. A feeling of panic came over her as she recalled Nicholas telling her that his flight was at 4:25pm. With an increasing feeling of dismay, she realised he must have misheard. He had mistaken 14:25 for 4:25. She checked her elegant Piaget wristwatch, which confirmed her worst fears; it was now 12:30pm. The airport was an hour's drive, but only if the traffic was not backed up. On a bad day, it could take a lot longer. Nicholas was still in his office, oblivious to the fact that he was in real danger of missing his flight.

Melanie wasted no time, hammering on his door, "Nicholas," she called urgently, "you have to leave now."

Nicholas opened the big heavy door of his office looking irritated. "Melanie" he began, but got no further as he recognised the real distress on his wife's face.

Melanie waved the airline ticket in his face, "14:25 Nicholas," she said, "NOT 4:25, you're going to miss your flight if you don't go NOW," she said breathlessly.

Nicholas was not a man, given to drama or extreme emotions, but he let out a yell of exasperation as he shouted, "Call a taxi and be quick about it." Melanie left him gathering up papers and dashed to the phone. Thankfully, Nicholas was a regular customer, and the operator assured an agitated Melanie that the driver would be there in five minutes. Melanie ran back to the study, dragging Nicholas' suitcase behind her. If she had forgotten to pack anything, it was too late; he would have to improvise.

"Got everything?" she asked anxiously; "Here's your passport and ticket," she added handing the documents to a harassed Nicholas.

"How could this happen Melanie?" he asked crossly, as he continued to grab randomly at things, "I mean, why did we not know the flight was 14:25?"

Melanie did not bother to reply. She knew the fault would be placed at her door, and at this moment, she did not care. "Hurry up," she said by way of an answer, "the taxi's on its way."

Nicholas strode purposefully out of his office, briefcase in hand; "See you in a week," he said as he kissed Melanie hastily on the cheek, and left the house still muttering to himself. Melanie exhaled, and out of the corner of her eye noticed that the door to Nicholas' office was still in the process of closing. In his haste to get moving, he had flung it open so wide, that the self-closing mechanism was taking longer than normal to close the door. Before she could move however, the door clicked shut and the Yale lock secured it. *Well THAT was an opportunity missed,* she thought wryly to herself as she went back into the kitchen to dry the dishes.

At that moment, Melanie heard a crash and Nicholas reappeared looking even more harried than ever. Before she could speak, Nicholas was fumbling with the lock to his office door shouting, "Glasses, where are my damn glasses?" He did not wait for an answer, but barged clumsily back into his office, re-emerging seconds later, glasses in hand. "Right," he said briskly, "this time, I'm off," and like a passing whirlwind, he was gone.

Melanie Bishop was nothing if not a fast learner; before the door to Nicholas' office could close for a second time, she stepped forward and tossed the tea towel she had been holding, neatly into the gap. "Oh no you don't," she said, smiling as she watched the heavy door come to rest on the offending article.

She was in.

***

Rose Bailey was crying. Though she tried to be quiet, her muffled sobs woke her husband of 40-years. The darkness of their bedroom pressed down upon them both like a suffocating wet blanket. William reached out and touched his wife's shoulder in a show of solidarity and sympathy. William understood all too well the complicated situation they were in. He cursed his ignorance regarding the truth of their son's lifestyle in Thailand and asked himself for the hundredth time, how he could have been so naïve, especially in light of the incident in the shed all those years ago. He could understand Rose's feelings for her son; she and Nate had always been very close and she had a blind spot where Nate was concerned. It had been Rose who was the driving force in them making the trip to Thailand to support Nate. She had protested his innocence, and defended him with righteous indignation. Even now, with the full force of their reality staring them in the face, Rose was struggling to accept the actuality of the whole debacle.

In the next room, the child who used to be Darcie Taylor let out a whimper. Immediately, Rose stiffened, stopped crying, and got quickly out of bed to go and check on her. William lay staring blankly into the darkness until Rose finally returned. "She okay?" he asked quietly.

Rose sighed, her voice thick with her recent tears as she answered, "No, she's not okay William, she frightened and confused. She wants her folks and she wants to go home, how can she be okay?" The enormity of her part in Darcie's misery provoked a fresh onslaught of weeping from Rose. "William, we HAVE to help her, we have to do something," she said through her tears. "I can't endure it another day, first the little boy, and now this poor wee girl, it's too much to bear."

William took a deep breath, "Rose, you know we're in too deep now," he began, "you know what they'll do to Nate if we dare to speak up, and don't forget, we had a part in that little boy's situation too. I'm as upset as you are, but the fact is my dear, we made this uncomfortable bed for ourselves, and now I'm afraid we have to lie in it," he said with finality.

Rose clasped her hands to her face and shook her head, "God forgive us William," she whispered, "what have we done?"

***

As Ethan guided *The Lady Elizabeth* easily across the open water, Diane was in the galley preparing lunch for later in the day. The weather was about as perfect as it could be for diving, but Ethan was not feeling good about the day ahead. Ethan tried to push aside his feeling of unease, but they stuck with him, pulling at his mind like a nagging toothache. Ethan surveyed the group of four men who he was taking for a day of diving. The Thai men were locals but Ethan did not feel comfortable with them. They presented as shifty and nervous; they didn't make eye contact and seemed to be avoiding any attempts Ethan made at conversation. They had however been engrossed in what seemed to be an animated discussion with the two British men, who Ethan knew had only been in Bangkok for two days and had travelled down to Pattaya for this trip. Since getting onto the boat, the four men had been as far away from Ethan as possible, and had been deep in conversation ever since.

Ethan checked his waterproof watch and called over to the men who were still in a huddle at the far end of the boat. "If you guys want to gear up, we'll be reaching our first prime spot in about ten minutes." One of the men looked over, with a look, which surprised Ethan. The man looked distinctly annoyed at the interruption; "Everything okay there buddy?" asked Ethan with concern. Usually, his clients were animated and enthusiastic about their day's diving off his boat.

The man immediately put a smile on his face as he answered, "Absolutely," he enthused, "can't wait to get going, can we gents?" he asked of his companions. The remaining three men exchanged glances before looking across at Ethan and murmuring their agreement as they began to gear up for the dive. Ethan found himself making a mental note of where he had left his dive knife. Whatever was unfolding here, Ethan got the distinct feeling that it had nothing whatsoever to do with diving, and the thought made him very uneasy. He felt even more troubled as he thought of Diane down in the galley. If there was going to be any trouble, the last thing he wanted was to place Diane in harm's way. His mind worked overtime as he tried to work out what the men's real agenda might be.

***

Standing in line, Claud Berlioz and his family were waiting to check in for their impending flight to Thailand. As seasoned travellers, Claude and Robyn were well versed in the process of flying, and were patient and composed. The same could not be said for Angelique. Containing

Angelique under such thrilling circumstances was akin to taming the wind. The little girl bounced around in a frenzy of over stimulation, and demonstrated her unreserved enthusiasm about the holiday. Fabien, on the other hand was outwardly stoic, and quietly restrained. Inside however, he was in a turmoil of well-disguised excitement; he was, after all, going to learn to dive and he could not wait.

"Angelique," warned Robyn, "I will tell you one more time now. If you do not stop wriggling and jiggling, I will get daddy to pick you up and hold you like a baby." Angelique froze for all of five seconds, before it all got the better of her and she danced a jig on the spot. Robyn rolled her eyes and looked pleadingly at Claude for support.

However, she was met with that crooked smile and a shrug. "She is a child Robyn, allow her the freedom of her feelings," he said indulgently.

Robyn scowled to hide the strength of her love for her family, "Oh you and your passionate French genes," she accused, "You have passed them directly to Angelique; what a good thing I have Fabien to be sensible like me." They both laughed and shuffled forward as the line gradually moved on.

As the gate was about to close, a frantic Nicholas Bishop approached at a run. "Hold on there," he called with authority, "I'm here." The flight attendant checked his ticket, "Only just made it sir," she smiled as she waved him through. Neither the Berlioz family, nor Nicholas had any idea of how intertwined their paths would become in the days ahead.

Chapter 13

Ethan made a seemingly casual visit to Diane in the galley where he quickly, and without ceremony whispered his unease concerning the four men on the boat. Diane became upset, as Ethan suspected she might in her fragile state; it took a few minutes of gentle reassurance from Ethan to calm her down. Diane took a deep breath and resumed her preparation of lunch for the six of them; making a note of Ethan's plan should things go awry. Diane had access to the Marine VHF radio, and at Ethan's instruction, had set the channel to 16, which was the internationally recognised "calling and distress" channel. Should there be any trouble; Diane was prepared to alert the coastguard to their potential predicament. She bit her lip anxiously as Ethan went back up on deck in readiness for the dive. She had failed to talk him out of entering the water with the men, and could not hide her apprehension concerning Ethan's safety. Though the men had done nothing outwardly untoward, other than for one of them to display some annoyance at Ethan's interruption of their discussion, Ethan's gut feeling for potential trouble was rarely wrong. Like Diane's social work antennae, Ethan seemed to have a built in system for picking up on the possibility of a challenging situation.

Back on deck, the men were shuffling about in a half-hearted effort to ready themselves for the dive. Ethan observed them for precisely one more minute before deciding to take the bull by the horns. He strode over to the group and asked pointedly. "Gentlemen, is there a problem?" In response, the four men exchanged more glances, and eventually, the older of the two English men spoke up.

"Mr Montana, you are clearly an intelligent and observant man, and have by now realised that perhaps our intentions here today are not solely related to diving from your beautiful boat." *Here we go*, thought Ethan, as he prepared himself for what might follow, though he had a bad feeling that he already knew. Ethan said nothing, but waited for the man to continue. The man was clearly the ringleader of the four; average height, middle aged, with a receding hairline of thin sandy hair, and cold grey eyes in a face, which was unfortunately scarred with acne. He was conservatively dressed and exuded self-confidence. He was obviously well educated and here for a specific, purpose.

"Mr Montana, or should I say, Ethan, may I call you Ethan?" the man asked politely. "My colleagues and I have a little proposition for you," he continued with a hint of menace.

Ethan raised an eyebrow, "A proposition?" he said sarcastically, "let's hear it then," he added flatly. The man moistened his lips, pausing for a few seconds before he spoke again, realising that this may not be as straightforward as he had anticipated.

"Mr Montana," he continued, "Ethan, why don't we sit down, it would be more comfortable."

Ethan straightened up defiantly, "I'll stand," he said decisively folding his arms and looking the man in the eye, "and you can call me Mr Montana." This action took the man off guard and he decided not to press the matter.

"Very well," he continued pleasantly, "I will come straight to the point. It would seem that you are now the new skipper of *The Lady*

Elizabeth. My colleagues and I were well acquainted with her old skipper and were somewhat surprised to find someone new in charge. However, we have made a few enquiries, and have been assured that you are a man of integrity and honour, and as such, we would like to offer you some very lucrative work, for very little effort. I am talking about a significant amount of money Mr Montana, more than you could possibly earn, in a whole season here." The man paused to allow his words to hit home; he failed to notice Ethan's eye's narrowing. "Of course," he continued, "In exchange for being generously rewarded for your co-operation, we would expect a certain level of, … how shall I put this?" he smiled to himself, "A certain level of, shall we say discretion."

Ethan looked down, concealing his disgust at the man who was occupying space on his boat. Inwardly cursing the friend of a friend who had done the deal on the rental of the boat, and who had led him into undeniable danger, he took a few seconds to get his emotions under control. When he looked up again, his expression was neutral, though his eyes were filled with undisguised contempt.

"Drugs," said Ethan bluntly. "I assume you want me to run drugs?" The man looked momentarily startled at Ethan's direct manner, but managed a reptilian smile as he replied, "Why no Mr Montana, nothing so mundane and grubby. What we require of you, is that you move a package of a different sort for us."

Ethan studied the man, and considered his options; he took into account the fact that there were four of them in total and he was outnumbered and most likely outgunned, as he did not doubt for one moment that at least one or more of the group were armed in some way. Added to this, Diane was also on the boat, and could be in significant danger, if Ethan acted impulsively, or, if he gave them men cause to think that he would report their proposition to the police. Ethan knew that he was walking a fine line here and had to play them at their own game, and play it safe.

Forcing a smile onto his face he continued, "Ah well, that may be different then, I want no part in any drug trade, Mr? What is your name?" he asked pleasantly.

The man visibly relaxed, "You can call me Ronnie," he replied, "And I am pleased to hear that you recognise a lucrative proposition when you hear one Mr Montana."

Ethan continued smiling, "Oh, call me Ethan," he said easily. "Now, why don't we sit down, and you can tell me more."

***

Melanie finished her chores in the kitchen. As she dried the last of the dishes, she began to fully contemplate her audacity in wedging open Nicholas' study door. *So now what?* She thought to herself, *Nicholas would be furious if he knew.* Having acted on impulse to prevent the heavy office door from closing, Melanie's apprehension as to what she might find in there was acting as a powerful preventative in her actually taking any action. Eventually, she ran out of chores and knew that she had to stop procrastinating, face her fears, and go in there, or take away the tea towel, which was acting as a provisional doorstop, and let the door close. *I have to know*; she said to herself, and with a decisive spring in her step entered the hallowed territory. She allowed herself a few minutes to take in the surroundings, which were unfamiliar. Nicholas did not allow her in the room, even to clean. It was the one part of the house, where he actually did any housework, dusting, and even taking the vacuum in there once a week. He told Melanie that his work was too sensitive for her to stumble on anything, even by accident.

The room smelled of Nicholas. It was a powerful masculine smell, with the unmistakeable scent of his aftershave hanging in the air. All the furniture was polished walnut. Papers were neatly stacked here and there in small piles. Each pile had a note on top of it, and Melanie stepped forward and read them. She felt nervous and guilty, and realised that she was sweating lightly. The notes on top of the piles were simply dates, which Melanie assumed were reminders as to when the paperwork was due to be somewhere. The soft chime of the Grandfather clock in the corner politely reminded Melanie that it was now 1:00 p.m. Nicholas had inherited the clock from his great grandfather and it was one of his most prized possessions. A well-worn leather chair in the corner was host to a casually thrown cardigan, a University scarf, and more papers. The rug on the floor was business-like and functional with a dark stain where Nicholas had spilled his coffee and failed to clean it up effectively. On the walls were fine oil paintings, most of which were originals, also courtesy of great grandfather who had an acute eye for fine art.

Over on the leather-topped desk, which dominated the room, a brass paperweight stood aloft on another pile of papers, and a matching brass lamp offered a restrained light over the rest of the table. In his haste to leave to catch his plane, Nicholas had left the lamp on. Allowing her gaze to scan over the desk, Melanie realised with a start that the lamp was not the only thing, which Nicholas had left on. A warm luminous glow emanating from the middle of the desk announced the unbelievable fact that Nicholas Bishop, the epitome of Organisation, had left his laptop on. Melanie stepped forwards in an almost trance like state, not realising that she was holding her breath. The tropical fish wallpaper swimming lazily on the screen confirmed the almost inconceivable fact that the laptop was indeed unlocked.

***

Ethan and the man called Ronnie sat uneasily across from each other in the small confines of the boat's galley. His three companions occupied the remaining space and sweated in the increasing heat of the day. Ethan had asked Diane to go up on deck, assuring her that he and the other men had much to discuss. Diane had complied, but looked highly anxious. As she left the galley, Ethan had managed to shoot her a glance and the almost indiscernible shake of his head warned her not to do anything foolish. "Not be long darlin," Ethan told her brightly, "just a few business details to sort out and then we'll be on our way."

Ethan took his place at the small table and smiled around at the men. "So gentlemen, let's talk."

Ronnie rubbed his hands together before speaking, "Ethan, what we have is a nice little earner for you, and all we ask is that you do the job, keep your mouth shut and no questions asked," he began. "Of course, if that's going to be a problem," … he left the rest unsaid but Ethan was wise enough to pick up on the unspoken threat immediately.

"I can't see why there should be a problem Ronnie," he said smoothly, "I mean, who doesn't like to earn a bit on the side eh? I'm sure I can be of assistance."

Ronnie and the other men exchanged knowing glances. "What is it I'm required to transport?" asked Ethan with as much disinterest as he could. "Not that it matters, I mean as long as it's not drugs, not with the jail sentences they hand out here."

The men looked nervously at Ronnie and the other English man spoke up, "Hang on Ronnie, are you sure you can trust him?" he said hastily, "I mean, we don't really know him."

Ronnie shot the man a look of contempt, "Listen to me Tony, we're on a bit of a tight schedule in case you'd forgotten. The Mover is anxious to transport his package as quickly as possible and I'm sure Mr Montana here is the right man for the job. As an unknown associate, it makes it harder for anyone to make the connection between him and us."

Ethan stretched back in his chair and put his arms lazily behind his head, in an effort to appear unperturbed, "I don't see why there should be a problem Ronnie, as long as I get the pay, which you tell me is due, everything should be fine; so tell me, what's the package?"

Ronnie smiled and Ethan was disturbingly reminded of a snake stalking its prey, "It's not so much what Ethan, ... as who."

Chapter 14

The following day dawned bright, hot and clear. Down on Cha-Am beach, 5-year-old Angelique was experiencing an overload of pleasure. She could scarcely contain herself, such was her excitement at being on holiday. True to her promise, Robyn had bought her daughter a bucket and spade, and laughed along with her as they mixed the freshly brought seawater with the fine dry sand to mould the castles. "No, no, maman," bossed Angelique, "do it this way," she instructed, demonstrated her technique, which consisted of flipping the bucket over and hitting the base hard with the spade. "See?" she said with satisfaction at the resulting castle, "It is the best way." Robyn looked at Claude and they both laughed at their daughter's antics.

"How's our little diver getting on?" asked Robyn of her husband. The family were staying in Bangkok, but had made the two hour trip down to Cha-Am in order that Fabien could go diving.

Claude nodded, "He's in his element," he replied, "The instructor said to go back for him in an hour, he will be finished then."

"Okay," said Robyn, "one hour and we will collect Fabien. Then we can enjoy a nice picnic on the beach before we go back to the hotel."

Angelique tugged at her mother's arm, "Yes but we still have to build more sand castles," she said with determination, "we must make a really giant fairy castle before we go."

Robyn smiled, "Then we had better get on with it," she agreed and applied herself to filling more buckets with sand as Claude relaxed, laid back and continued reading his newspaper. Both parents winked at each other, knowing that their children were having the time of their lives.

The hour passed quickly, and Robyn helped her daughter to clean up before they set off to collect Fabien. As they left the beach, Angelique twisted her head to get a better view of something she had never seen before.

"Maman," she asked, "Why is that man sat in a chair with wheels on it?"

***

Nicholas unpacked his case in the five-star hotel room, which would be his home for the next week; his razor sharp mind had a sudden disconcerting thought. *I don't remember logging off the laptop*. He shook his head to eradicate the nagging doubt, reassuring himself that it did not matter as his study door was locked and only he had a key. Nicholas was due at an important conference on child trafficking later that morning and did not have long to shower and make himself presentable. He had been invited once again, by the Thai Government as a key speaker at the conference. Amongst other things, Nicholas was an authority on child trafficking and had written several highly acclaimed research papers on the subject. With its ever-growing reputation as a magnet for depraved tourists, and an equally unenviable notoriety for human trafficking, Thailand needed all the help it could get and Nicholas Bishop was just the man for the job.

The strong connections, which Nicholas' father had to the country due to him owning the clothing factories in Bangkok, meant that Nicholas came to view his visits to Thailand as routine. However, his recollection of those years were corrupted by dark memories, which, when dwelt upon, were like peering through smoked glass at someone else's life. However, his early experiences in Thailand had been key in focusing his mind on his goals for his life; a path from which he had never wavered. With his knowledge of the country and his ability to speak the language, Nicholas had been an appreciable asset to the ongoing relations between the two governments.

The conference could not have come at a more appropriate time, occurring only three days after the disappearance of British born Darcie Taylor whose forlorn little face continued to stare out of the major tabloids. Darcie's parents had rarely been off the television, making appeal after tragic appeal for information, sadly to no avail. The child simply seemed to have vanished. Nicholas had a private meeting scheduled with the Taylors later in the day. He had requested the face to face as soon as he realised he would be in the same vicinity. Nicholas was anxious to offer more than empty condolences to the distraught parents. He was hoping to glean information from them about the day Darcie went missing, information, which was desperately lacking thus far. With this on his mind, he selected one of the crisp white shirts Melanie had so carefully packed, laid it out ready, and went for his shower.

***

Fabien could not have been happier. His inaugural one-hour experience of diving had lived up to all his expectations. Fabien knew without a shadow of a doubt that he would follow his heart and work towards a career as a marine biologist. Even at such a young age, Fabien could not imagine a better life, than one lived in the mysterious and wonderful world under the sea. He had been in an almost dream like trance since his parents and sister had picked him up. His dive instructor had enthused about Fabien's abilities, telling his parents that he was a natural. Fabien glowed with pride; he had found his niche in life and could not imagine doing anything else. Robyn and Claude had been encouraging and happy for him. Fabien talked enthusiastically all the way back to the hotel, which for once meant that Angelique did not get a word in. She bounced up and down in the back seat of the hired car, as far as her seatbelt restraints would allow.

"Maman," she demanded, interrupting her brother, "Fabien is talking too much."

Robyn adopted a patient look as she regarded her dynamic youngest child, "Cherie, do not be rude," she chided, "Fabien has had an exciting day and it is only polite to listen and let him enjoy his experience." Fabien nodded solemnly and continued his tale of the biggest fish he had ever seen, while Angelique rolled her blue eyes in silent protest.

Once back at the hotel, the family showered, changed and went down for dinner in the hotel restaurant. Angelique, tired of listening to her brother, did her best to monopolise the conversation. "Papa, what are we doing next?" she asked in her politest voice.

Claude finished the last of his chocolate gateau and regarded both his children with an indulgent smile. "Well," he began, "maman and I thought we might go down to the square and listen to some music. There is a band playing tonight, and you my angel, can dance to your heart's content."

The thought of being officially permitted to dance, brought a huge smile to Angelique's face, "Oh merci papa," she cried, reverting to her father's native tongue as she often did when she was excited, "can we go now?" She demanded.

Robyn and Claude exchanged an amused glance; they knew that at the mention of music and dancing, their quiet meal was over, as Angelique's elation would now afford them no peace. With the maximum of fuss and noise from Angelique, the family left the table and made their way out into the darkness completely unaware of the horror, which lurked in the shadows of that sultry holiday night.

***

The conference had been well attended, and Nicholas felt satisfied that his speech had been appropriately received and understood. Headlining the day's events had been the recent kidnapping of Darcie Taylor. Nicholas spent over an hour following the conference, talking to various Thai officials, all of whom were eager to glean more information and advice from him, before he returned to his hotel. Glancing at his watch, Nicholas realised that he had less than two hours to get ready for his meeting with the Taylors. His face became grim as he thought about the impending rendezvous; he stepped into the bathroom and sluiced his face with water to refresh himself. He then lay on the bed and closed his eyes for a 20-minute power nap prior to the meeting, knowing he would require all his wits about him for this one.

Down in the lobby of the hotel, Verity and David Taylor were a sorry sight. Exhausted by recent events, and strained to breaking point, they waited anxiously for Nicholas to appear, not knowing quite what to expect. With them, was a police appointed family liaison officer, who had flown out from the UK; a pleasant softly spoken Scottish woman by the name of Elspeth Duncan, who was fighting a losing battle in her efforts to offer solace to the grief stricken couple. Elspeth glanced at Verity and felt a stab of pain for the woman, whose face was cloaked in unspoken agony. Elspeth knew that it was only a matter of time before Verity broke down completely. She knew that Verity was hardly eating and had not slept properly since the dreadful day her daughter had disappeared. Like most families Elspeth had been involved with, both parents were wracked with guilt about Darcie's disappearance, with Verity shouldering a burden of disproportionate blame, which threatened to engulf her. Elspeth reached out and touched Verity's hand in silent sympathy; as she did so, the lift doors opened, and Nicholas strode across proffering his hand as he did so.

"Mr and Mrs Taylor?" he queried as they stood up, "I am Nicholas Bishop, and I am deeply distressed to hear of your situation. Please, follow me, I have a private room where we can talk."

Once ensconced in one of the hotel's conference rooms, Nicholas ordered drinks for everyone and once they had been served, he turned his full attention to Verity and David. "So," he began grimly, "tell me everything you can remember about what happened."

Overwhelmed with relief at having someone in authority to talk to, Verity immediately broke down and sobbed. David put a protective arm around her shoulders and looked frighteningly angry. "My wife is not coping with this situation at all," he said shortly, "Our world has come to an end and we feel we have no one to turn to."

Nicholas nodded in sympathy, "I completely understand how you feel," he said, "However, as difficult as it may be, we must try to concentrate on the situation and establish as many facts as we can." David Taylor inclined his head in agreement as Nicholas continued; "Mrs. Taylor" he said gently, "Can you tell me as much as possible about what you can recall from the day Darcie went missing."

Verity Taylor composed herself, looked directly at Nicholas and said, "I remember every single detail of that day Mr Bishop," she said quietly "every, single, thing."

Chapter 15

Ethan carefully guided *The Lady Elizabeth* back into the marina where she would be moored for the night, just as the sun was setting. He tied her up and nodded to his four passengers as they disembarked. "We'll be in touch then," said Ronnie with a shrewd grin as he left, "don't go far will you?"

Ethan managed to laugh as he answered, "And where would I be going Ronnie? I'm here for the summer, remember?" As the men walked away, Diane opened her mouth, with a hundred unanswered questions waiting to pour out. Ethan cautioned her with a stern look and whispered to her without moving his lips, "Not yet Di, not yet." Diane complied and with a huge effort smiled and gave the men a cheery wave.

Once they were well out of sight and earshot, she turned back to Ethan, her eyes ablaze with unspoken fear, "What on earth happened out there?" she demanded.

Ethan's face was terrible as he replied, "We need to talk, but not here; come on," he said catching hold of her hand "let's go back to the flat, you need to hear this and then we need to think."

The couple were silent on the two-hour trip back to Bangkok. Ethan's eyes were fixed firmly on the road ahead, his mouth a thin determined line, and Diane knew better than to start asking questions. Once they had parked the 4x4 in the underground car park and got back to their one-bedroom apartment, they showered, changed and sat down with a bowl of Nachos, some chilli dip and a bottle of white wine and only then was Ethan ready to divulge what had happened on the boat. Diane impatience was getting the better of her now, and she had already fired a round of questions at Ethan as he was gathering his thoughts. He held up his hands for silence, and then took both of Diane's hands in his, looked into her eyes and told her the truth of what had happened on the boat.

"They asked me to move a package for them," he began. Diane opened her mouth to interrupt but he silenced her, "Let me finish," he said quietly. "It would appear that they used to do business with the previous skipper of the boat. It was him they were expecting today, not me. Wait till I see Gary," he said, referring to the friend who had put him onto his own friend who owned the boat. "Whoever Gary's mate is; is the guy they were after. He's landed me in a real mess. Naturally, I thought they were looking for someone to move drugs, but they have another kind of package in mind." Ethan paused as he searched for the right words, knowing the impact they would have on his already fragile girlfriend. "Di, they want me to move a child and have offered me a great deal of money to do so."

Diane listened in horror as Ethan outlined the bald facts of what Ronnie and his accomplices had asked him to do. Her eyes burned with righteous indignation and she leapt to her feet in anger. "For the love of God Ethan, we have to go to the police immediately," she said with passion, "they can't be allowed to get away with this.

Ethan took a deep breath, "Diane," he began slowly, "these are very dangerous people who will stop at nothing to accomplish their goals. Though he never said it in as many words, Ronnie made it crystal clear to me that we would both be in danger if I did not comply, or if I reported this to anyone. We dare not risk going to the authorities as we have no idea how far reaching this network is. For all we know, the authorities may be in on it."

Diane's fervour left her and she sank back in her chair deflated. "Then what?" she asked, "What's the solution Ethan?"

Ethan sighed heavily as he contemplated the question, "I have no idea," he said wearily. "I have a strong suspicion that the child they have in mind may be the missing girl from the UK, Darcie Taylor, though they didn't say exactly. It's vitally important that they think I'm going to cooperate with them. The alternative consequences do not bear thinking about. One thing's for sure Di, we need a plan and quickly, but who in God's name can we trust?"

***

Darcie Taylor lay on her neatly made bed staring up at the ceiling. So much had happened in her little world, in which she no longer knew who she was or what was real any more. The two people looking after her were nice and kind, but she did not know them, and despite their efforts to get her to call them nanny and granddad, she simply could not do it. She had a nanny and granddad at home, and it felt wrong to apply the familiar and much loved names of her real family to these strangers. Darcie had become withdrawn; she ate very little and slept even less. She pined for her parents and brother and cried most of the night. She had a constant pain in her tummy, which would not go away and her head ached all the time.

A soft knock on the door made her jump; the smiling apologetic face of Rose Bailey peeped around, "Ah there you are pet," she said with affection. "Will you come and have some tea now?" she asked. Darcie turned over to face the wall, ignoring Rose's efforts to bring her out of her room and the depths of her depression.

Undeterred, Rose approached and sat on the edge of the bed, "Holly, she began, at which, Darcie rolled over and with startling ferocity said,

"DARCIE, my name is DARCIE, I am DARCIE Taylor and I want my mummy."

Rose was taken aback, the child had always been so quiet, so sad, but now, she was beginning to show some spirit. Rose considered the fragile little person in front of her and cursed herself for the thousandth time. She knew that one day she would have to atone for the sins she had committed against this innocent child, but knew also that her own son's life depended on her total compliance.

"I know pet," she said kindly, "but it's better for us all, if we call you Holly; you know what the man said," she added with a sigh.

Darcie sat up, her tear filled eyes ablaze, "I HATE the man," she shouted, "I HATE the nurse lady, I HATE the shouting smacking lady, and I HATE YOU," and with that, she turned her face to the wall and began to sob.

Rose closed her eyes and knew that she could not continue. Despite Nate's predicament, she knew that she could not carry on being part of this heinous labyrinth of deceit and wickedness. She stood up decisively and made her way back to where her husband was sitting in the living room. "William," she said abruptly, "we need to talk."

***

The Old Man was nothing if not careful with his investments; he had many hundreds of useful contacts, in all four corners of the country. Where he could not have a person in place to report back to him, The Old Man still found a way to make sure he had eyes and ears on a situation. As Rose and William Bailey discussed their dilemma in great detail, they were blissfully unaware that every word they said was being recorded and transmitted via the many high tech devices, which The Old Man had made sure were fitted in the safe house. Every element of their conversation was at that moment, being relayed back to a control room, which was hidden in Chan Chai's opulent home.

***

Back in Bangkok, by the side of the Chao Phraya River, a local fisherman was bringing in his nets. He pulled a face as he felt the all too familiar snag, which signified that his nets had caught on something deep under the water. Straining with effort, he managed to haul in the reluctant catch and bring it onto the bank. Cursing at his misfortune, the man upended the net and shook it to see what had weighed it down so deep in the water. His irritation turned to shock as he found himself staring at the bloated and disfigured corpse of a man. A man he knew to be a fellow fisherman by the name of Sunan Simsek. The man dropped the nets and ran as fast as he could to the local village where he gabbled out his story to the police man there who happened to be the dead man's cousin. Prasert Simsek nodded as he took down the details of the discovery and then turned away smiling; how unfortunate that his cousin had drowned while fishing, how very careless of him.

***

Charn Chai dialled the familiar number and waited for The Old Man to pick up. He spoke briefly and kept to the point. "It is done," he said without ceremony, "his body was discovered this morning. No, no one suspects, but there is a new problem. The child's carers are getting too emotionally involved with her and seem to be developing a conscience, which is as dangerous as it is untenable. Action is required." He listened intently before answering, "I understand, of course, your instructions will be followed to the letter," and he quietly hung up knowing what he must do, not realising that his hand was about to be forced with regard to just how quickly he would have to act.

Chapter 16

Verity composed herself as she began to relate the details of that dreadful day to Nicholas. She recounted the fact that her husband David had gone for a swim, leaving her with both children. She had been building a sand castle with Darcie, when Jack had wandered off and fallen. Leaving her daughter for only a minute, while she attended to her son, Verity had returned to find that Darcie had disappeared. No one had seen anything, let alone Darcie. Nicholas kept the emotion from his face. It was a story he had heard before, and one he hoped never to hear again. He nodded to show he was listening, but Verity's eyes had glazed over at the memory of the moment she became aware her daughter had gone.

Nicholas turned his attention to David and asked, "So, Mr Taylor, you were swimming, and saw nothing of any of this, is that correct?"

David put his arms protectively around Verity again before he answered, "That's right, I had gone for a swim; Verity said she'd be okay with the kids, I mean, I wasn't gone long, who could have known this would happen?" he said with unnecessary defensiveness.

"So you saw nothing," Nicholas pressed the point. David looked up bewildered by the events which had befallen his family, "No, nothing," he confirmed.

Nicholas paused before asking his next question. "I want you both to think very, very, carefully about what I am going to ask you next. At any time that morning, did either of you notice anyone sitting at the edge of the beach in a wheelchair?" David and Verity looked at each other, and scowled with the effort of casting their minds back. David shook his head and was about to answer when Verity's hand flew up to her mouth.

David stopped in concern, "What? What is it darling?" he asked, his voice tight with concern.

Verity stumbled over her words, "Yes, yes, there WAS someone like that, an Old Man, I only noticed him as he had a straw sun hat on exactly the same as the one I bought for myself. I thought it odd that a man would wear a woman's style of hat." Nicholas leaned forward, his eyes burning with anticipation, "Describe him to me Mrs Taylor, think back and tell me what you can remember about him."

Before Verity could answer, David interrupted, "What has this man to do with Darcie? Are you saying he was involved? How can a man in a wheelchair be responsible?"

Nicholas held up a hand, "Please, Mr Taylor," he said urgently, "allow her to think."

Verity sat quietly, with her eyes closed, trying to force her mind to remember. Finally, she opened her eyes, "He was old, really old, and thin too, in fact, he looked quite unwell now I think about it. I didn't see much of his face because of his hat, which was pulled down, but I saw enough to know he was old." Nicholas nodded again; his expression grim.

Unable to contain himself, David spoke up again, "Mr Bishop, you owe us an explanation, who is this man, and what does he have to do with our daughter's disappearance?"

Nicholas sighed and placed his hand on David Taylor's arm, "You're right David, you are owed an explanation. I will tell you what I know, but I ask that you divulge this information to no one, particularly the police. "Ms Duncan," he added addressing the startled family liaison officer, "that goes for you too, this goes no further than these four walls, Darcie's life may depend on it."

Nicholas took a deep breath before he continued, noting the grave expression on all the faces before him. "I cannot give too many details, the reason for which will be obvious to you as I go on. However, suffice to say I have been coming to Thailand for many years now for personal and business reasons, and I have made certain useful connections with regard to the trafficking of children. I, and other interested parties, have reason to believe that one of the main operations is run by an Old Man, who is known to use a wheelchair. We are not certain if this is genuine or simply a front, a disguise. What is important is that this Old Man has been seen at several sites where children are known to have been abducted. This has been going on for many years now, and we are highly anxious to apprehend, not only this Old Man, but his associates.

I am afraid to say the authorities here cannot be trusted. There is corruption and bribery at the highest levels, which leaves me and my other contacts somewhat at a disadvantage."

On hearing this, David Taylor leapt to his feet in unbridled anger, "What!" he exclaimed, "are you telling me that we can't trust the very people who are supposed to be looking for our daughter?"

Nicholas held up his hand in a placatory gesture. "David," he began grimly, "I'm afraid that you and your family are caught up in something much bigger than you can imagine. The tentacles of this operation are like the threads of a spider's web, which are so intricately woven, and so well hidden as to be almost invisible. These men, whoever they are, cover their tracks well. They are dangerous and evil. They have no conscience and will stop at nothing to promote their empire. I know this from experience and am afraid that wherever Darcie is, she is in a huge amount of danger. If anyone in authority does know of her whereabouts, it is highly likely that they will either be handsomely bribed for their discretion and silence on the matter, or, if they are foolish enough to try and come forward, quite frankly, they will never be seen or heard from again. We are dealing with a band of ruthless individuals and I am sorry to have to tell you that the chances of ever finding your daughter are slim."

On hearing this, Verity let out a cry, which sounded almost inhuman. It was primeval and raw and generated from deep in her soul. David glared at Nicholas and spat out his words, "God damn you man, did you have to be so blunt? Couldn't you have given her a bit of hope?"

Nicholas saw that the muscles at the corner of David's eye was twitching; he was a man on the edge of his own sanity, an emotion Nicholas understood only too well. "I'm so sorry David," he offered, "I truly am, but there is no point in my lying to you. I hope to God that Darcie is found, but these people have networks extending worldwide, and to be brutally honest, she may not even still be in the country."

This was the last straw for Verity, and she collapsed in her husband's arms, as a pale faced Elspeth Duncan looked on impotently.

***

William Bailey looked up from the newspaper he was trying unsuccessfully to read. Like his wife, he was having great difficulty in applying himself to anything of late. He was fully aware of his wife's increasing guilt over their terrible role, but he had not expected this.

He shook his head as if trying to dispel the startling words from his ears, "What did you say?" he asked in disbelief. Rose stood, hands on hips, with a determined look in her eye, which William knew of old. Once Rose had that look, he knew that any argument he could present to change her mind was pointless.

"You heard me William Bailey," she replied with considerable force, "I said enough is enough and I said we are going to return this child to the proper authorities, who in turn will reunite the poor wee soul to her family, which is where she belongs. How DID we get caught up in this William, how can we live with ourselves anymore, knowing the misery we're a part of?" Rose's speech was impassioned, but she stood dry eyed and totally resolute in her demands. "We will explain everything to the authorities William; we will go to the British Consulate in Pattaya, and take Darcie with us. We can disclose everything, including the fact that we have been blackmailed. If we go to prison, then so be it William, God knows we deserve to be held accountable, but I cannot, no, I WILL not have this child's future destroyed at my hands."

Fixed with the steely stare of his wife, William knew that she was right. They would have to suffer the consequence of their actions, and knew Rose was right. This could not go on. Their health was suffering, neither of them slept or ate properly, and given the stress of their untenable situation he was surprised neither of them had suffered a heart attack. With a deep sigh, William stood up and took Rose by the hand. "We're in this together," he said softly, "just like everything we've shared over the years, good and bad, we'll get through it together. Now," he said with an assurance he did not feel, "let's think of the best way to go about this."

***

Back in his hotel room Nicholas shrugged off his jacket, and sat on the bed staring at his own reflection in the mirror. His disclosure to the Taylors had shaken them to their core, as he knew it would. *So what now?* He asked the face, which stared back at him, *what now old boy*? Feeling suddenly weary, Nicholas lay down on the bed as he tried to focus on a plan. However, the fatigue of his long flight, coupled with the emotionally draining issues he was trying to deal with soon overtook him and he began to doze off.

As his body surrendered to sleep, the nightmare returned; the one, which Nicholas had been having for the past thirty-six years. The one about the country, which at one time had been his second home, the one with the Old Man in the wheelchair who wore a straw hat. The one where his life had been changed forever.

Chapter 17

Thailand 35 years ago – The Young Man

At nineteen years old, the young man seemed *too* young to be in a position of such authority. However, he was about his father's business, and well versed in the ways of the clothing industry in Thailand. With two factories producing the highest quality silk shirts, and with a successful export business to the UK and worldwide, the young man was in Thailand to oversee performance at the factories and to ensure that things were running as smoothly as they always had. His father enjoyed a lucrative partnership; co-owning the business, as the law demanded, with a native born Thai man. The man was the son of a lifelong friend of his own father, the two men having forged a bond many years ago.

The young man had been making solo trips on his father's behest for the past ten months, constantly reassuring his father that there was no further need for him to make the arduous journey as he had things well in hand. Having proven himself beyond doubt, the young man's father was content to allow his brilliant son to take up the reins of power, knowing that it was a matter of time before he ran their entire portion of the business at home and abroad.

However, the young man had an ulterior motive for his desire to travel alone, one which had little to do with running a business. For the past six months, this young man had been leading a double life, a life he knew, that despite their connections to the Thai people, his parents would never understand, and would certainly never approve of.

Quite simply, the young man had fallen in love.

It happened so quickly that he had shocked himself. Never in a million years could he have predicted such an absolute 180 degree change of direction in his life. A life, which had been mapped out for him from an early age. It was accepted that he would follow his grandfather and father into the family business, eventually taking over and running the empire himself, and one day turning it over to his son.

That was before Lily Rose.

The young man had been attending a business meeting of important future clients. As is the custom in Thailand, there had been small talk and tea. The young man had been outlining the benefits of investing in his father's company when a young lady had entered the room to serve the tea. While the young man was no different to any other young man when it came to a pretty face, this one had captivated his heart without any effort or intention. On the day in question, which he would eternally remember as the 19th of September, his words had stuck in his throat, and his chest had constricted as he beheld her. As beautiful and delicate as her namesake flower, 18-year-old Lily Rose had respectfully lowered her eyes and with the slightest inclination of her exquisitely dainty head, she had bewitched him. He continued to stare, stupidly, open mouthed. Her eyes were a mysterious green; slanting in an intoxicatingly oriental manner. Her mouth was a tiny red rosebud, which he immediately wanted to kiss. She lifted her lashes for a micro second and delighted him by blushing when she realised the intensity of his gaze. As she poured his tea, he could smell gardenias.

That, had quite simply, been that.

The young man had courted and won Lily Rose, and in a moment of utter madness reserved for the young and carefree, he had married her only a month later. Lily Rose's family had been honoured and delighted that their eldest daughter had made such a fortuitous marriage and had offered what the young man knew was a lifetime of savings as her dowry. While the young man had no need of his bride's fortune, he knew that to refuse it would be an insult, which would cause a devastating loss of face for her parents. Instead, he accepted it with gratitude and immediately gave it to Lily Rose to spend as she pleased.

Their lives had been almost perfect. The young man's family knew nothing of their son's marriage, which meant that he had to continue with the charade of travelling back to the UK after each trip to Thailand leaving Lily Rose behind. Eventually however, he had convinced his father that with such expansion, the business needed him in Thailand full time. The New Year, saw the young man leave the UK behind and make his home with Lily Rose. Within a year, Lily Rose had given birth to a daughter, another precious jewel of great beauty, named Misumi by her doting parents. *Now* life was perfect.

However, the Gods of fortune, ever cruel, decided that the young man had had his share of happiness, and so plotted to remove it from him, which they did in the most brutal and heinous fashion.

He had not even been there when it happened.

Lily Rose had been out with Misumi while the young man was at work. Shopping for new shoes for their fast growing daughter, who was now three years old, and an almost perfect miniature of her mother, Lily Rose had been momentarily distracted by an Old Man; an Old Man in a wheelchair, she had told him later. The Old Man had stopped her with a whispered plea for help in reaching a garment from a high shelf; *for my granddaughter* he had explained. Lily Rose had smiled her exquisite smile, and with manners born of her good family, she had graciously assisted the Old Man. It took only a minute, but in that minute, their precious child had disappeared, never to be seen again.

The horror of the aftermath would remain with the young man all his life. The guilt he felt at not being there, and the absolute heartbreak of a loss from which his lovely Lily Rose never recovered. He found her six months later, after she had lost all hope of recovering their child. She looked as if she were sleeping, an alabaster doll, still perfect, still so beautiful; all the harsh lines of fear and worry gone from her face in death. An overdose, the doctor had said, such a shame, such a terrible tragedy.

People had come and gone, sympathies had been given, but the young man felt nothing. He was numb and dead inside. It was a loss he could not share with his parents as they had never known his graceful wife, or their angelic child, and now they never would.

Retreating into himself, the young man had gone back to the UK and resigned from the family business. He had thrown himself into the dark and terrible world of missing children; with dozens of trips back to Thailand in a never ending quest to find Misumi. He had eventually discovered a way to continue his search for his daughter and to help others similarly affected by this nightmare. It hadn't been his idea, but had been on the advice of a good friend. Initially, the young man had thought it a joke in poor taste until he realised that his friend was absolutely serious. After some research, which confirmed that he might well be qualified, the young man had approached MI6. Fearing rejection or ridicule, he had told his tale bluntly and without a hint of self-pity; he had then offered his services as an undercover operative in the world of missing children. His knowledge of the country, coupled with his ability to speak the language and his undeniable contacts and ties made him an attractive prospect. The men in shirts had listened, and after much deliberation told him he was "in." There was however, one stipulation; he had to find an ordinary job as a cover.

What could be more ordinary than a social worker?

It seemed like many lifetimes ago for the young man, who despite several promising leads, had never found his lost daughter.

Nicholas Bishop however, had never given up hope.

Chapter 18

Thailand Present Day

Nicholas woke up sweating from the nightmare, which had haunted him for all these years. Sitting bolt upright on the bed, he found he was shaking, and moved quickly to the mini bar where he steadied his nerves with two small overpriced bottles of whiskey. He closed his eyes and allowed the liquid to burn his throat, forcing himself to come back to the present and leave the memory of his, all too familiar, nightmares buried, as he had done for so long. Angrily, he pushed his fingers through his hair and with a grunt, made for the shower where he attempted to wash away the remembrance of it all. It was all so long ago, it almost seemed unreal.

Once showered, Nicholas still felt restless and uneasy. He decided to take a walk, and headed for the busy city streets. As he walked, deep in thought, he failed to notice the woman approaching from his right hand side.

He was therefore startled when he felt a hand on his arm and an enquiring voice asking, "Mr Bishop? Is that you?" Looking up, he was even more surprised to see social worker Diane Foster staring at him with about the same amount of incredulity as he imagined was showing on his own face.

"Ms Foster," he said in complete surprise, "what brings you here?"

Nicholas was not in the habit of knowing the names or faces of many of the social workers in his area. He was too far removed from the front line for that. However, he knew Diane Foster – practically the whole of the UK knew Diane Foster. He was aware that Diane was off sick and still suffering from the impact of Daniel Thompson's death. However, the very last place he had expected to see her was here in Thailand.

Ethan looked questioningly at Diane as she and Nicholas exchanged pleasantries. "This is your boss then?" he asked, interrupting their small talk.

Diane turned back to Ethan and apologised, "Sorry Ethan, yes this is Nicholas Bishop, Director of Social Services in our area. Mr Bishop, may I introduce my partner Ethan Montana. Ethan is a dive instructor and we're here for the next few months. Ethan has a boat and organises diving trips for tourists."

Nicholas and Ethan shook hands before Nicholas excused himself saying, "Good to meet you Mr Montana, and nice to see you recovering Ms Foster. I'm sorry to dash off, but I have to be somewhere else." Then, recalling the trauma Diane had suffered as a social worker in his area, he felt a small stab of guilt and added, "Look, I'm at The Millennium Hilton, why don't you both drop in at say 7 tomorrow evening and we can have a drink." Diane and Ethan glanced at each other and both nodded their agreement and thanks. Nicholas was already walking away as he called, "Right then 7 it is, see you there," and he was gone.

Ethan raised his eyebrow as he whistled softly, "So THAT'S the one and only big shot Nicholas Bishop eh? What's HE doing here Di?"

Diane screwed up her nose at Ethan's appraisal of her boss. "Don't be ungenerous Ethan, Mr Bishop is a brilliant man. I don't really see much of him, but he has a reputation for getting the job done and he's totally dedicated to stamping out child trafficking. He's a bit of a specialist, and no doubt he's here for some sort of conference. I know Glenda used to tell me he often flew out to Thailand to advise their Government. God knows it's got a big enough problem, as we both well know."

Ethan took Diane's hand as they resumed their walk through the bustling streets, "Ah well, I'll let him buy me a drink then. It shouldn't be too arduous a task to go to the Millennium Hilton," he grinned.

Diane punched him good naturedly on his arm, "Ridiculous man," she said without any real conviction. Ethan smiled back at her, but then suddenly stopped dead in his tracks and whipped round to face Diane. "What's up?" she said, somewhat startled at his wide eyed appearance. Ethan gripped Diane's hand, looked around furtively and pulled her off the main street to a standstill.

"Ethan, what on earth"? She began, but he interrupted her, "Diane," he said urgently, "do you trust him?" Diane was at a loss as to what Ethan was talking about,

"Do I trust who?" she asked, bemused by his actions.

Ethan looked exasperated, "Nicholas Bishop of course," he retorted, "who do you think?"

Still not grasping where this conversation was going, Diane continued to look dimly at him as she fumbled for words. "Well, I don't really know him Ethan, I hardly ever see him, I mean, he IS the Director, and Directors don't as a rule consort with minions such as me." Diane could see that this was not the answer Ethan was hoping for, so she pressed on, "Well, I'd have to say I trusted him, yes, why wouldn't I? He's done some great work and is so committed to working against the child traffickers ..." her words tailed off as she finally understood where Ethan was heading. "Oh," she added softly as she ran out of words.

Ethan looked relieved, as Diane caught up with where he was. He nodded, “Yes, precisely, he fights against child trafficking; IF he can be trusted, and it’s a big IF, then he could be just the man we need to talk to about Ronnie and his unsavoury friends. What do you think? It’s a risk, but who else can we turn to?” Diane considered the enormity of their situation. She bit her lip; “Oh God Ethan, what a dilemma, I need caffeine to help me think; come on, let’s go grab a coffee and talk about it.”

Chapter 19

After his discussion with The Old Man, Charn Chai decided to pay a visit to one of the many establishments owned by their Organisation. They would not be expecting him, and he smiled at the thought of the consternation his visit would cause; it was good to keep the proprietors on their toes. As he walked, the busy city centre was alive with the noise, smells and sights of a thriving metropolis. He was in the notorious Phat Phong district of Bangkok, or as the farang (tourists) called it Patpong; it was an assault on his senses. Catering mainly, but not exclusively, to expatriates and tourists, Phat Phong's reputation as a sink hole of depravity was well deserved. A stone's throw from the BTS Sky train Silom line, the area was all too handy for those wishing to pay a discreet visit, or stay longer in one of the many bars and clubs. With establishments catering for every taste, from the gay bars to the high class places with Thai hostesses, whose clientele were limited to Japanese men, the area had something for everyone – that is if you were looking for a good time.

Before 1946, the area was no more than an underdeveloped piece of land with a dirty canal running through it. By the late 60's a few night clubs had developed and it became popular with the US troops who were serving their time in Vietnam. Phat Phong quickly established itself as Bangkok's premier nightlife area, famous for its sexually explicit shows. If you wanted to watch well-trained young women do creative projectile things with ping-pong balls, Phat Phong was the place to go. If Lady Boys were more your thing, that was catered for too. However, though the area offered a cornucopia of debauchery, caution was needed. Many a tourist had been stung with a wildly inflated bar bill, and threatened with physical retribution if it were not paid. While the local police were supposed to assist in such illegal dealings, they rarely did. More often than not, the police were in the pay of the establishments and organised crime gangs, and earned more than enough to look the other way when the farangs were being scammed.

Charn Chai ducked off Silom Road and knocked on a heavy ornate door, which was the side entrance of his destination. The door opened, and Charn Chai enjoyed a moment of satisfaction as he noted the momentary look of panic on the face of the door man.

The man opened the door hastily, clasped his hands together above his head and bowed reverently to Charn Chai, as he entered. "Will you take some tea," he asked politely.

Charn Chai declined with an equally polite shake of his head. "I would speak to Madam upstairs," he instructed the man.

Bowing again, the man answered, "I will advise her at once of your magnificent presence."

There was not a hint of sarcasm in the man's flowery response; Charn Chai was a legend in these parts and there were many who aspired to be like him, or if they were very ambitious, to *be* him, and take his place.

As he waited, a woman approached; she too bowed on recognising him and asked,

"Would you like some tea eminent one?"

"Thank you Madam, I have already been offered tea, which alas I must decline on this occasion."

The woman lowered her eyes respectfully, "Then, may I be so honoured as to make arrangements for you to meet one of our girls?" The woman turned and softly clapped her hands. As if by magic, girls and women, aged from about 16 up to around 25 materialised. Mainly Thai, but with European, Cambodian and some Chinese girls in the group, they all had the same aura of hopelessness about them, despite their brightly painted smiles. While prostitution was technically illegal in Thailand, it was tolerated, and the Organisation, to which Charn Chai belonged, took full advantage of the laxity in enforcing this particular law.

Charn Chai regarded the Madam, who was a Thai woman of around 28, and undoubtedly a past hostess of this self-same place. Now past her prime, she was in charge of the domain, in which, she had sold her body too many times to recall. Small, neat and immaculately turned out, he noted that she was a credit to the establishment and would be praised when he reported back to The Old Man.

"I am not here for my own pleasure Madam, but to speak with Madam upstairs." The woman clapped again and the girls and women melted back into the shadows to await the next punter, who would undoubtedly have more use for them than Charn Chai.

"Another time perhaps," she said softly as she too blended away like an ethereal being.

The door man returned and led Charn Chai up the dimly lit flight of stairs to the first floor. The place smelled of patchouli incense and sex and was a totally different world to the one downstairs. This was where the *real* money was made. The Madam who ran things up here was a hard faced Thai woman in her 40's called Pakpow; aptly named thought Charn Chai wryly to himself. Chosen not for her looks, but for her iron hand in running another illegal operation, but one where penalties for indiscretion were far more punishing. She was harsh, unforgiving and brooked no nonsense from any of the children in her care, for children is what they were.

The girls were lined up along the corridor waiting for clients; with ages which ranged from 11 to 15, many had been sold into what amounted to a life of slavery simply because their parents were too poor to keep them. Maybe they had a doctor's bill they could not pay, maybe a debt they owed to a neighbour. The Old Man had tentacles, which reached far into the poorest of communities; his contacts sent whispers to him of this family and that, all of whom had debts they could not hope to pay. The Old Man would generously step in to help these poor families, paying their debts, and telling them that the only thing he asked was that their daughter be allowed to come and work in his house as a servant. With promises of an education and a good life, these simple farming families, were trusting and grateful. Sending the girls away to what they thought was a better life, they had no idea that they would never see them again. They did not realise that their daughter's lives were effectively over and now belonged to The Old Man.

There were others here too who were lost children, taken from their families here in Thailand, or from families who came on holiday and entered into a nightmare. High risk children like Darcie Taylor, who would never stand in a line as these girls did, but who would be kept hidden away, going only to the very highest bidders, and then disappearing without a trace once they had served their purpose.

All these young girls could earn more money in a single night than some of the older women downstairs, for young flesh was what the depraved tourists and locals alike demanded. On seeing Charn Chai, the girls immediately pasted smiles onto their painted faces, smiles that only ran skin deep. None reached the eyes or came from the soul. Charn Chai noted with approval that all the girls had been tattooed on their left shoulder with the insignia of their Organisation - a tattoo of a tiny pair of handcuffs; indicative of their life of captivity and slavery. The girls were all too thin; a combination of a lack of food, plus their almost non-stop expenditure of nervous and physical energy. They were given a cocktail of drugs to maximise their waking hours and performance. Depending on their age, each of the girls had a quota to meet, and on a typical night, might be expected to service 30 or more men. It was an impossible task and as a result, their life expectancy was not a long one. All would be discarded in some way or another before they left their teens. Some would succumb to disease or violence at the hands of the men they served, some would die from botched abortions, and some would simply be thrown out onto the streets to fend for themselves.

Madam was walking up and down the line of girls, muttering complaints as she went, prodding one here and poking another there. One girl was slapped hard across the cheek for no reason Charn Chai could discern. She did not flinch, but stood blank faced, lost in her own private world of misery. From somewhere in a distant room, Charn Chai heard a scream. It died away quickly, but Madam's eyes narrowed on hearing it, and he knew that the unfortunate girl who uttered it would meet with swift and merciless retribution when her client had left.

Madam bowed stiffly to Charn Chai. "It goes well?" he asked.

Madam made a gesture with her hands as she spoke, "I have two new girls," she said, "they are ill-disciplined and headstrong; peasants from ignorant farming stock. They will have to be taught in our ways and quickly; they must accept their destinies and submit to my will or there will be serious consequences."

Charn Chai listened with interest and without emotion. He felt no sympathy for any of the girls, like Madam said, it was their destiny and they either had to work, or the consequences would indeed be severe. The girls themselves would feel Madam's wrath, but their families would also be made to suffer if they did not comply.

"Where are these girls?" demanded Charn Chai.

Madam shrugged, "One is in there screaming, and will be dealt with when she comes out again, and one is in the cellar thinking about her poor attitude to work."

"Take me to her," he instructed.

Madam clicked her fingers and another stern faced woman appeared, "Watch them," she snapped, "I am taking our revered guest downstairs." She hesitated, "And when the new girl comes out of that room, bring her straight to me, I will teach her the value of screaming when she is supposed to be working."

The woman nodded grimly, enjoying the unexpected power afforded to her by Madam, even for a short while. She busied herself immediately in bullying the line of girls, delivering scathing remarks accompanied by spiteful nips and slaps.

Charn Chai followed Madam down into a damp cold cellar. Stepping on rubbish as he went, he spoke softly but with meaning as he said, "I do not expect my feet to step on garbage when I visit one of our establishments."

Madam's back stiffened at the rebuke, "Apologies excellence, it will be rectified swiftly and not repeated." Madam seethed inwardly and made plans as to who she could punish for this disgrace.

"Where is the girl?" asked Charn Chai. Madam indicated with a nod of her head,

"She is in there; as I explained, she is thinking about her poor attitude." Charn Chai saw a wooden box, which resembled a large wardrobe; it measured 5 feet high and 4 feet wide and made an effective prison Madam took the heavy set of keys, which jangled at her waist and selecting one, opened the box.

"Stand up slut, you have an important visitor," she ordered. Inside the box, was a girl, who Charn Chai estimated to be about 10 years of age. She was pitifully thin and wore only a stained cotton shift dress. As she struggled to her feet, he noticed that her face was puffy with tears and fresh bruises; her arms also bore witness to Madam's particular brand of justice and her bare feet were cracked and raw.

Charn Chai regarded her as he would produce at the market. "Why is she so filthy?" he demanded, "No client wants a girl looking like a neglected rag doll, get her cleaned up."

Madam looked at the floor in embarrassment, she was not accustomed to being on the receiving end of criticism. "At once excellence," she fawned, anxious to redeem herself, "but she has been particularly wilful and has had to spend many hours in here to adjust her thinking."

Charn Chai reached out and grabbed the terrified child by the front of her dress; leaning in close he spoke to her. "Do you love your family?" he asked seductively. The child shook with fear and a spurt of urine shot down her leg as her bladder gave way. Charn Chai exclaimed in disgust and shook the child hard. "Answer me daughter of a whore, do you love your family?" The child nodded, but could not speak, such was her terror. "Then, you had better begin to work for your living or they will suffer in your place. Do you understand me?" The child managed to nod again, her legs giving way under this new onslaught of abuse. Charn Chai continued, "You will work, or you will starve here; is that clear? You are here because your family owe a debt, one which they agreed you will work to pay. Do you wish to disgrace them by not being an obedient daughter? DO YOU" he added in a shout. The child gave a wail and fell at his feet. He delivered a kick, "Get up," he ordered harshly, "get up and decide; you will work or you will starve and your family will suffer also."

Turning to Madam he issued more orders, "Get her clean and put her back to work and make sure she is tattooed this week," he added noting that the girl's shoulder was devoid of the Organisation's insignia. "She is not to be fed until she has met her quota." Madam's eyes gleamed, this was music to her sadistic ears. As she bent down to take hold of the unfortunate child, the other woman appeared from upstairs; with her was another girl, not much older than the one who still grovelled in terror on the floor.

"Here is our screamer," said the woman with satisfaction, as if she had caught a thief red-handed and not a screaming child who was being raped by a grown man.

"Leave her," said Madam crisply, "I will deal with her, you return to the others."

The woman turned to go, adding without sympathy, "She is bleeding again."

Madam sighed as if this was a huge inconvenience. With a lightning fast movement, she punched the girl hard in the chest. There was a noise as the breath went out of her and she doubled over clutching her injured chest.

"Why must you scream?" demanded Madam, "You have been told and told and yet you continue to disobey. Do you know who THIS is?" she said indicating Charn Chai. "He is your patron and is most displeased to visit here and find ignorant and disrespectful girls like you making trouble. What have you to say? You disgrace us all," Madam panted with the effort of her anger, Charn Chai said nothing.

The girl was clearly in some pain; blood seeped down her legs in rivulets, like scarlet tears, evidencing her recent brutal treatment at the hands of some vile individual. Madam clucked in annoyance, "Get on the bed," she ordered and the girl responded as if on automatic pilot. Climbing onto a metal framed bed, it was obvious to Charn Chai that it was not the first time she had been up there.

The child began to weep pitifully, and found her voice. "Please Madam," she begged in a whisper, "I will be alright and I promise not to scream anymore," Madam ignored her pleas and continued her preparations, "I have heard it all before," she said disinterestedly, "now lie back and be still." Turning to Charn Chai, Madam spoke, "I must stitch her again," she said apologetically, "it should not take long."

When the needle bit into her softest flesh, the child broke her promise and screamed before the pain overwhelmed her and she passed into blissful darkness.

Chapter 20

Down in the old part of the town, Robyn and her family took in the sights and sounds. The music from the live band was loud, and Robyn could feel the beat resonating right into the core of her being. Cupping her hands around her mouth, she spoke to Claude, "It's a good band, but very loud," she said above the noise. Claude nodded in response and looked around for the children. Fabien was stood close by, watching a group of local boys dancing in the street. He was silently impressed and knew he could never attempt such a thing. For one, he was no dancer, but more than that, he did not have the confidence to act in such a way in public. His little sister on the other hand was in her element. Angelique had run over to where the boys were dancing and was desperate to join in.

Claude followed quickly and took her by the hand with a mild admonishment, "Cherie," he warned, "do not run off like that, it is very busy here, and I need to know where you are at all times." Angelique's hand squirmed in his as she tried to liberate herself. Claude swept his wilful daughter up into his arms and looked directly at her. "Angelique, I am quite serious," he said more sternly this time, "do not run off again. You must stay where maman or I can see you, do you understand?"

Angelique's bottom lip trembled; she was not accustomed to her papa being stern with her. He could usually be relied upon as an ally. She assumed a downcast expression, "Yes papa, I understand," she said dutifully, "I will stay where you or maman can see me."

"See that you do," said Claude less fiercely as he set her down, hiding a smile, which rose unbidden to his lips. Claude knew that Angelique required a firm hand at times, in order to keep her safe, but he could not help his feelings for her. He loved her free spirit and often cheered her on in her efforts to be independent, but he knew he had to keep her safe and on this occasion, she could not be permitted to wander so freely.

He stood and watched as Angelique joined the boys, and even above the noise of the music, he could hear her piping tones, as she took control, "Like this," she shouted to the oldest boy, "you're doing it all wrong, you should dance like this," she bossed. Claude joined the laughter as he watched the boy's surprised expressions at the firebrand in their midst. They shrugged, and ignored her, carrying on with their own routine, much to the chagrin of Ms Berlioz. Undeterred, she continued to dance, mimicking the moves the boys' made, and slowly worming her way into the group. Eventually, the boys laughingly accepted her, and Claude knew without any doubt that his daughter would grow up to be a leader, not a follower. *She just needs channelling in the right direction*, he mused to himself as he watched her ongoing efforts to take charge of the group.

Suddenly, Claude's thoughts were interrupted by a noise so loud; it carried above the rock and roll number being belted out by the band. As he turned to see what the commotion was, he distractedly, recognised the song as Johnny B Goode. Claude's thoughts of music were however short-lived as without any warning, a fountain of fire shot up into the night sky, illuminating the scene on the ground. Angelique's silhouette as she danced with the boys shimmered momentarily against the dramatically incandescent backdrop of flames. The scene reminded

Claude of a still from an old movie he had once seen about Rome burning. The children were shocked into a frozen tableau and Claude desperately yelled to Angelique, but his voice was lost; snatched away in a melee of noise and confusion.

With no clue as to what had occurred, Claude ran towards his daughter, while looking wildly around at the unfolding drama in an effort to locate the rest of his family. There was pandemonium as people screamed and scattered in all directions.

Claude's efforts to reach Angelique were abruptly thwarted as his vision was filled with the horrific spectacle of a person on fire. Claude was unable to determine if it was a man or a woman, but stood transfixed as they ran past him, their arms flailing silently as they ran, with their hair ablaze. Someone screamed again, and the sound jolted Claude into action. Without another thought, he ran at the person and rugby tackled them to the ground, rolling them over and over in the dust and beating at the flames with his bare hands. He felt no pain, but was acting on instinct and adrenaline. He pulled at his sweater which had been tied around his waist, and wrapped it around the person's head extinguishing the flames. Somewhere in the distance, he could hear sirens, trumpeting their arrival, "We're coming," they seemed to say, "hold on, we're coming," though Claude realised that for this person, it was a false hope.

He felt the person under him convulse, and then relax. Claude immediately rolled them over and felt for a pulse. He found none and closed his eyes in anguish as he realised that the person, who had been a man, had died from his appalling injuries. It had been less than two minutes since the explosion. Claude sat on the ground in total shock, and could not speak. His ears were ringing from the force of the blast, but slowly, he became aware of someone talking to him, but their voice seemed far away and hollow.

He looked up to see the familiar and worried face of his beloved wife. She was shaking his shoulder and talking to him, "Claude, oh God Claude, are you alright?" she asked, her voice awash with anxiety and concern. "He's dead," was all he could manage.

Robyn took in the situation in an instant and drew a sharp breath. "Right," she said decisively, "come on Claude, we must find a medic and tell them what happened here. You can do nothing more for this person Cherie, come on, we need to go, there may still be danger."

Claude allowed himself to be led away, but suddenly stopped short, "Where are the children?" he demanded, his voice hoarse with emotion. Robyn looked around her and immediately saw the familiar sight of their son Fabien who was running towards them in panic.

"It's okay son," she soothed, "papa is alright, do not be alarmed." Fabien was crying and trying to say something, Robyn put her arms around him and tried to calm him. Fabien was unlike Angelique, he was sensitive, gentle, and tender hearted. This incident would have upset him greatly.

Robyn attempted to stroke his hair, but Fabien struggled free of her, "Maman," he began, but Robyn interrupted him, "shh my love, it's going to be alright, Papa is not hurt and we will soon all be back at the hotel together."

Fabien's face was a mask of fear and horror combined, he opened and closed his mouth, and it was clear he was struggling for words.

Claude realised that this was more than a reaction to the explosion and stepped forwards, "Fabien," he said firmly, struggling to master his own emotions, "son what is it?" On hearing his papa's voice, Fabien seemed to lose what little self-control he had left.

He collapsed into his father's arms and sobbed. "Papa, oh Papa, Angelique, it is Angelique." At this moment, both parents realised with a shock that while it was now probably less than three minutes since the explosion, neither of them had any idea where Angelique was.

"Don't worry son, we will go and get your sister right now," said Claude starting off in the direction of the street dancing, where he had left Angelique, not more than a minute or two ago. "She was dancing with the other children and I am sure she is still there," he said with more conviction than he felt. The explosion and ensuing fire had been extreme and very dramatic and would have startled even the usually stoic Angelique. Fabien continued to weep and was trying again to talk to his parents. This time, it was Robyn who comforted him as Claude strode ahead the 200 yards to where the dancing had been going on. He had to push his way through the crowds of people, who were still in a state of total panic. Screams continued to ring out through the night, and in some places, bodies lay on the ground, seriously injured, or obviously beyond help.

"Cherie, please be calm, everything is okay," Robyn urged. She was becoming more and more worried about her son's frantic presentation. He was usually such a calm and sensible boy.

They caught up with Claude who was bellowing Angelique's name into the crowds of people. He began to catch people by the arm and demand if they had seen a little girl with long blonde hair. However, the people were far too focused on their own friends and relatives to concern themselves with others. The fire had not yet been brought under control, as the first on the scene was an ambulance rather than the fire brigade.

"Claude, where is she?" asked Robyn as she joined him.

"She can't be far," Claude assured her, "she was just here, only minutes ago," he stated as he continued to shout Angelique's name.

Fabien broke away from his mother's hold on him and ran to his father, grabbing his arm. "What is it son? Asked Claude distractedly, "what's the matter?"

Fabien regained some composure, and took a deep breath. "This is what I am trying to tell you Papa, Angelique is gone. I saw a woman take her hand and lead her away, Papa, someone has taken my sister."

Chapter 21

Ruang Sak Yunram was in his most favourite restaurant in Bangkok eating his most favourite dish of Tom Yam Goong soup. He savoured the delicious blend of lemongrass, chilli and lime juice, which was enhanced by fish sauce and large juicy prawns and straw mushrooms. Slurping it into his mouth with chopsticks, Ruang Sak sighed with deep pleasure and congratulated himself on yet another successful outcome. He had anticipated that the old square would provide him with ideal cover for his operation, and, once again, he had been right. He allowed himself a moment of pride; was he not the best in his field? No one could doubt it. Ruang Sak knew the square well of course, but when he had been advised that there would be live music and crowds of people, specifically tourists, he knew he could not fail. He knew from experience that when on holiday, people let their guard down. They drank too much, and relaxed – allowing their children far more freedom than they would ever allow at home. This was always a grave error if Ruang Sak Yunram was around.

He had a target already in mind; a child with hair so blonde as to be almost white. Young and pretty and clearly on holiday with her family; she made an ideal target in Ruang Sak's heinous game and he knew she would command the highest possible price. He had spotted the child earlier in the day on the beach in the south, and his mouth had almost watered at the sight of her; there was no doubt, he had to have her and he had immediately given orders that the family be followed and their whereabouts relayed to him. He had been delighted when told that the family were staying right here in Bangkok, where he himself lived. He had thought they might be staying in the area he had seen them, close to Pattaya. This was excellent news, as the other child had been taken from that area, and it would have been a grave risk to attempt another abduction from the same location.

Hurrying back to Bangkok, the Old Man had been unobserved by the crowds last night, no one took any notice of an old man any more, and an old man in a wheelchair was almost invisible. He had with him, his trusted companion masquerading as a nurse, as well as one of his six sons who would one day take over his sordid little business. The "nurse" was a pretty little thing by the name of Suzy Meesang; at 23 years old, she was of course, past her prime, but Ruang Sak still had a use for her. Suzy had been one of his conquests from long ago, before he had started to target European children, who were of much higher value than local children. The men, and occasionally, the women, whose demands kept Ruang Sak in business grew more exacting by the week, and Ruang Sak had adjusted his business accordingly, taking only those children he knew would bring the best possible prices. After all, his was a world of risk taking, and if he was going to take a risk, he may as well be well paid for it.

No one bothered to look for the Suzy Meesang's of this world, but they looked very hard indeed for the Darcie Taylor's, which meant that Ruang Sak had to pay close attention to every detail. He trusted no one, not even those who considered themselves his most dependable companions. He did not even trust his sons, knowing that they were greedy to take the reins of this most lucrative business as soon as they could wrest it from his hands. However, Ruang Sak was not quite ready to hand over power of his empire just yet. He craved another white haired little girl, and now he had her in his sights, he was ready again for the chase.

He could not have planned the evening any better if he had paid for the diversion of the explosion. It was a heaven sent opportunity – a gas canister from one of the many food stalls exploding and causing a serious fire, which resulted in the loss of two lives and the grievous injury of many more citizens. Ruang Sak however, gave thanks for the incident as it had provided the perfect cover for him to make his move. He had been sitting patiently awaiting his moment, when the explosion occurred. Quickly, with the instincts of the hunter, he had signalled to Suzy to act. Smoothly and seamlessly, she had approached the group of children whose dancing had been arrested by the sound of the blast. Singling out the girl, Suzy had whispered her lies into the child's unsuspecting ear, and as all children do, the child had innocently and trustingly acquiesced and followed without question.

The Mover had been waiting nearby in the van and the child was now in a safe house awaiting her next move. Firstly, however, Ruang Sak had to negotiate Darcie Taylor's move, or should he say Holly Bailey. The stupid and incompetent Ruby Wong had ruined the child's looks, so it was proving more difficult to gain the high price he had originally been asking. Ruby Wong had been punished for her stupidity, and Ruang Sak was confident there would be no repeat of such behaviour. A visit had been undertaken to her family, and one of Ruby's younger sisters had paid a high price for Ruby's unasked for blunder. Ruby had been presented with a photograph of her sister following the assault; the sight of her sister, lying naked and weeping had been enough to assure her obedience for the foreseeable future at least. If not, there were plenty more Ruby Wong's to be had. Yes, thought Ruang Sak, I have much to do before I am ready to step down, and my sons had better not forget that.

***

Almost 6000 miles away and unaware of the horrors taking place in Thailand, Melanie sat alone in her kitchen. It had gone dark over an hour ago, but Melanie was oblivious to this fact. She sat staring at the floor, clutching a cup of tea, which had long gone cold, trying to make sense of what she had seen in Nicholas' study. Shaking her head, she sighed, and tried to force her mind to focus on the disturbing information she had uncovered. She wished with all her heart that she could turn back time. If so, she would never have tossed that tea towel into the door, which allowed her access to Nicholas' study. She would not have pried into a world, which she now realised, she had lived in blissful ignorance of ... until now.

***

Robyn and Claude Berlioz were completely exhausted. Like their unfortunate counterparts, the Taylors, they had been subjected to the harsh reality of the Thai justice system. In the police station, which only a few days ago had seen the Taylors pouring out their story, the Berlioz family were now doing the same. Claude was like a man in a trance. The trauma of his daughter's disappearance, coupled with the death of the man he had tried in vain to help had rendered him almost mute.

Robyn on the other hand, with the advantage of speaking the language and the strength of maternal ferocity was proving to be an incredible force to be reckoned with. She had given her story umpteen times to the police officers and had reached a point of exasperation and anger. "I am NOT repeating myself again," she had said loudly when asked for her account of what had happened for the fourth time. "You should be out there looking for Angelique, can't you people see there must be a connection? First one child, and now our daughter. For God's sake WAKE UP will you, this is an organised thing. People are taking children and it's happening right here in your own back yard."

The officer in question had pursed his lips in disapproval of this loud and coarse foreigner. Thai women were so much more compliant and well mannered. "Madam," he said drawing himself up to his full five feet four inches of height, "we are looking into the possibility that your daughter is simply lost in the aftermath of the terrible tragedy, which occurred last night. Your son insists that your daughter was taken by a woman dressed as a nurse. Now I ask you, does that sound like a suspicious activity? I am of the view that this woman was indeed a nurse, and took your child to a place of safety, and that in time, she will be located. Until then, I must ask you to calm yourself and desist from making wild accusations about organised child abductions."

Robyn used every scrap of will power she had not to punch the pompous shrimp of a man right in the face.

She looked him in the eye, "Then, we can go?" she asked with absolute determination, which brooked no argument.

The man looked offended again, "Yes" he said reluctantly, "you can go." Robyn was out of the door in seconds, and had located Claude and Fabien in minutes.

"We can go," she said bluntly, "they're treating it as non-suspicious, they're convinced someone was genuinely trying to help Angelique, and that she will turn up. I don't buy it. Come on, we have a lot to do."

Claude allowed himself to be led back to the hotel by his wife. He had no fight in him; depression had fallen on him like a cloud and all he wanted to do was close his eyes and sleep. Fabien was suffering too; overwhelmed with misplaced guilt, he was haunted by the sight of his sister being led away by a woman dressed as a nurse. Robyn was the strong one, she knew she had to be. If she allowed herself to give in to her deepest fears regarding what may have befallen her precious child, she knew she would not endure. For the sake of Angelique, she had to stay strong.

The Taylor family were still in Bangkok along with their family liaison officer Elspeth Duncan. Robyn had asked to see them, and in a hugely emotional meeting, which both sets of parents refused to allow to be televised, they came together in shared misery. The women clung to each other, the men shook hands and sat looking withdrawn and angry. Fabien and little Jack were over in a corner playing quietly together, Fabien glad of the distraction of a younger child to take his mind away from his own personal nightmare, even for an hour.

During the discussions, Verity Taylor had told the Berlioz family about their meeting with Nicholas Bishop.

"He's really good you know," opined Verity, "and I do believe that sadly, he will affirm your fears about Angelique having been abducted. It's not for us to say any more other than Mr Bishop has a world of experience and I urge you to meet with him."

Robyn took all the information in, "Thank you," she told Verity with one last hug, "I believe we will."

***

Charn Chai sat cross legged in the living room of his opulent home. Bought with the ill-gotten gains of his life of depravity, the house was a magnificent villa, carefully screened from prying eyes by the large hedge around it, not to mention the high security measures, which were always in place. Charn Chai had just come from yet another meeting with The Old Man, and was now contemplating his next move. The Old Man had been clear in his instructions; the Bailey's could no longer be trusted, and the Taylor girl was to be moved quickly and The Bailey's were to be "retired." However, it was less than a week since she had been taken, and Darcie was still considered too hot to handle by most of Charn Chai's regular contacts. He frowned in concentration as he applied his sharp mind to the problem. He would not return her to Ruby Wong's incompetent care, neither would he risk bringing her to his own home, though he had, on occasion, been forced to bring children here in certain circumstances. Darcie Taylor was still headline news; moving her would be a test of all his skills and cunning. He smiled a self-satisfied smile; he was not called The Mover for nothing. No one else could be trusted with this delicate task; it was up to him.

After some quiet meditation, Charn Chai knew he had the answer; the girl would have to go to one of their most trusted operatives. Apart from himself, who was naturally, the best in the field, there was a woman who was now around the age of 37 years. With looks bestowed upon her by her beautiful but long dead Thai mother, and brains from her long departed European father, the woman's real name had been lost in time. Known only as Shakiya, the woman had proved invaluable over the many years he had known her. Shakiya lived alone now in a small but comfortable house bestowed upon her by the surprising benevolence of The Old Man, who seemed to have a soft spot for her. Charn Chai had heard through the grapevine that she had been one of his first conquests, but The Old Man never talked about it and Charn Chai did not ask. Retired from her lifelong role as one of The Old Man's sex slaves, Shakiya seemed to have accepted her retirement with remarkable gratitude and grace. However, her usefulness was still in occasional demand as a carer for high value packages in challenging situations.

Today was Sunday; too quiet a day to blend in easily. He was due to visit the Baileys anyway on Wednesday, to check up on the girl, and on them. Maybe Wednesday would do ... maybe. He dug his latest burn phone from his pocket and dialled Shakiya's number.

Shakiya had been about to get into a deep hot bath when her phone rang. She froze at the sound as she always did, and felt the familiar slide of apprehension in her stomach. *What now?* She asked herself wearily, *what do they want of me this time*? Picking up the phone, she said nothing, but listened intently to the terse instructions, which were delivered without preamble in less than a minute.

Once clear of her role, she spoke only to confirm that she had understood, and hung up with a sigh. Shakiya's second name, like her birth name, was lost forever; she liked to call herself Shakiya Wattana, though she knew that this was not her real name. Everyone simply called her Shakiya. With a dubious reputation in her younger days of being one of the highest paid whores in Bangkok's old quarter, Shakiya could remember nothing else but a life spent in the sexual servitude of men. From as far back as she could recall, The Old Man had been in her life. Her mouth twisted upwards without mirth as she recalled how she naively used to think he was her grandfather; ha, what kind of a grandfather did those kind of things to a child? More to the point, what kind of human being allowed other people to do the things, which Shakiya had been subjected to, and demanded a cash payment for it? Returning to her bath, Shakiya hesitated before getting into the water, studying her reflection in the full length bathroom mirror instead. She considered her ageing frame without emotion, knowing that her once greatest asset had also been the prison, from which she had never managed to escape. The body, which had been so sought after by a lost count of groping hands, had sealed her own fate.

Shakiya was a woman without a history, other than the one she had been given, and the other scant bits she could remember in the vague and distant past. Her earliest memory was of crying bitterly and being comforted by a woman who was not her mother. She remembered The Old Man in his wheelchair visiting her and crooning over her. The rest of her memories concerning The Old Man were better forgotten. As she got older and asked questions, Shakiya was told without sympathy that her mother had died at the hands of her father, who had fled the country after committing the crime, abandoning three-year-old Shakiya to her fate. She was told that The Old Man, in his kindness had taken her in and given her a home, a home for which she ought to be grateful. Shakiya doubted that the word grateful had ever been used so inaccurately. Oh they had their "gratitude" out of her alright, and the older she got, the more gratitude it seemed was required.

At only 12 years old, Shakiya had been expected to work in one of The Old Man's many whore houses, entertaining visiting tourists who came to the country for sexual amusement, which was provided in spades by The Old Man and his Organisation. Shakiya knew that many of the girls had been taken from their real families, and forced into this shameful existence. Shakiyak knew nothing else; escape was a futile hope, and she had long ago resigned herself to the bald facts of her pitiful life; she would never escape The Old Man's clutches, many had tried and had met with his terrible form of justice. The one redeeming thing in her favour was that she seemed to be The Old Man's favourite, for reasons she could never fathom. This appeared to have saved her from being put to work on the streets, and eventually saw her run her own upmarket brothel; an esteemed madam with girls working under her eye. She had tried in vain to liberate some of the younger victims, to no avail. She was watched, they were all watched; it would never end.

Shakiya studied her face; yes, she had once been a great beauty with large brown eyes, hair as black and smooth as the sheets where she had been forced to perform again and again. A pleasingly small nose and perfect white teeth, which never smiled. Though showing the inevitable signs of aging, she knew she was still good to look at, though she had outlived her usefulness as a sex worker. Her value now, and her survival, was based on her ongoing obedience to The Old Man and his occasional demands that she provides a safe house for some unfortunate child, who Shakiya knew only too well was destined to relive the life she had lived. Worn down, and with a lifetime, where obedience was the norm, Shakiya continued to acquiesce to The Old Man's requirements, knowing that to refuse would mean certain death. However; downtrodden as she might be, Shakiya was a survivor, and still held a flicker of hope in her heart. *One day,* she thought to herself, *one day, I will leave this all behind.* Allowing herself at last to sink into the bath, which was growing cold, Shakiya lay emotionless and stared at the high ceiling, hiding her hope like a precious jewel, safely out of sight, in a place where no one could steal it from her. She sighed deeply and refused to cry. She had promised herself never to cry again, when, at only 7 years old, an English tourist, sweating from nerves and fear of discovery, had bid the highest price for her virginity. The searing pain of that memory, both physical and emotional threatened to bury her, and she shook her head to rid her mind of it. "NO," she declared aloud, "I will not cry, never again," and she set about scrubbing herself, a little more harshly than was necessary.

Chapter 22

Angelique sat up and considered her surroundings. Her head reeled from the events of the previous evening. She had been dancing, but then had come the explosion, the noise, fear, blood and panic. She recalled the woman who had appeared out of the chaos; her voice soothing, reassuring; promising Angelique that she was taking her to her mummy and daddy. Angelique had followed of course; complicit, trusting, betrayed. Once she realised the truth, she had fussed and shouted, loud and long, but to no avail. The woman, who had appeared so kind and caring had silenced her with a hiss and a raised hand. Angelique was thunderstruck. No one in all her short life had ever hit her, and the shock of the threat of it was enough to render her silent ... for now.

Unaccustomed as she was to being ignored, Angelique's silence did not last for long. Jumping off the stained bed, she ran to the locked door, lifted her considerable voice and shouted, "Maman, Papa, Fabien, where are you?"

Almost immediately, the door was unlocked and flung open; the woman occupying the space stood, eyes wide in disbelief, "Are you crazy?" she demanded, "Do you WANT to be in trouble?"

Angelique tilted her head on one side and answered with all the honesty of her five years, "No, I do not wish to be in trouble, I wish to be with my maman and my papa and brother, NOT here with you." The woman nodded, her mind racing; this little firebrand was quite different to the crying, hopeless children who usually passed through her hands. She pursed her lips to avoid smiling. This one might, just might, have what it would take to survive what lay ahead of her.

Shrugging away any personal feelings of sympathy, which she knew were futile, Suzy Meesang fixed Angelique with a glare, "Well little one; that is not possible at the moment. We are looking for your maman and the rest of your family, but alas, it would seem they were lost in the explosion."

Emotion flitted briefly across Angelique's face; "Lost? Like no one can find them you mean?" she asked in heart-breaking innocence. "Well, I can help, I know where we were staying, the Hotel Plaza, that is where you will find them I am sure. Please can you ring up and tell them I am here and then they can come and get me?" she finished as bravely as she could.

Suzy held her breath to maintain control as she looked down at the pleading little face. How much longer could she do this? Suzy knew only too well what this child was experiencing. Having been snatched from a supermarket many years ago when her mother's attention was diverted by an Old Man in a wheelchair asking for assistance. An Old Man she now knew all too well; her life had been one long road of misery in which she replicated the sins visited on her and subjected other children to the same horrors. Oh she knew she had no choice; that had been made perfectly clear, but it did nothing to assuage her conscience. The Old Man had threatened not only her life, but that of her parents and younger siblings. Her compliance had been easily bought, and Suzy wondered for a moment, if her mother still looked for her. It was a lifetime ago and so far away, for The Old Man spread his nets widely, and who would ever think to look for her so many hundreds of miles from her original home. No one it would seem.

In a rare show of affection Suzy reached out her hand and cupped Angelique's face under her chin. "You have to forget them little one," she said with a heavy heart, "they are gone forever." Then, closing her eyes to the lie and to the devastation, which she could not bear to see spreading across the child's face, she left the room leaving Angelique to face the horror of desolation alone.

***

Rose Bailey twisted her hands together, unable to quell the nerves she was feeling. Smiling reassuringly at Darcie, she spoke with forced brightness, "Well pet, it's a fine thing that we can go out today isn't it?" Darcie regarded her with eyes that were no more than sunken hollows, dead and lifeless. Not even the mention of a totally unexpected day out could lift the child from the pit of misery she was living in. She shrugged her thin shoulders and returned her gaze to the floor. Rose bit her lip and whispered under her breath, "Not long now pet, not long." From the other room, she heard the sound of her husband as he packed the last remaining things. "Hurry William," she called, you know that the Consulate closes at twelve on a Tuesday."

William appeared looking flustered and not at all at ease with what they were about to do. Lowering his voice to avoid Darcie overhearing, he spoke urgently to Rose. "Are you sure we can pull this off?" Rose levelled him with steel in her eyes, "We have to do it today William, you know who is due to visit tomorrow," she reminded him, leaving it unsaid. William nodded, Charn Chai was due to call in to check on them and Darcie tomorrow. They had to act on their plan today but after so long in hiding away from the world, it seemed an almost impossible task, even to walk out of the front door and into the awaiting taxi. Swallowing hard against his anxiety, William took one last look around the place, which had been home for the past few months; whatever the outcome today, he knew they would never return here. "Ready?" he asked as he held out his hand to Rose, "Come on my dear, let's put this to rights."

As they walked to the waiting taxi, William noticed that the driver was speaking on the phone. He hesitated, all his senses on alert. The driver looked out of the window to see the couple and the child. He smiled with a mouth full of bad teeth and called to them, "Next fare, hurry please, I got another fare."

William exhaled, that was all it was. The man had taken a call about his next pick up. Opening the back door for Rose and Darcie to get in, William sat beside the driver, and with a cursory nod said, "British Consulate please," and they were off. Sinking back into their respective seats, neither Rose nor William noticed the self-satisfied smile on the face of the driver as he considered the handsome reward he would receive for such priceless information. The Old Man could be so very generous when the need arose.

***

Charn Chai was not a man who was easily surprised, neither was he one to overreact. However, at this precise moment, his heart was pounding and he had broken out in a sweat as he gripped the phone tightly and listened to The Old Man's quavering voice repeat what he had already said, but what Charn Chai's ears refused to accept. The Old Man had it on good authority that the Bailey's had taken Darcie in a taxi and were heading for the British Consulate in Pattaya. This was a disaster on a magnificent scale and Charn Chai knew he had to act faster than he had ever done before in his life. Despite the listening devices in the Bailey home, Charn Chai had not been in his home to replay any discussions, which had taken place most recently. He was now paying the price for his absence.

Speaking tersely now to The Old Man, and regaining control of his treacherous emotions, Charn Chai hung up and immediately called another number, one he did not call very often.

The man who answered his call was softly spoken, which belied the violent nature of his profession. He listened without comment to Charn Chai's predicament, before answering. "It can be done," he said without ceremony, "but given the short notice and the risks involved, it will cost you dearly my old friend."

Charn Chai's face grimaced in distaste, "The cost is immaterial," he snapped, "just get it done and leave no trace." There was a pause of no more than a heartbeat,

"Have I ever left a trace?" the voice at the other end of the phone demanded with a hint of offence, and with that, he hung up. Charn Chai knew that there was nothing he could do but wait, and he was not accustomed to waiting.

***

The taxi carrying Rose, William and Darcie was caught up in an horrendous traffic jam, common to the area. William's anxiety was at an all-time high, and for the third time, he asked the driver if he could take them by a different route. The man simply shrugged his shoulders and said nothing. William neither liked nor trusted the man; he had shifty eyes and a knowing smirk on his face. William turned to Rose and Darcie in the back seat and saw that they were both white faced with stress and fear.

The sound of the man's phone ringing made them all jump. He spoke in Thai, so neither William, nor Rose understood the content of the brief conversation. However, immediately after he hung up, the man turned to William with a thoroughly ingratiating smile and declared, "I take you another way," and with that, swung the car hard left, and began to wind his way through the back streets of the City.

In the back seat, Rose felt a cold hand of unease grip her heart. "William," she said quietly, hoping the man could not hear her, "Where is he taking us? I'm sure we're heading the wrong way now."

William shared his wife's fears and asked the driver in as level a voice as he could muster, "Are we nearly there?" the man grinned, treating William to another flash of his blackened teeth.

"We go new way," he nodded, "not far now."

The taxi was leaving the hustle and bustle of the City behind and William and Rose now knew for certain that wherever they were going, it was certainly not the Consulate. As they broke free of the traffic, the area became more rural. Swallowing his fear, William tried a different tactic, "Now see here, I asked to be taken to the British Consulate, and I insist that you return to the City and fulfil the request." It did not work. The man continued to drive, staring straight ahead at the now quieter roads. From the back seat, Rose stifled a whimper and pulled Darcie closer to herself. "It'll be alright pet," she soothed unconvincingly, "the taxi driver has got a bit lost, that's all."

As the taxi rounded a sharp bend, a metallic black four-wheel drive Mercedes with tinted windows and no plates, came out of nowhere, skidded to a halt and effectively blocked their path. William Bailey's only surprise was that he wasn't surprised.

Chapter 23

Melanie suddenly realised that she was cold. She shook herself from the trance like state she had been in for the past few hours and wearily went into the kitchen to make herself another cup of tea, replacing the one in her hand, which was stone cold. She was still wrestling with the enormity of the information she had discovered from her illicit foray into Nicholas' study. A naturally honest person, Melanie was trying to balance the guilt she felt for prying, with the absolute shock and confusion she felt on her discovery. It had been a complete bombshell to her and despite almost short circuiting her brain in thinking of plausible explanations for the information she had uncovered, she was left with only one conclusion.

For entirety of their marriage, her husband had been leading a double life.

With her tea made, Melanie picked up the phone, and despite the lateness of the hour, dialled a familiar number and waited for someone to pick up. On hearing the sleepy, "Hola," at the other end, Melanie closed her eyes and choking back the tears said, "Livvy? Oh Livvy, I need to talk to you."

1500 miles away in her villa in southern Spain, Olivia De Santiago sat bolt upright in bed, her black hair all awry, and her satin nightgown falling from her shoulders. Fully awake now, she gripped the phone; placing a gently restraining hand to settle her husband who was stirring beside her, she swung her legs over the edge of the bed and whispered hoarsely, “Speak Carino, tell me everything, I am listening, I am here for you.”

***

When the black Mercedes had skidded to a halt in front of their taxi, Darcie had not known what to think. Her world, already forever changed, had been a series of nightmares. This was just another episode. She remembered Rose’s arms around her, hugging her tightly and saying over and over, “It’s okay pet, it’s okay,” but even at four years old, Darcie knew that this was a lie. The driver had jumped out, the instant the taxi had stopped. Darcie never saw him again. He seemed to disappear into thin air. The front passenger door had opened and there had been a funny noise, which reminded Darcie of the whip of the circus master she had once seen, as it cracked. On hearing this noise, Rose had cried out in horror and Darcie had looked with detached interest at a snake of blood, which trickled slowly down William’s face and wondered why his eyes were so wide open.

Within seconds the rear door was ripped open and rough hands had pulled her and Rose out of the car. Rose had fought bravely, but the men were too strong for her. She heard her shouting, “Not the bairn, not the bairn, don’t hurt the bairn.” Darcie knew that bairn meant child, Rose had told her so. One of the men laughed as he answered Rose, “Oh don’t worry lady, she’s the most important person here, I can guarantee *her* safety.” Then there had been the same noise, the whip cracking noise and Rose had stopped shouting and fallen on the floor.

Before she could look at Rose, someone had picked Darcie up and bundled her into the Mercedes. She did not resist, she had no more to fight with. As the vehicle sped off into the night, Darcie simply closed her eyes and waited for the next chapter.

***

Diane sat in the shade of a small acacia tree and tried to focus on reading the news on her IPad. At that moment, Ethan came into the room and smiled disarmingly, "Anything interesting?" he asked.

Diane sighed, "It's all bad news," she replied with a frown, "did you read about that Scottish couple who were killed near Pattaya?"

Ethan shook his head, "No, what happened?"

Diane studied the story before replying, "Well it appears that their taxi was waylaid by a gang of thugs. They were robbed and then murdered in cold blood, though I understand that the driver got away unharmed. God Ethan, there was no need to kill them, I mean, they were in their 60's, what harm could they have done?"

Ethan came across to Diane and put his arm around her shoulder, "It happens darling," he said sympathetically, "sad to say, it's all too common round here, tourists get robbed all the time." Diane fought back the tears, which seemed to spring to her eyes almost unbidden these days and wondered why she should care so much about a couple she did not know, but whose heart breaking plight had touched her gentle heart.

***

Despite pacing the floor in anticipation for several hours, Shakiya jumped when she heard the soft, but urgent knock at her door. Pulling her silk robe more tightly around her, she hastened over and asked quietly for confirmation of who was outside. Once satisfied as to their identity, she opened the door and allowed her visitors entry. Indicating the small comfortable sofa, her visitors sat down, or more accurately, the man sat, the child was pulled down with more force than was necessary.

Shakiya did not know the man, which was no surprise; The Old Man seemed to have a never ending supply of goons who took care of his dirty work for him. The child however was a different matter. Unless you had spent the past week on Mars, no one in Bangkok, or for that matter, the world, could fail to recognise the pale pinched features of little Darcie Taylor. Ignoring her emotions with a skill borne of many years of practice, Shakiya simply nodded in the child's direction before asking, "And the plan?"

The swarthy features of the man's sweating face broke into an ugly scowl. "How do I know the plan?" he growled, "I'm just a delivery boy; it was a rush job. You need to sit tight till you hear from The Old Man." He stood up abruptly, leaving Darcie frozen in silent terror on the sofa. Eyeing Shakiya's barely hidden curves through the silk of her gown the man hesitated. "How about a bit of your famous hospitality before I go?" he suggested with a lewd wink.

Shakiya regarded him for less than five seconds before responding, "I will be sure to report to The Old Man that you repay his generosity by disrespecting one who is like an adopted daughter," she said with contempt. The man regarded her, considering for a heartbeat whether or not to slap the whore and wipe the self-righteous look from her face.

Swallowing his anger, he knew that despite the satisfaction is would give him, he would be a dead man before the day was out. No one crossed The Old Man and lived to talk about it. "Another time then," he said with forced pleasantry, and with that, he was gone.

The silence in the room was like an invisible weight. Despite having been in this position several times over the years, Shakiya was, on this occasion, almost lost for words. The enormity of her situation could not be underestimated and she knew she must act accordingly. Gaining control of her emotions, she approached Darcie with a practised smile. "May I sit with you?" she asked kindly. Darcie neither spoke, nor moved, but sat like a miniature mannequin, with even her breathing so superficial as to be almost indiscernible. Shakiya sat; "It's Darcie isn't it?" she asked gently, ignoring the fact that Charn Chai had renamed her

Holly. Again, the child showed no response other than to stare straight ahead at the wall. Shakiya knew that the child was in shock, not only from her brutal abduction, but also from recent events. Shakiya knew very little about what had happened on the road but she did know that the child's former caretakers were now dead, and that Darcie Taylor was now a liability of epic proportion.

Shakiya regarded Darcie with detached interest. She could not afford to get involved, and she most definitely could not allow herself the luxury of feeling sorry for the child. Shakiya knew that her own survival in this most heinous game, had been based on her ability to maintain an inner strength. She had, by necessity, forsaken her emotions and disassociated herself with the atrocities, which she herself had suffered over the years. She had, by bitter experience, trained herself to abandon her feelings, to remove herself emotionally from every situation she had been in and only by doing so, had she managed to endure.

Adopting a casual approach, she took a deep breath, stood up and without a backward glance at Darcie said, "In your own time then," and went into her bedroom, where she began to do battle with her duplicitous feelings, which at this precise moment were threatening to betray her.

Chapter 24

Nate Bailey lay sweating in the 90-degree heat of the notorious Bang Kwong Central Prison, seven miles north of Bangkok, where he had been a prisoner, or as he preferred to think of it, a guest, for the past four months. His dirty blonde hair tied back in a thin greasy pony tail did little to alleviate his discomfort. Nate did not occupy much space; though at only five feet six inches, he was taller than the average Thai inmate. His once good looks faded, Nate rubbed his hand bad temperedly across his sallow unshaven face, which now sported two days growth. Wiping the resulting sweat on his already stained shorts, Nate cursed aloud at no one in particular. "Fuck this heat," he said, "fuck it."

Nate Bailey's ugly mood was as a result of this morning's visit from an official from the British Embassy. Initially, hopeful of news about his release, or at worst a transfer to a UK prison, Nate's expectations had been dashed. The sombre faced man who stood before him told him bluntly that both his parent's had been killed in what looked like an ambush and robbery gone wrong. He gave him the bald facts of the matter, and explained that his parents had been identified by their passports, which they had on them when their bodies had been discovered. The man added that he was sorry for Nate's loss, got him to sign some papers and left. Nate's emotions on the matter were entirely narcissistic. His relationship with his parents, particularly his father, had been strained. He had little to do with them since moving to Thailand, though his mother had continued to try to smother him long distance. However, their presence in Thailand had meant a glimmer of hope for him, as they had at least been fighting his corner. With their deaths, Nate's confidence of some genuine support evaporated. He found that he had no grief, and very little compassion, despite the violent manner in which they had met their deaths. Like all psychopaths, Nate cared only for himself, no one else really mattered; they never had.

Almost immune now to the clouds of mosquitoes, which swarmed constantly, Nate squinted his pale blue eyes against the lights, which were never turned off and once again abandoned all hope of sleep. He was in one of the large holding cells, crammed in with 50 other inmates, all of whom were sweating as freely as he was; the stench of unwashed bodies, coupled with the stink from the one open toilet, was truly nauseating. Many of the men around him were naked, or almost so, partly due to the heat, but also to allow them to display their ornate and intricate body art and tattoos, which they did themselves to alleviate the boredom. Nate noticed some of the men in leg irons; "Newbies" he thought with a grimace as he remembered his first three months in them. He tried not to think about the hunger, which was a constant presence; the one bowl of thin greasy soup with rice which was his allowance for the day, did little to alleviate the griping pains in his stomach. He was lucky in having a job in the laundry, which allowed him to earn enough to supplement his diet with food from the prison shop. Despite living in Thailand for five years, it had taken him weeks to adjust to prison food, suffering almost constant diarrhoea and vomiting for longer than he cared to recall. Adjust he did however, determined to survive in this hell hole of a prison, which was nicknamed The Bangkok Hilton by inmates and others who knew of its charms.

Nate closed his eyes against the heat, noise, overpowering smell and mosquitoes and tried to think. With his parent's dead, he needed another plan, a contact on the outside who could help him. He could not believe he had been caught, after so long in Thailand; he was usually so careful. It did not occur to him that his capture had been brought about by his own arrogance and stunning ego, which led him to believe he was above the law. Nate had built up a considerable network of like-minded men; men whose main pleasure in life was the victimisation of children, either through the vile photographs which littered the Internet, despite the best efforts of the cyber police, or directly. Nate had always preferred the direct approach, the younger the better. He had a solid reputation in the underworld for being able to supply young children, though it was getting increasingly difficult in the current climate. Nate Bailey had no scruples whatsoever, and saw his line of work simply as one of supply and demand, and there was demand aplenty, especially here in Thailand. When he had lived in the UK, Nate had a similar network of contacts, but conducting his business in the UK, was problematic, as the police and other agencies were way too conscientious and determined. He had fled the UK following an unfortunate incident involving the child of his then girlfriend. The child had made certain allegations, and Nate, anxious to maintain his unblemished police record, had left for Thailand within the week. He still had his UK network though, and at times, would email them, offering tempting opportunities, for online entertainment, or the real thing, if only they cared to come out to Thailand, which they did of course, in droves.

Nate's day of reckoning in Thailand had come after the police had raided the apartment he was living in, and found him there with two small girls. Nate smirked at the memory of them. Boys or girls, it mattered little to him, but these two had been quite special. They were four-year-old twins, who Nate had been watching for some time. The children of an impoverished basket maker, Nate bided his time, befriending the man and had slowly, slowly gained his trust. In this city, money talked and for the amount of money Nate Bailey was offering, the man would probably have included his wife and grandmother into the bargain. Nate had assured the man that he would not hurt his daughters, which was of course a lie. The man had eventually been won over by the cash, which Nate waved in his face one day as he began to lose patience. "There are other children," he had said pleasantly, "maybe I will go to the fish merchant, I hear he has a daughter who is quite willing." The man had cracked, taken the money and sold his daughters and his soul for a handful of baht. However, the man had not reckoned with the fury of his wife, who had demanded the truth from him when he returned home without their daughters. The man had tried to show her the money and explain how long they could live on this large amount. He pleaded with her that their daughters would succumb soon enough to sexual advances, and they might as well be paid for it. The wife had responded by hitting her feckless husband with her cast iron frying pan, rendering him unconscious, but not before she had identified the whereabouts of her daughters.

With the local police in tow, one of whom was her distant cousin, the woman had stormed into Nate's apartment screaming and waving the frying pan, which she had brought along just in case. Thankfully for Nate, the police were quicker than she was, and managed to intercept her as she swung for him, still screaming. The Thai police were well aware of Nate Bailey and his depraved lifestyle; however, in the past, they either did not have enough evidence to arrest him, or, the police were on his payroll and received handsome bribes for looking the other way. On this occasion, Nate's luck ran out as they were unable to ignore the fact that he had literally been caught in the act with the children's mother as an irate witness, and off to prison he had gone to await trial.

Nate cursed some more at his misfortune, and despite the discomfort of his situation, eventually succumbed to a bone weary tiredness and slept.

Chapter 25

Morris Powell rubbed his round paunch of a belly, a habit he always fell back on, when deep in thought. A prolific sex offender, Morris had now recovered from the beating administered to him by Steve Blake, and had been lying low for some time though he had not been idle. Several months ago, Morris had victimised Steve Blake's daughter Daisy, within what should have been, the sanctuary of a church attended by the family. Morris had carefully infiltrated the Waters of Life church, on the Deacon Hill Estate in Millbrook, and had posed as a member of the congregation. He had then waited a long time for his opportunity to get Daisy alone and subject her to a frightening indecent assault in the kitchen of the church. Unfortunately for Morris, Daisy's father, Army Captain Steve Blake had got to hear of it and Morris had paid a heavy price. He had spent several weeks in the hospital, but had always denied he knew his attacker; a denial which the police viewed with a high degree of scepticism. Given his track record of child abuse, it had been a matter of time, before some angry parent accorded Morris Powell his just desserts, and the police had not wasted too much time on investigating. Steve Blake's presence on the periphery the Deacon Hill estate had served as a deterrent for some time. Morris recalled with some discomfort the words, which Steve Blake had hissed into his ears after he had beaten him.

Touch her, or any other child again, and believe me, I WILL kill you.

With these threats of further retribution ringing in his ears Morris had laid low, for a short while. However, the Blake's had now moved away from the area to avoid painful memories for Daisy, leaving Morris free again to engage in more nefarious behaviour without the fear of reprisal. When Morris had been released from hospital, he had received an interesting visit from the Pastor of the Waters of Life church, Alan Slater. The Pastor had not been fully appraised of Morris' actions by the Blake family, as Steve Blake trusted that his more direct method of Karma would be a lasting incentive for Morris to change his ways. However, the Pastor had put two and two together; the attack on Morris and the sudden departure of the Blake's from the area, and he had come to an accurate conclusion. He had then made some preliminary police checks using his status as a church pastor, and had discovered that his conclusions had been correct. Morris Powell, was indeed a known and registered sex offender. Alan had almost hugged himself with delight, knowing that it would not take much to bring Morris into his own particular, private fold.

Morris had not been prepared for what followed. He had almost laughed out loud, when, after some cautious discussions, the Pastor had revealed his own true nature to him. It turned out, that like Morris, Pastor Alan Slater, had a criminal record for the abuse of children. However, Alan Slater was a cunning and intelligent man. He had changed his name, moved hundreds of miles out of the area of the offences, and had taken an online course in becoming a religious leader. It had worked; Alan Slater had been covertly leading the church for the past three years. Adopting a genial and compassionate persona, he had easily gained the trust of his flock, forming profitable friendships and researching his new opportunities. With his owl eyed sympathetic presentation, complete with thick rimmed glasses, and quiet speech, Alan looked for all the world like a friendly bumbling pastor. However, Alan Slater was a wolf in sheep's clothing and a man after Morris Powell's degenerate heart.

After their initial discussions, Alan and Morris had met on a regular basis to engage in their mutually revolting shared interests. Alan proved himself to be the leader of the two, with Morris his simple minded follower. Morris had been impressed beyond words when Alan had shown him into his study, and with an air of the dramatic had asked, "What do you think of this then Morris?" Pushing a button, the panel wall at the back of Alan's study had clicked softly to reveal a hidden door cunningly concealed in the intricate woodwork of the panelling. As the door opened, Morris could see a smaller room contained in a space of no more than six feet by nine feet.

Morris watched open mouthed, feeling as if he was in a movie. "A secret room," he had marvelled, feeling a pang of jealousy that he had not thought of something like this. Alan had nodded and invited Morris inside. Closing the panel door behind him, Morris had been agog at the array of technology in the room. With three computers, several cameras, microphones, TV screens, CCTV and a network of wiring, Morris was amazed.

"What have we here Alan?" he asked laughing through his surprise, "It looks like NASA control." Alan basked in partner's praise, he had known that his secret room would impress Morris.

"Not bad eh Morris," he agreed. Alan had then taken Morris further into his confidence and deeper into the covert underworld of the voyeuristic and thoroughly perverted online community of sex offenders.

Online voyeurism was a whole new world for Morris. With his limited intelligence, and lack of finances, Morris had never really managed to gain access to this furtive underground community. Granted, he did have a computer at his mother's house, and of course, he had managed to get some indecent images of children on there, but these were mainly blurry photographs and of frustratingly poor quality that had come via email from old friends. Morris had no idea how to break into the bigger world of the online sex offender, but he was a more than willing student.

"How does it all work then?" he had asked with nauseating eagerness.

Alan turned on a few switches and said softly, "Watch and learn Morris, watch and learn." He had then regarded Morris solemnly and asked, "I can trust you can't I Morris? I mean, you can keep a secret can't you?"

Morris had laughed, "Alan, I'm a registered sex offender, secrecy is my keyword."

Alan seemed satisfied and continued, "I'm part of a syndicate Morris," he confided. "There's a group of us and we communicate using the latest technology and secure websites; we share information which is of interest to us all." Morris was all ears, thrilled at the new opportunity, which seemed to be opening up for him.

"Go on," he said almost salivating at the very thought of it.

"There's a cost involved," Alan warned, spreading his net a little wider, "We all pay a monthly membership fee into an offshore bank account, it can't be traced. In exchange for this, we get unlimited access to some of the best entertainment you can get, aside of the real thing." Alan Slater's eyes had taken on a glittering, slightly unfocused look as he talked about his detestable passion.

"How do I join?" pleaded Morris with the fervour of a convert. Alan Slater hid his triumph, he knew that Morris would be up for it, and it was all more money in the bank for him, as naturally, Alan would take a cut, an introductory fee. Morris' enthusiasm reminded Alan of a school boy not wanting to be left out of playtime games.

Putting him out of his misery he answered, "It's easy Morris, all you need to do is give me the cash and I can put it through on my account. Save you going to any bother and risking getting caught, what with the police keeping a watchful eye on you."

Morris nodded vigorously, "Whatever you suggest Alan," he said, his gratitude at being included in something this big shining through.

"Well, there's no reason we can't sort it out now Morris; that is if you've got the money on you," Alan added casually. Morris looked crestfallen; dependent on benefits, he never seemed to have enough money and he did not have any now.

Hesitating for only a second, he spoke up again, "I'm a bit short right now Alan, but give me twenty minutes and I can be back with … how much did you say it was?" Alan repeated the amount, and Morris tried not to look too shocked. He nodded as if it was the best bargain he had ever struck. He had to buy into this, he simply had to, and he knew all too well where to go for the funding. "Twenty minutes Alan," he affirmed, "Twenty minutes, and I'll be back."

Alan Slater smiled, "No problem Morris," he said soothingly, "I'll be here, a pastor's work is never done you know."

***

Morris was as good as his word. In twenty minutes, he was back at the Waters of Life church. Sweating with the exertion of rushing home and back again, he clutched the required cash in his sweaty hand, grimacing at the memory of the scene he had left behind. He knew his mother had cash in the house; she'd always been the same, never trusting the banks, she had it hidden all over the place. As a rule, she denied she had it, or refused Morris's never ending demands to be given some. However, on this occasion, Morris had been so forceful and insistent that it had frightened the old lady and she had hardly put up any argument. Disappearing into the bathroom of her warden controlled bungalow, Gladys had rooted about in the plastic set of drawers where she kept her spare teeth and other knick-knacks. Knowing that Morris would never look in there, it had been a good hiding place, until now. Muttering as she came back into the living room, she had given Morris a bundle of cash and told him not to ask for any more, though she knew that this was a futile hope.

"You're up to no good again," she complained.

Morris winked insolently and replied "Mother, you know it's for a good cause, it's going to the church." Morris congratulated himself, as this was no lie. In effect it WAS going into the church, into Alan Slater's pockets. Humming to himself, Morris had hurried back to church.

With the money locked safely in his desk drawer in the secret room, Alan had paused dramatically before saying, "Are you ready then Morris? You've just bought yourself a real treat, all we have to do is wait a few minutes and we should have a connection." Morris waited with bated breath; seated now in one of the secret room's comfortable armchairs, he stared expectantly at the 50-inch TV screen in front of him. It was fuzzy with interference, but after a few minutes, the screen became clear and from thousands of miles away, in Thailand, the all too familiar sound of a child crying could be heard. "Here we go" said Alan his voice thick with undisguised lust, "This is what you paid for Morris, enjoy my friend, enjoy."

Chapter 26

Nate Bailey was awoken by the noise of a fight. He sighed disinterestedly, in-house fighting was an almost hourly occurrence, though the guards were never far away and broke it up with batons, feet and fists. With little else to do with his time, Nate Bailey reflected on the empire he had now lost. It had taken him years to build it up and now it was gone. *All those contacts, all that revenue* he thought bitterly, *gone for good.* Without a doubt the online business had been the most lucrative. With hundreds of dirt poor families in the area, who were literally willing to sell their souls for cash, never mind their children, it had been easy pickings for someone as sharp and motivated as Nate. In fact, it had been laughable easy. Nate had rented a private house, out of the way of prying eyes and nosey neighbours, and had equipped it with an impressive display of high tech gear. Using his local contacts to find willing participants, it had not taken long for Nate to find a steady stream of families whose needs were so great that they were prepared to sacrifice their children on the altar of desperation. For pathetically few baht, Nate had a regular flow of families visiting the house, all of whom brought children who were pitifully ignorant of what was about to befall them. It had surprised even Nate to see how sadly enthusiastic some of the families became, once they discovered they could have a regular income.

One of Nate's best customers had been the pastor of a church in the UK. An eager and seemingly prosperous man, he paid regularly to watch the online entertainment Nate could provide. Making himself as comfortable as he could within the confines of the prison, Nate brought to mind the last screening he had arranged. The pastor had another like-minded individual with him, which meant more cash for Nate. The subject had been a six-year old doe eyed Thai girl. Her family were new to Nate, and had incurred debts with their landlord; the consequence of which was that they were now in danger of losing their home and livelihood. Having been told by one of Nate's contacts about how easily they could relieve themselves of this needless burden of debt, the family had earnestly sought him out, agreeing to his terms with indecent haste. The child had been unsuspecting of course. As the cameras had begun to roll, the reality of her situation had become painfully apparent and she had begun to wail and cry. Silenced with a blow from her own mother, the child had submitted to Nate's attentions without another sound. Her misery and humiliation was broadcast live across the deep cess pit of the Internet and watched in the comfort of the good pastor's private rooms. The memory of the abuse brought Nate the quick sexual release he was looking for. Sighing with sated lust, Nate mourned the loss of his business, but recalled that on that occasion, everyone had been satisfied, everyone that is apart from the nameless victim. She had not been consulted.

***

Following on from their perverted viewing session, Alan had revealed to Morris that he had big plans for a trip to Thailand and had asked if Morris wanted in. Never one to miss out on an opportunity for depraved behaviour, Morris had jumped at the chance. Alan had then told him, that he had a contact, known only as NB. A man high up in the network of equally corrupt individuals, for whom, the abuse of children was a career choice. NB was the brains behind the online abuse of children, including the tragically graphic, long distance screening they had both recently enjoyed. Alan had never met NB, and he knew of no one who had. Communicating via secure email, NB was due to contact him when a live opportunity arose. Naturally, this would come at considerable cost, and Alan's extension of seeming generosity in including Morris, was partly a financial one. He needed someone to share the cost, not only of the trip, but the payment, which would be due on arrival for whatever NB had lined up for them. Advising Morris to embark on a course of inoculations for the forthcoming trip, Alan had reeled Morris in with no effort whatsoever.

What Morris and Alan were not aware of however, was that the National Crime Agency and police had been working for many months now on Operation Firefly. They had gathered intelligence on several individuals, including Morris and Alan, and were biding their time in making a solid case, before acting. The information had been shared with the social worker who had been involved in discovering the paedophile ring, namely Diane Foster. Information on NB was scant; other than his initials, no one had any suspicions who NB was, no one, that is, apart from Diane's Old Manager Glenda.

In the aftermath of baby Daniel's death, Glenda had been attending to the paperwork, which Diane had been unable to complete. She had come across a "Post It" note signed in haste by their Director Nicholas Bishop. Glenda's heart had skipped a beat as she had read the quickly scrawled note and initials – *keep me appraised of this one, NB* – however, Glenda had told no one about her suspicions, and neither would she, unless she had more concrete evidence that her Director was involved. Though an arrogant and ambitious man, Nicholas was also focused and extremely good at his job. Glenda had difficulty in imagining that Nicholas was involved in something as abhorrent as the organised abuse of children. She knew only too well the impact of inaccurate accusations, and had no intention of sharing her doubts unless she had more to go on, which at the moment, she did not.

***

The man known as The Mover sat once again facing the one known as The Watcher. The pleasantries had been exchanged, and they were down to business. "It is done? The old couple are retired?" asked Ruang Sak, though confirmation was not really necessary, as he knew everything about the workings of his Organisation. However, formalities had to be observed.

Charn Chai inclined his head, "It is done," he affirmed.

"And the child?" demanded Ruang Sak sharply.

"The child is safe," replied Charn Chai, "However, if I may be so bold as to mention, that in my humble opinion she should be moved as quickly as possible. She is commanding the highest level of attention at home and abroad. She is going to be extremely hard to place unless we find a solid contact."

Ruang Sak narrowed his wrinkled eyes and considered this before giving his answer. "A visit," he crowed decisively, "you must make a visit to the prison to visit the son. Find out all he knows and make him an offer, a generous offer; one he cannot possible refuse. We must know of his contacts and use them to our advantage."

Charn Chai had expected this but responded graciously, "As always esteemed one, your plans are masterly."

Ruang Sak curled his lip, "Do not assume to flatter me Charn Chai, I am aware that my plans are the right plans, which is why I am still in charge."

Ruang Sak was well aware of Nate Bailey and his lucrative affairs and had long wanted him out of the way; coveting his operation in Thailand and wanting his UK and online contacts for himself. Bailey was a nuisance; no more than a farang tourist who had come to make a quick buck and satisfy himself in the bargain. The Old Man had worked decades building up his empire and contacts, and he took an extremely dim view of the Nate Bailey's of this world, who came to Thailand looking for fast money and cheap thrills. The Old Man, had of course heard of Nate's arrest through his web of police spies. The fact that Nate's parents had arrived in Thailand shortly afterwards was almost too good to be true, and Charn Chai had worked wonders in securing their co-operation, albeit, reluctantly. It was a pity that their involvement had ended so abruptly, but then, in this game, one always had to be ready for change.

The Old Man met Charn Chai's eyes and said softly, "Then it is decided; you know what to do. Now leave me as my chef has prepared my favourite dish of Tom Yam Goong soup and I wish to enjoy it undisturbed." Charn Chai knew that his relationship with The Old Man would never get to a point where he would be invited to remain and eat lunch with him. His non-Thai paternity and bastard status assured him of that. Swallowing his bitterness at The Old Man's blatant rejection, he stood and bowed politely. The Old Man did not look up, but dismissed him with a wave of his gnarled old hand as he applied himself to his soup.

Chapter 27

Less than 24 hours after her phone call in the early hours of the morning, Melanie Bishop and Olivia De Santiago were seated together in the privacy of one of the golf club's member's booths. Set right back away from the other tables, the booths were semi-enclosed and offered the opportunity to speak without the risk of being overheard. Given that it was a weekday and raining, there were few other members in the room, affording them even more intimacy to discuss the issues at hand.

Sipping her cappuccino, Melanie reached for her friend's hand, "Oh Livvy, I can't tell you what it means to me to have you here. I'm sorry to ring you in the middle of the night, but who else could I turn to?"

Olivia shrugged; "It is nothing," she said with the nonchalance of one accustomed to having the wealth to do exactly as she pleased. "As soon as I heard of your terrible situation I knew I had to come. I had Diego bring me in the jet, and here I am my friend, here for you as always." Melanie sighed a deep heartfelt sigh of desolation.

"I don't know where to begin Livvy," she said, trying not to cry again. Olivia patted her hand and in a voice heavy with empathy said, "Begin where all good stories begin carino, at the beginning."

Taking a deep breath, Melanie explained to Olivia how she had finally gained access to Nicholas' study. On hearing how she had thrown a tea towel into the door to prevent it closing, Olivia had clapped her hands and interrupted, "A glorious move my friend, truly inspired," she said with a smile.

Melanie returned her own weak smile, "I disagree Livvy, and I wish with all my heart I had never done it. I've unearthed information, which I wish I'd left alone. I looked on his laptop Livvy; how could I be so underhand and act like such a spy? On my own husband." Melanie put her head in her hands in shame and in horror of what she had discovered.

Olivia allowed her compose herself and then said, "Melanie, you have a right to know, now, tell me what you found."

"I found a file marked *Thailand*," she began in a low voice. "I know Nicholas has ties to the country, he's there now on business. In fact, he's been many times. He can speak the language and I know he likes it there. He even took me there once for a holiday four years ago. However, I thought it odd that he should have a file about the place, so I opened it." Once again, Melanie's emotions threatened to overwhelm her. Getting a hold of herself she went on. "It would appear that Nicholas has been in Thailand many, many times before he met me. In fact, it looks like he lived there for quite some time when he was a young man. That's not all though Livvy; you've not heard the worst of it." Melanie began to cry, causing her friend to reach out in sympathy.

"What carino? Tell me, it surely cannot be that bad."

Melanie's next words came out in a rush, "He was MARRIED Livvy, MARRIED. How COULD he not tell me about this?"

Olivia's hand flew to her mouth, "WHAT?" she gasped, her usually calm exterior cracking on hearing the news, "What?"

Melanie went on, "Yes, he was married, but I can't find out any more information about who she was or what happened. I just found a marriage certificate. I do know that her name was Lily Rose, and she and Nicholas were very young, but apart from that ..."

Melanie's voice trailed off. The friends sat in silence for a few minutes, until Melanie composed herself enough to continue. "I feel like I don't know him Livvy, like I'm married to a complete stranger. I feel as if my whole life has been based on a lie. The thing is, that a secret wife is not all I discovered. There is far more going on with my husband that I could ever have imagined."

Olivia's eyebrows shot up, "What, you mean there's more?" Melanie laughed, "Oh I've only just begun," she said sardonically.

"It would also appear that he is mixed up in some sort of child trafficking ring." She waited to let the enormity of this latest statement sink into Olivia's mind. She watched as her friend's brows creased together in consternation.

"Surely not," Olivia declared stoutly, "Nicholas is a man dedicated to fighting child trafficking is he not? I know he gives talks all over the world, surely to God you cannot think he's mixed up in something illegal?"

Melanie made a fluttering gesture with her hands. "I know Livvy, I know, it's horrific, but the documents I found talk about men in Thailand who are known to have links to missing children. He writes as if he knows them intimately. He's got names, personal details, email addresses and a whole lot more. How can that be? I'm terrified Livvy, absolutely terrified that he's some sort of insider, like everything he's done is a front for some sort of abominable child trafficking ring and he's the mastermind. You know how secretive he is; if it was all above board, why the need to keep it so hidden away? Who knows, maybe that's why he had, or maybe still HAS a Thai wife?"

Melanie's voice trailed off into a wail of despair. Olivia got up and went round the table and sat beside her, putting one arm around Melanie's shoulder. She gave her a small shake and said, "Now listen to me carino, whatever you have discovered is obviously of great importance. What matters now is what you are going to do with the information? Who can you tell, who *should* you tell?"

Melanie came upright in one fluid movement, "Tell? Tell? Oh my God Livvy, are you kidding? I can't tell anyone, Nicholas would know I'd been snooping, he'd kill me, well not literally, but you know, it would mean the end for us. He'd never trust me again."

Olivia shrugged, "What then?" she asked with a hint of sarcasm, "What then Melanie? You ask for my help, for what? To tell me a story like this and then to do nothing? Listen to yourself, how can you not act? It is your duty; if your husband is some sort of two faced genius, masquerading as a Director of a service dedicated to the wellbeing of children, and going around the world lecturing on a subject you think he might be involved in, how can you NOT act?"

Melanie's eyes reflected the enormity of the situation as the reality dawned on her. Her voice fell to a whisper, "Oh Livvy, I feel like I've opened Pandora's Box, and now, there's no going back is there?"

"No," replied Olivia a little too harshly, "there is not; now then, what are you going to do?"

Chapter 28

Nate Bailey was awake again and sat cross legged playing chequers with another inmate, when one of the prison guards shouted his name across the cramped room. With little enthusiasm, Nate looked up; the last time the guard had summoned him, it had been to tell him he had a visitor; that visitor had then told him that his parents were dead, crushing his hopes of release or transfer. *What now?* He thought bitterly as he sat glaring back at the guard.

The guard gave a jerk of his head, indicating that Nate should follow him. The effort of rising to his feet was an irritating distraction, and he made a show of taking his time, while the guard's repeated and impatient shouts grew louder. Nate sauntered over, displaying a blatant disregard for the guard's authority. However, his interest piqued when the guard told him in one short terse sentence that he had another visitor.

The visiting area in the prison could not have been less private, housing dozens of men at the same time, all of whom were receiving visits. Nate was shown to one of the phones, which were used in communication. He stared in puzzled surprise at the man who sat calmly in front of him. He was a total stranger to Nate, a bald headed man with a distinctive scar on his face, who introduced himself as an interested party offering help.

The Man enjoyed the look of consternation on Nate's face when he explained the purpose for his visit. Without ceremony, the bald headed man revealed to Nate that he had known his parents, and had been working closely with them to try and secure his release. Nate could not help but grimace in surprise. That did not sound like his parents at all. They had been quiet, people who kept to themselves. He found it hard to believe that they would offer any assistance to a Man such as this. *Bully for you mum and dad*, he thought to callously to himself, still suspicious.

The Man went on to offer his condolences on the loss of his parents. After allowing a moment for his sympathies to be received, The Man had then smoothly told Nate that though his parents were gone, HE could assist him, not only in being released, but, more importantly, in keeping his business going. The Man, skilled in negotiations such as these, paused again, to let the information hit home.

Nate's interest was aroused, though the cautious side of him told him not to trust this smooth talking stranger. He was more than a little alarmed about the fact that the man seemed to know about his operation. How? Nate knew that he had evaded the police for many years, and would have continued to fly under their radar had it not been for the fact that he had been stupid enough to get caught.

If nothing else, Nate Bailey had learned to think on his feet and think quickly. Already neck deep in trouble, his main concern was that this man was a Government agent, sent undercover to glean information about his operation. However, something in the Man's presentation and words were compelling. If this guy was a Spook, then he was the best he'd ever met. The Mover could see Nate's hesitation, and played his trump card. Fixing Nate with an intense gaze, he spoke so quietly that Nate had to strain his ears to catch what he said.

On hearing the whispered name of Ruang Sak Yunram, it took Nate less than 30 seconds to make up his mind. The Old Man was a legend, and few people outside of certain circles even knew his real name. Nate had never met The Old Man, but had heard his name spoken with reverence, and with fear, for many years. He was a main player in one of the biggest child trafficking Organisations in Thailand.

Nate had been prepared to take any opportunity to save his business, no matter the risk and now it seemed, he had his lifeline. He leaned into the phone and in an almost imperceptible whisper began to negotiate with the stranger.

It took less than ten minutes for Charn Chai to convince Nate that he had highly influential contacts in his pay. A few well-placed bribes would see Nate released quickly, after which time, he was to await further instructions, which would lead to an ongoing and lucrative joint business venture with The Old Man. Appealing to Nate's over-inflated ego, Charn Chai assured him that The Old Man was looking for people to hand the reins of his empire to when he was no longer able to play the game. With years of practice, Charn Chai made his story so plausible, that by the time he left the prison, he had Nate's secure email address and most of his contacts in the UK and Thailand. Charn Chai was well aware that he would be richly rewarded when he told The Old Man of his success in securing such a great advantage for them.

The Old Man liked to have an edge, and thanks to Charn Chai, he had exactly that. If The Old Man had anything to do with it, he would make sure that Nate Bailey stayed exactly where he was ... well out of his way.

***

Back in his comfortable house, Charn Chai retrieved his laptop from the safe in his control room. Cunningly hidden in a false book case behind a copy of *The Life of Buddha,* Charn Chai immediately logged into Nate Bailey's email account. He scanned the contents, noting without surprise that there were hundreds of unread emails. Quickly promising himself he would return to read the messages in detail when he had more time, Charn Chai knew that he had a more pressing task in hand. Choosing his words carefully, he composed a short email to one who Nate Bailey had assured him would respond most eagerly in regard to the child. Having written the message, Chan Chai signed it as he had been instructed to – a sure sign to those receiving the message that it was genuine.

Charn Chai simply signed it NB.

***

In the sanctuary of his secret room, Pastor Alan Slater logged onto his laptop and checked his private emails. His heart leapt when he saw the one he'd been waiting for, for so long. It was short and to the point.

Package secure and awaiting collection, NB

Alan smiled to himself; cryptic as the message was, he knew exactly what it meant. "I think it might be time to book a trip," he said out loud to no one in particular. Reaching for his phone, he dialled an all too familiar number and hummed quietly to himself as he waited for the call to connect. "Morris?" he said when he heard a voice at the other end, "Morris, it's me, Alan, everything's in place, how are you fixed for a nice little trip to Thailand my friend?"

***

In the Child Exploitation and Online Protection division (CEOP) of the National Crime Agency, (NCA) analyst Sally Palmer was about to go to lunch, when an intercepted email was red flagged. Sally skim read the content, printed the email and walked briskly to the office of the Head of Division; knocking briefly, she went into Jim Cooper's office, "I think this is the one we might have been waiting for sir," she said grimly as she handed him the print out.

Jim Cooper considered the email for no more than 30 seconds before reaching for his phone. "You may be right Sally," he said as he dialled the number, "Leave it with me, and well done."

Chapter 29

Ethan was on his own at *The Lady Elizabeth*, when he heard the sound of soft footsteps approaching. Diane had pleaded a headache and asked to be left in Bangkok to do some serious thinking. She and Ethan had spent hours talking about Ronnie's proposition and whether or not they could trust her Director Nicholas Bishop. Diane's head was spinning with the implications of what they were caught up in, and desperately needed to think clearly. Ethan had agreed; he had no dives planned that day, and only needed to do some routine maintenance, which would take him no more than three hours. It would also give him time to spend in trying to work out the best way forward.

On hearing the stealthy approach, he slowly placed his hand over the six-inch titanium dive knife he kept close by. Casually slipping the sheathed knife down the back of his shorts, he turned to see two men, who he recognised immediately as Ronnie and Tony.

Forcing a smile onto his face, he called out in greeting, "Long time no see, I was wondering if you two had got lost." Ronnie gave him a bleak look, "You wish," he said without humour. "No my friend, we're here to bring you up to date on business. Shall we go on board and be a little more private?" With the comfort of the knife in the waist band of his shorts, Ethan agreed and the three of them got onto the boat.

Later on back at the flat, Ethan filled Diane in on the day's events. "Two days," he said flatly, "they want me to move this package in two days." Diane looked aghast, "Oh God Ethan, this is really happening isn't it? "Yes it is," he replied grimly; "They're meeting me at the boat at midnight in two days. They've given me the co-ordinates of where I'm to drop this package." Ethan looked at the floor, he felt sick to his stomach. "So; are we going to trust your Mr Bishop? Time's ticking Di, and I don't feel we have many other options. I sure as hell don't trust the police and if we went to the Embassy, you can guarantee they'd be watching us. However, an innocent drink in a hotel with your boss won't arouse too much suspicion. What do you think?"

After more discussions and a lot of agonising, he and Diane agreed that they *would* confide in Nicholas and tell him all about Ronnie and his gang approaching Ethan to move "A package" which they suspected was a child or children. "Let's hope Nicholas comes through for us Di, if not, then God help us."

***

When Charn Chai had sent the email to Pastor Slater, he played the final card in a game, which would culminate in a lucrative pay day for him as well as The Old Man. Slater had predictably taken the bait, believing that Nate Bailey had sent the email, and had consequently agreed to make the trip to Thailand for receipt of "The Package." He was bringing a friend with him – *all the better* thought Charn Chai, *more profit for us*, he smiled to himself. Alan Slater and his friend would arrive in Thailand two days hence. Charn Chai would now have to live up to his reputation as The Mover and ensure that the package was in place. Nothing must go wrong, there must be no mistakes, though as always, they would be anticipated, and back up plans would be in place.

Charn Chai picked up his burn phone and waited for someone to answer, "Ronnie?" he asked when a voice finally answered, "Is everything in place?" When he hung up the phone, Charn Chai was smiling like a smug cat. How he loved it when things went according to plan. He dialled again and the phone was answered immediately. "It is done," he told The Old Man, "the deal goes down in two days," and he could picture him smiling too.

***

For Morris Powell, life could not get much better. He hummed tunelessly to himself as he prepared for his trip to Thailand; packing another loud shirt into his shabby suitcase and daydreaming of the depraved pleasure to come. It had taken a fair bit of organising, which he hoped would be worth all the effort he had gone to. Because his name was on the Sex Offender's Register, Morris had to go to his local police station and make notification that he was going abroad. He had smirked when the officer raised an eyebrow on hearing that his destination was Thailand.

"Thailand Morris?" he had asked sarcastically, "Seriously?"

Yes, seriously thought Morris, though out loud he said, "Yes, why not? I've heard it's a very beautiful place." The officer scowled and made a note of his travelling dates and that was that. Then there were the injections he had to have, which given his needle phobia were pretty traumatic. Never mind, everything was now in place and he was looking forward to it with shameless lust. He smiled, a wolfish smile as he congratulated himself, *Morris, old lad, you're going up in the world.*

Alan Slater was due to meet him at the airport in Bangkok when he landed the following day. They had agreed to fly separately, thinking that if they did so, no one would be able to connect them. Their thought process, especially in light of their collective experience of such matters, was no less than stunning in its naivety.

Less than one hour after Alan Slater's passport had been swiped at Manchester airport, the information was flagged up in the Child

Exploitation and Online Protection division of the National Crime Agency, and precisely two minutes later, Jim Cooper knew about it. "That's one of them," he said cynically to his assistant Sally, "now, let's wait and see if old Morris is going to join him?" They had not had long to wait and once Morris was airborne, Jim Cooper had made a few well-placed phone calls to his contacts in the UK and in Thailand. "Now we wait," he said grimly, "let's hope that this time we can snare the bastards."

Chapter 30

"Hurry up Ethan, it's almost seven." Diane's voice floated through to Ethan who was still wrestling with a shirt decision.

"Blue or white?" he called to Diane, who on hearing his query, came through to the bedroom.

She studied the choices, frowned briefly before declaring, "White," and then shook her head in exasperation as Ethan put the blue on one.

He shrugged apologetically, "What?" he said, "I think I prefer it."

Diane sighed, "Then why ask me?" she said tartly, "I don't really care which one Ethan, just hurry up, we need to leave." Ethan fastened the last button, grabbed his jacket against the cool of the evening breeze and with a final wink at himself in the mirror, he and Diane made their way to The Millennium Hilton for their rendezvous with Nicholas Bishop.

Though he would never admit it, Ethan was nervous. As they approached the hotel, he stopped and hesitated. "Are we absolutely sure about this?" he asked Diane, whose face reflected his own doubts.

"No my love, we're *not* absolutely sure," she answered honestly, "How can we be? But what else can we do? Who else dare we tell? Come on, before we change our minds," and with that, they made their entrance through the lobby of the rather grand Millennium Hilton.

Upstairs in his room, Nicholas had just finished speaking to one of his contacts in the UK. He had known Jim Cooper for many years, and had listened with grim faced concentration as Jim outlined the latest information they had. With the phone call completed, Nicholas glanced at his watch and realised with a frown, that he was ten minutes late for his drink with Diane and Ethan. Hurrying down, he found them waiting in the lobby looking awkward.

"So, here we are," he said more cheerfully than he felt as he greeted the pair. "Sorry I'm late, shall we go up?" and with that, he moved towards the lift. Diane and Ethan followed and gasped in amazement as they came out in the most splendid executive lounge either of them had ever been in. With views over the impressive Chao Phraya River, which dominated the vista below, the room offered a stunning panoramic view of Bangkok by night. Nicholas enjoyed their reaction to the room and smiled, "Not bad eh? So, what's it to be? What are you drinking? It's on me." Diane would have liked to order a glass of wine the size of a bucket, such were her nerves, but she ordered a plain tonic water with ice and lemon, not trusting herself to have alcohol flowing through her veins, not tonight. Ethan joined Nicholas in a beer and for half an hour or more, they chatted about Bangkok, the weather, the conference, diving and other day to day topics. Diane could see that Nicholas was probably reaching the end of his interest in sharing drinks with them, and she knew he had another conference in the morning.

She fixed Ethan with a look, and he shifted uncomfortably in his seat. The exchange was not lost on Nicholas, "Something the matter?" he asked in genuine concern.

Ethan took a deep breath, "Mr Bishop," he began, "is there somewhere we can speak to you more privately? There is something we think you ought to know about."

Nicholas frowned, but was enough of a judge of character to see that both Diane and Ethan's discomfort was genuine. Signalling to the waiter to charge the drinks to his room, he stood up and spoke softly. "How about we go to my room? We can talk freely there." Ethan nodded in relief at having been taken seriously and all three took the lift to the 28th floor where Nicholas had his room. He closed the door and invited them to sit in the two lounge style chairs, while he sat himself on the edge of the bed and fixed them with a concentrated look. "Now then you two; what's this all about?"

***

Darcie sat on the settee in the lady's apartment where she had been left. The lady had gone off into another room and Darcie wondered if she would come back, and if she did come back, if she would be mean to her like the shouting smacking lady where she had first been taken. She tried not to think about Rose and William; they were just two more people who had disappeared from her new and confusing life. She waited, and after a while, when the lady had not come back, she braved a glance at her new surroundings. The room was warm and smelled of hot candles. It wasn't quite dark, but wasn't too light, having four soft lamps, one in each corner of the room, which gave the room an orange glow. The wallpaper was dark red, which made Darcie wonder if this was why the room glowed an orangey colour. There was a table in the middle of the room with some magazines on it, a box of tissues and a pen. Next to the pen was another candle, which was all melty and soft.

The settee that Darcie sat on was covered with a big white soft throw, like the one her mummy had at home. Darcie tentatively reached out her hand and felt how soft it was. The small action and the memory of a comfort now lost, brought unbidden tears to her eyes, which overflowed and ran down her cheeks. She licked the tears away as they passed her mouth and sniffed quietly. She had learned all too quickly that crying was futile and usually made people cross. She stuffed her emotions way down where she could not feel them anymore. Opposite the settee were two chairs, arranged together side by side as if they were about to hold hands – if they had hands that is. They had covers on them too, but they did not look quite as soft as the one Darcie was sat on. Darcie crossed and uncrossed her ankles, in a small anxious repetitive action, which betrayed her highly strung state.

An almost imperceptible movement in the corner of the room caught her eye. She turned her head and to her surprise, she saw a black cat. Her nanny had a black cat once, but it got knocked down on the busy road outside nanny's house. Everyone had been sad and nanny had cried a lot. This cat was almost the same, apart from the fact that this cat had white paws, all four of them, as if it had walked in white paint. Darcie watched with a frozen watchfulness as the cat strolled over and arched its back as it made contact with her legs, which dangled over the edge of the settee, not quite reaching the floor. "Oh," said Darcie, uttering the first words she had said in many hours, "Hello kitty..." She leaned down and in a gesture as old as time, scratched the car's ears. The cat responded as cats do, by rearing up on its back legs and purring loudly. When Darcie withdrew her hand, the cat reached up with a velvet paw and tapped her gently, politely demanding that she repeat the action. Darcie felt a strange sensation; she felt the beginning of a smile for the first time since she had been abducted. Granted, it was a ghost of a smile, a mere twitch of her mouth; it felt alien to her and somehow wrong.

As she continued to fuss with the cat, the lady came back into the room. She said nothing, but sat down quietly next to Darcie on the settee. Darcie ignored her and pointedly focussed on the cat. After a few more minutes of silence, in which Darcie continued to acquiesce to the cats' ongoing demands for attention, the lady spoke up. "I see you've met Mr Whiskers," she said with a smile in her voice. "My name is Shakiya, can you say that? I know it's a bit hard to say." Darcie regarded the woman with her huge solemn eyes and replied slowly and quietly as if awakening from a dream.

"My nanny had a black cat once, his name was Marmite, but he got knocked down and everyone was sad." Her words came out in a tumble, like the inspired words from a writer's pen.

Shakiya's face remained solemn, "Really?" she exclaimed, "poor Marmite, poor nanny, I should be quite devastated if anything happened to Mr Whiskers," she said picking the ecstatic cat up off the floor and hugging him. "He's my best friend you know," added in a conspiratorial whisper, "but don't tell anyone will you?"

Darcie considered this for a moment before declaring, "Well I think that it's okay to have a cat for a best friend. My daddy's dog was his best friend when he was a little boy," she began, but at the mention of her daddy, Darcie lost her new found confidence and choked, as her tears sprung up once again.

Despite herself, and despite knowing the futility of it, Shakiya reached across the void to Darcie and asked softly "Darcie, would you like a hug? With me and Mr Whiskers?" Darcie nodded, gulping back the grief of her long days in captivity, the loss of her family, the deaths of Rose and William who had been kind to her. For the first time since her world had crashed down around her ears, she allowed herself to be comforted. The dam wall burst, the flood gates opened and this precious lost child sobbed a lifetime of tears into the arms of a stranger who understood, because she had once been that same child.

***

Darcie lay in Shakiya's arms; she was spent, and amounted to little more than a damp, crumpled defeated ball of grief. She had cried her heart out for a very long time, howling for her mummy and daddy like an abandoned wolf cub. Shakiya had held on as her little body rode the storm of anguish, feeling every emotion with her and allowing her own tears to run unashamedly down her face. Her body ached with the effort of sitting in an awkward position for so long. Mr Whiskers, startled by the noise, had stalked offended out of the room, but was now back, prowling suspiciously. Shakiya sat upright to ease her muscles, a movement, which jolted Darcie out of sleep. Mr Whiskers moved in, anxious to rebalance the emotions in the room. He patted at Shakiya enquiringly and she rewarded him with a smoothing of his fur, prompting a new outbreak of contented purring.

Darcie blinked and sighed deeply as she sat up and began to refocus on her surroundings. Shakiya ruffled her hair in a gesture of affection and asked, "Feel better now baby?" Darcie regarded her with solemn eyes and shook her head sadly.

"I want my mummy," she whispered.

Shakiya put her hands on Darcie's shoulders, "Listen to me now poppet," she began in a serious but kindly tone, "there are some things I need to tell you. I know you're only little and you may not understand everything I say, but you need to listen to me, okay?"

Darcie shifted nervously on the settee. "Please can I go to the toilet?" she asked in a hardly audible voice.

Shakiya sat back, "Of course you can sweetie, here, let me show you where it is, and how about a drink and something to eat too? Then we can talk."

Once Darcie's most basic needs had been taken care of, and with Mr Whiskers picking delicately at a bowl of tuna, Shakiya sat once again on the settee with Darcie, face to face. "Right baby doll, you need to listen to what I say now." Shakiya paused to let Darcie focus before she continued. "What's happened to you isn't right, I know that, and I'm so sorry to be involved in your unhappiness, but there are things you don't know about me, so for now, you'll have to trust I am on your side. I know you want your mummy and daddy, but the thing is kitten, I can't help you, no matter how much I want to I can't. You see, what happened to you, happened to me when I was a little girl, and there are bad people in charge of us both Darcie, very bad people and we have to do what they say or we will get hurt. Do you understand me so far?"

Shakiya could see from the look on Darcie's face that she didn't really grasp the enormity of her words, but she battled on. "Very soon, someone will come and take you away again, away from this house and away from me. I can't sugar coat it, but there are things that will happen to you that you won't understand and you won't like, but you HAVE to be strong, do you hear me, you MUST endure. Now I know that you have a new name, your name isn't Darcie now, but Holly Bailey, right? Well, the chances are, it will change again now that ... Well, now that you're not with the Bailey's anymore. Now then, listen, here's the most important thing. Are you listening? No matter what happens, no matter HOW bad it gets, and it will get bad, don't you EVER forget your real name. Your name is Darcie Taylor, not Holly Bailey, not anything else and you MUST NOT forget that, promise me? Every day after you leave me, I want you to wake up in the morning and whisper to yourself, *my name is Darcie Taylor, I have a family and they love me and they are looking for me.* Then, before you go to sleep, say it again, and then again. It's really, really, important Darcie, you MUST NOT forget your name. Don't let anyone hear you saying it or even thinking it, but in your heart, you must believe you are and always will be Darcie Taylor."

Shakiya waited as Darcie thought about her words. "Can you remember all that sugar?" she asked eventually, "remember your name."

Darcie nodded slowly and repeated, "My name is Darcie Taylor, and I have a family, they love me and they are looking for me."

Satisfied, Shakiya hugged her and said, "Well done little one," and to herself she thought, *God forgive me for being part of this, let this one survive, oh please, let her survive it.*

Chapter 31

Nicholas ran his hand through his hair, a gesture he tended to make when deep in thought. "You did right to come to me," he told Ethan and Diane. The pair had spent the last hour, spelling out their predicament to a stern faced Nicholas. He had listened without interrupting, grunting now and again, but not speaking. "Right," he said decisively, "Now it's your turn to listen, but first, I think we could all use a drink, am I right?" Ethan and Diane nodded in relief. He had taken them seriously, and not written them off as complete nut cases, neither had he called the police, which had been another of their fears. Once they all had a drink in their hand, Nicholas resumed his poker faced countenance and began talking.

"Ms Foster, you are a professional social worker, one who is more than capable of keeping confidential information to yourself. Mr Montana, though I don't know you, I feel I can place my trust in you, as you have in me. What I am about to divulge is known to very few people and I would be obliged if it were not repeated to anyone outside these four walls. Am I clear?" Diane and Ethan regarded each other, before nodding their agreement. Nicholas went on, "If either of you were to divulge this information to other parties, you would be jeopardising many, *many* years of intelligence gathering and it would be a lot of damn hard work gone to waste. I would not be telling you this, if I did not consider it a matter of life and death, which it is, ... Darcie Taylor's life."

Diane and Ethan sat in stunned silence, as for the first time in decades, Nicholas Bishop revealed the truth of his situation to people who were practically strangers to him. He told them of his past, of his marriage to Lily Rose, his missing daughter and his years of searching for the Old Man. He explained how he had approached MI6 and now worked for them as an operative, gathering intelligence and sharing it for the common good under the cover of his position as Director of Social Services. He told them that for reasons of security, he had to keep it from his wife, who knew nothing of his past life, or his involvement with MI6. "I think she might pass out if she knew," he added wryly, "poor Melanie, I hate to keep secrets from her, but I cannot risk her repeating anything. As it is, she tells that damn Spanish friend of hers way too much, though she thinks I don't know it."

Diane had tears in her eyes when Nicholas described the loss of his daughter. "I'm so sorry," she offered when he spoke of it, but Nicholas shrugged. "It's so long ago now, it's almost like a dream; you never give up hope you know, and I understand only too well what the Taylors are going through." He hesitated before continuing, "I gave DNA you know," he added quietly. Ethan and Diane regarded the man they had only just come to know and who was letting down his barriers and sharing his most intimate secrets with them.

"DNA?" asked Ethan questioningly.

Nicholas nodded, almost embarrassed, "Yes, someone at the Agency suggested it when it became available, you never know, one day she might be found, and you can't argue with DNA can you?"

There was an awkward silence as Ethan and Diane considered everything Nicholas had told them. He had bared his soul in the most personal way and now he had finished, there seemed to be nothing to say. Ethan was about to speak when Nicholas beat him to it.

"I realise that the information I have shared will have come as a huge revelation to you both," he said seriously, "But I shared it for a very good reason. It is vitally important that you understand my background and how deeply I am involved in the situation we now find ourselves in, both here in Thailand and at home. You must appreciate that am in a position of great influence and can indeed offer the help you are both seeking. However, before we get to that, I have more information to share, but the same confidentiality must apply."

Nicholas paused and felt a stab of sympathy for Ethan and Diane as they tried to make sense of the unfolding drama they were now involved in. He pressed on regardless, "I had some information today from my agency, which will be of great interest to you Diane. There is a British born man called Nathan Bailey who has been living here in Thailand for several years. He has been on our radar for some time, but we have never had enough evidence to make anything stick. He fled from the UK after a child made some serious allegations against him and has been here ever since. The local police have had their suspicions; many are paid to look the other way and the honest ones have never been able to catch him doing anything illegal; that is up until now. I have been told that he is currently in prison awaiting trial for the abuse of two local children. His house was searched and his many computers revealed thousands of indecent images of children. There is no doubt that he will remain in prison for many years to come. However, what was of great significance were the contacts on his computer. Diane, do you recall meeting with DC Jill Fletcher and other professionals when you were working in England?"

Diane frowned at the memory, "Of course I do, we met to discuss a possible paedophile ring. The police were undertaking covert intelligence gathering, called Operation Firefly as I recall."

Nicholas nodded, "That's right; you may also recall that there were a number of names which cropped up again and again, men we knew were involved. However, the ring leader, the man who sent the emails, set up the online abuse of children and seemed to be running the show, was known only to us as NB."

Diane's eyes flew wide open as she made the connection, "Nathan Bailey?" she asked, "Nathan Bailey is NB? The guy who is currently in prison?"

Again, Nicholas nodded, "One and the same," he said, "furthermore, I have been advised that lady he received a visit not long ago from a local man, who we have also been watching for some time. We suspect that this man is working for The Old Man. He signed into the prison under a false name of course, but we will be keeping a very close eye to see if he visits again. What was even more interesting was that following this man's visit to Bailey, an email was sent to a contact in the UK and signed NB. Now we know it could not have been from Nathan Bailey, and yet it came via his usual secure email address. We are assuming that somehow, the man who visited him in prison now has Bailey's personal details and is using them to his own ends."

Diane got to her feet and began to pace the small room, "This is unbelievable," -she exclaimed, "I mean, what are the chances? The case I was involved in when I was working in the UK has reached Thailand, in the very area Ethan and I are in. You couldn't make this up. What do you intend to do?" she demanded.

Nicholas drew in a deep breath, "Well, firstly, we will of course be speaking with Mr Bailey and seeing what, if anything, he has to say. When I say we, I mean the local police. With my government contacts, I can almost guarantee that we can identify some genuine officers who will do everything in their power to get to the bottom of what he knows and who his contacts are here and back in the UK. We have a good idea of most of them, which brings me to my next bit of news.

I was told only this evening before I met with you both, that two of the men we suspect are embroiled in all this, are here in Bangkok as we speak. Alan Slater, who is the pastor of the Waters of Life church back in Deacon Hill, and Morris Powell a registered sex offender.

It was Alan Slater who received the most recent email from NB; it is no coincidence that within days of the email, Slater and Powell were on their way here. Sad to say, we lost track of them after they landed. We suspect that the police officer assigned to follow them is in the pay of the Organisation responsible for abducting the children. He is currently under surveillance in the hope he may lead us to them or others of interest."

The NCA intercepted this email and as I said, I was informed of the content of it in a phone call just before I met with you two. The email spoke of a package awaiting collection; the package is undoubtedly a code word for a child, who we suspect is either Darcie Taylor or Angelique Berlioz. I have no doubt whatsoever having listened to what you two have had to tell me, that the package you have been asked to move Ethan, is the same package referred to in the email from NB and a code word for a child. The NCA are not yet aware of the information we have on the real identity of NB, but I understand that my superiors will be sharing this information with them first thing in the morning."

Diane stopped pacing and whipped round to face Nicholas, "Hang on … Powell? Morris Powell?" Her face turned white, "My God Nicholas, I know him," she said in astonishment, "Well, I don't know him personally, but I was involved with his brother and family as they were allowing Morris to visit the children. Morris Powell is the guy who got beaten up by some local vigilante and the police suspected it was linked to the abuse of a child, though they could never prove it. And you're telling me that he's here too, oh this is too much." She sank down into her chair again, "I can't take it in, my old caseload is following me," she said with a wry smile.

"I was aware that you had some involvement with Powell," said Nicholas, "how about Slater, do you know anything about him?"

Diane thought for a moment, "No, nothing apart from his name coming up as a suspected sex offender in the professionals meeting."

Nicholas nodded, "Well, we're well aware of them now and if we can only locate them here in Thailand, they will be placed under the closest surveillance possible. It is imperative that they are found and quickly. We can't arrest them unless they have committed a crime, which as yet, they haven't. What we DO know from you Ethan, is that you are expected to take your boat to a certain rendezvous at a specific time. What we need to do now, is formulate a plan of action. Here's what I'm thinking."

Another hour went by and more drinks were consumed, with Diane permitting herself that glass of wine now. Eventually, they had thrashed out a plan, which they all agreed would be their best opportunity for rescuing Darcie, if in fact it WAS Darcie who Ethan was expected to move, which given all the information Nicholas had been given was highly likely. Nicholas told them that he would make some highly placed phone calls for back up, and also arrange for some high tech listening equipment to be fitted on Ethan's boat under cover of darkness tomorrow night. Diane was to wait it out back at the flat and be ready to call the Embassy immediately if they had news. "So," said Nicholas recapping on their plan, "you'll go to the rendezvous as planned Ethan, pick up the package, whatever, or whoever it might be, and take it to the drop point, for which you already have co-ordinates. I will have my people in place at the drop off; don't worry, you won't know they are there, no one will know they are there until it's too late. You will be arrested along with the rest of the gang to make it look authentic and to prevent any suspicion falling on you. Diane, you will wait at the flat for the phone call to say that there has been a positive outcome. Any questions?"

Diane felt lightheaded, and not just with the wine. "This feels unreal," she said, "just unreal. I feel like I'm in a play." Nicholas shot her a stern glance, "I can assure you Diane," he said grimly, "this is for real and we had better all pray it goes to plan, or little Darcie Taylor may not be the only casualty."

Chapter 32

Charn Chai was an extremely busy man but was finding time to relax. He sat crossed legged in his luxurious home on a thick fur rug in front of a bronze statue of Buddha two feet tall. The smell of incense drifted pleasantly around him, though the strength of it stung his eyes. Charn Chai spent ten minutes centring himself and focusing on the days ahead. As he meditated, he applied his mind to the issue of moving Darcie Taylor, or should he say Holly Bailey. A frown creased his brow as he realised that with the Bailey's now dead, he would need to find her another name and also move her to another safe house. That was of course, after she had begun to earn her keep for him and The Old Man. He was not prepared to leave her with the old whore Shakiya. She was getting soft in her old age and the last thing Charn Chai needed was more problems. No, after the deal with the English pastor and his friend, he would look around for another safe house and put the child well out of circulation until she was required again. He went over the plan again in his mind, probing for any unforeseen obstacles.

He contemplated the new man who was now the skipper of the boat they had used in the past. Ethan Montana was a risk. It was always a risk bringing new people into the circle, but with Sunan Simsek shooting his mouth off to the police and then meeting such an unfortunate end in the river, they had had to identify someone else to make the drops, and quickly. The old skipper of *The Lady Elizabeth* had effectively gone off grid, no one knew of his whereabouts, but that was not an issue for now. Montana would be watched of course, and tested, but he would not be aware of that. The farangs from England were due to pick up the package (as the child would be known) tomorrow night. They would be waiting at a pre-arranged spot where Montana would make the drop. They would make a cash payment of one thousand English pounds for the opportunity to have the child for three hours. The child would then return with Charn Chai in the dead of night, though he doubted she would be in the same condition. The child would have to temporarily return to the old whore unless he had managed to identify a new safe house for her before then.

Charn Chai then applied his mind to the Organisation's other interests. As well as all the whore houses and individual children they had in and around Bangkok and Pattaya, the other package at the top of his list of priorities was Angelique Berlioz. While he was already well acquainted with Darcie, he had yet to meet Angelique. It would have to wait until he had dealt with Darcie. She was secure enough with Suzy Meesang in one of their other safe houses in the isolation of the countryside many miles from Bangkok. Meesang had strict instructions to keep her quiet and well-hidden until further instructions had been issued. Privately, Charn Chai felt that The Old Man had somewhat overstretched himself taking two European children within a week of each other. It showed a level of greed and desperation and was not befitting the reputation of such a well-run Organisation. Charn Chai was also of the opinion that in doing so, The Old Man had made them vulnerable, and that was where mistakes could be made. It was however, an opinion he would keep firmly to himself. Charn Chai had lost count of the children whose disappearance he had been involved in. Most were Thai or Cambodian children, but in response to the demands of the highly lucrative market he was immersed in an increasing number were American or European. The Thai and Cambodian children were easy to place and to move. From the poorest of families, who often had no idea of what they were sending their children to, they were not missed. The American or European children however were a different matter; their disappearance always created a media storm, which took months, if not years to die down. Charn Chai sometimes wondered if they were even worth the risk, despite the ridiculously high prices the Organisation could command for them. The stakes in taking a Western child were high, and you had to take them young to get a return on the investment. It took many months of planning and so many people behind the scenes to keep such an operation afloat that Charn Chai almost lost count. When he considered the corrupt police officers, judges and government officials, whose bottomless pockets were lined with hush money, he realised just how many people were involved and how high it went. Bringing his mind back to the issues in hand, he decided that the Berlioz girl would wait. She was going nowhere and there was no chance of finding her, not with his tangled web of hiding places.

Satisfied with his plans Charn Chai smiled to himself, bowed to the effigy in front of him and signalling to the small boy who waited obediently close by, he went to his bed to take his own particular brand of pleasure.

***

Nicholas made the long distance call while distractedly trying to focus on the ever growing problems in hand. He was midway into what he thought might work, when he heard the line connect. "Melanie?" he said a little too loudly, "Melanie listen my love, I need to stay in Thailand a while longer. No, you don't need to worry or do anything, I've cancelled my flight and will book another when I know when I'll be coming home. Yes, it's about the missing children, I know, terrible business. Well look darling, I must dash, got lots to do, yes, love you too bye for now, take care." Nicholas hung up, and at the back of his mind felt a tiny seed of disquiet. Melanie was usually effusive, and if he was honest, a bit too smothering at times. However, she had sounded subdued and unnaturally quiet. Maybe it was simply because he wasn't coming home, but Nicholas had the strangest feeling, that all was not well in his own camp.

***

Angelique was awake. Suzy Meesang rolled her eyes and groaned. The child was impossible, with her hundreds of questions, non-stop demands to be taken back to her family, and her overall high levels of energy. She was like a caged tiger, a tiny spitting caged tiger. Suzy had to admire her strength, most children simply cried for their parents and eventually gave up, but not this one, oh boy, not this little firebrand. The child had cried of course; she was only human, but she had such spirit that she recovered quickly from her tears, returning to anger, tantrums and shouting as a way of being heard. *Today is going to be no different* thought Suzy as she made her way into Angelique's bedroom where the noise had already begun.

Angelique was sitting up in her squalid bed, her hair like a silver cloud of candy floss all around her. She pulled a face when she saw Suzy, "Where is my maman?" she demanded immediately. "I will not stay here anymore, you must take me to my maman and papa, you are a wicked lady to keep me here like this, you must let me go home." Suzy steeled herself for another day of Angelique's insistent appeals.

She regarded the child with what she hoped was indifference, "I have told you many times now, you will not be going back to your family, no matter how much you shout and demand it. Anyway, they are no longer here, they went back home without you," she added cruelly.

Angelique took in this new piece of information with a frown of demonic proportions and yelled, "No they did NOT, my maman would never leave me, you are a nasty lady and you are lying to me," and with that she jumped out of bed and ran to the kitchen to get herself some breakfast.

Suzy followed, amazed at her independence. She hated to admit it, but she really could not help but feel some admiration for this little power house. However, Suzy knew all too well that she had better get over herself and pretty damn quickly if she didn't want to meet with the Old Man's justice. Suzy had been in the game long enough to have heard the horror stories of what happened to those who crossed the Old Man and his associates, and she was not about to be added to the casualty list. No, as much as she could feel sympathy for the child, she would not get involved. She had never got involved before and she wasn't going to start now. All their lives were in the hands of the Gods and this child would have to take her chances, just like she did, just like they all had.

Hardening her heart, she stepped in front of Angelique and reached up for a bowl for her cereal, "Here, let me," she said in an attempt to regain control.

Angelique took the bowl, but reached for the box of cereal herself, "I can do it," she said defiantly.

Suzy sighed and walked away thinking to herself as she went, *if only you knew what was ahead of you little one, I hope you can survive it.*

Chapter 33

Back in the UK, several professionals gathered around a table for a highly important and confidential meeting. It was chaired by Jim Cooper of the Child Exploitation and Online Protection division of the National Crime Agency. The meeting had been called as a matter of urgency, after the interception of the email from NB to Alan Slater. The local police were represented by DC Jill Fletcher from the Child Protection Unit. DC Fletcher had been a friend of Diane's when she had been working as a social worker. Together they had undertaken several joint visits to known sex offenders. It had been Diane and Jill who had uncovered much of the information, which formed the basis of today's meeting. Also present from Social Services, was Diane's Old Manager Glenda Rogers, resplendent as always in hippie type trousers, a bright orange flowing top, and lipstick to match. No one could ever accuse Glenda of under dressing. The rest of the meeting was made up of professionals from other Counties, plus men in suits, some from Organisations who were not identified, but who had a deep interest in the activities of the men who were the subject of the meeting.

Jim began by giving a synopsis of events. He outlined the uncovering of the paedophile ring, thanks to Diane and Jill. However, he explained that this network extended far beyond their own boundaries and was now known to be operating overseas. In particular, Jim had told them, there were known contacts in Thailand. One individual who they were all anxious to identify was the mysterious NB who they suspected was one of the ring leaders, and who was a common denominator in the UK and Thailand. NB was known to send emails to the other men in the network.

Jim shared the latest email from NB stating that "The Package" was ready for collection. "This email," he explained, "was sent from a secure email address in Thailand but was intercepted by our agency. The recipient was none other than Pastor Alan Slater whom we have had on our radar for some time now. We know that on receiving the email, the good pastor rang a member of his congregation; known sex offender Morris Powell. Both men are now in Thailand. Coincidence? We think not. We have reason to believe that the package they are discussing might be the missing Darcie Taylor. I have been in touch with our operatives in Thailand who are formulating a recovery plan as we speak. However, we are aware, that as well as NB, there is an organised crime syndicate in Thailand, who are involved in Darcie Taylor's abduction as well as other children, including Angelique Berlioz who was also kidnapped last week. They may well be the real brains behind the whole operation."

Glenda listened to the information, with a growing sense of unease. Her suspicions regarding the identity of NB gnawed at her and she felt that in light of the current situation, she must voice her fears. However, Glenda was no fool, and she did not intend to expose Nicholas Bishop as a potential suspect to the whole room of professionals. What if she were wrong?

When the meeting concluded, Glenda approached Jim Cooper and asked him quietly, "Could I have a word in private Mr Cooper?" Jim looked up from the papers he was gathering, "Of course Glenda, we can remain in here if you like, I think everyone is about ready to leave."

Once alone in the room, Glenda came straight to the point. "Look, this is very difficult for me to say Mr Cooper, but I cannot help but fear that somehow our Director Nicholas Bishop may be involved in all this and may even be the unknown NB. He is in Thailand as we speak, which I find disturbingly coincidental. He speaks the language and has strong ties to the country. I know he's an excellent Director, but I can't shake the nagging feeling that he's somehow involved.

Jim Cooper listened intently before nodding slowly and saying, "I think you'd better sit down Glenda. I know I can trust you with this information, which I would not share unless I felt it absolutely necessary. You see, Nicholas IS involved, but not in the way you think."

When Glenda Rogers left Jim Cooper, her view of the situation had undergone a radical shift. Her head was reeling from the information she had been given. She appreciated that Jim Cooper had only shared it with her due to her fears that Nicholas was involved in something illegal, and he needed to prevent her repeating that notion to anyone else. What she had NOT expected to hear was that Nicholas Bishop was actually working under cover, though he would not say for who or in what capacity. THAT was on a need to know basis. All Glenda needed to know was that their Mr Bishop was most definitely a good guy and NOT the illusive NB. Glenda felt an immense sense of relief. While she found Nicholas quite abrasive and arrogant, there was no doubt that he was good at his job, and she had not relished the idea of him being involved in a negative way. *Well, well,* she mused with some amusement, *Nicholas Bishop saving the day, who'd have thought?*

***

Melanie put the phone down, her lips pursed in thought. It was Nicholas, telling her he was staying longer in Thailand. *What do I do when he comes back? What then?* She asked herself, *what am I to do?* After her unauthorised visit to his study, Melanie had convinced herself that Nicholas was involved in the worst possible way in some sort of child abuse ring. Her discussions with her best friend Olivia had done little to reassure her; on the contrary, Olivia was insistent that she go to the authorities. *But who?* She had agonised, *who am I supposed to tell? He's the Director of Social Services for God's sake.* After a generous measure of gin and tonic and much thought, Melanie reached a decision. Steeling herself, she spoke out loud, "I'll challenge him," she said, "that's what I'm going to do, I'm going to come right out with it, admit I was in there and challenge him." She set her glass down with a decisive bang and knew in her heart that when it came down to it, she would probably change her mind. Closing her eyes, she reached out again for the gin bottle, though it wasn't really helping. "Oh damn you Nicholas and your accursed secrets," she said in frustration, "damn you to hell."

Chapter 34

Charn Chai put down his phone, which never seemed to be out of his hands of late. He had just finished giving instructions to the whore Shakiya with regard to the delivery of the package tonight. The whore would have the child ready by 11pm, when he, Charn Chai would collect her and take her to Ethan Montana's boat. He would trust no one else to make this delivery, though he knew there were risks involved. However, Charn Chai knew that Ronnie had made it quite clear to Montana that there would be severe penalties for anyone who double crossed him in this venture. Besides, people were naturally greedy and Ethan Montana was being handsomely paid.

He had spoken to the farang pastor from England and told him where to be and at what time. He had also reminded him with more than a hint of menace that he had better not forget the money. The farang had stuttered and stumbled over his words, giving assurances that he had every penny of the one thousand English pounds required for use of the package for three hours. *Yes,* thought Charn Chai, *it was all working out,* though he would be happier once he got the child into a more secure and remote setting. He cursed the Bailey's for the hundredth time. Theirs had been an ideal cover, but their over developed sense of conscience had ruined that plan. Never mind he thought, there would be others to take their place. There were always others.

***

Ethan was sweating. He had felt fairly confident until it came to leaving Diane alone in the flat, when the stark reality of their situation had hit him fully. He hugged a tearful Diane and cautioned her unnecessarily to make sure she locked their door and NOT to open it for anyone apart from him or Nicholas. Diane had held on tightly and begged him not to take any risks, but the die was cast and there was no turning back. Ethan was a strong and capable man, but suddenly, he felt out of his depth. Breathing deeply, he took hold of his emotions and managed to extricate himself from Diane. "See you later darlin," he managed, and with that, he walked out into the night to make the two-hour drive to his rendezvous with evil.

Meanwhile, Nicholas had also made the trip south and was seated with a small team of six handpicked specialists at the drop off point given to Ethan by Ronnie. The men, like him, were all working under cover and would evaporate into the night once the operation was over. Led by a capable veteran of many such operations, one of them had paid a silent visit to Ethan's boat last night and had fitted a tiny listening device on board. Two of the men with Nicholas were posing as local police, complete with fake IDs. These men would remain, and if all went to plan, would remove the perpetrators into the hands of justice. While many of the local police officers were indeed corrupt, Nicholas still held a few genuine contacts, including ones in high Government Office, who he could trust. However, on the instructions of his superiors, he had not included them in tonight's little ambush. There would be time to involve them later once he had the perpetrators in hand. He looked at the luminous dial on his watch; 00:15 – *Showtime* he thought grimly, *here we go.*

***

Ever since Shakiya had got the phone call to say that Charn Chai was coming for Darcie, she had felt sick. Sick with guilt and worry about this child who had got under her skin like no other. She had tried to talk to Darcie, to prepare her in some way for the terror and pain, which undoubtedly lay ahead for her, but the words stuck in her throat. All she had initially managed to do was to repeat her earlier mantra that Darcie should never forget her real name, nor forget that she had a family who loved her and were still looking for her. She had then told the terrified child that she was to be taken to meet some new people and that she would not like the things they wanted to do to her, but that she had to be a brave girl and accept it. Shakiya had hated herself the moment the words were out of her mouth. Accept it? Accept someone's prying, probing hands on her innocent and untouched body? Accept it when some unwashed stranger forced his disgusting body parts into your mouth? She bit down bitterly on her own lip tasting blood. The thing in her stomach which was like an oily snake, uncoiled once again and resettled itself as she continued in her euphemisms to the child.

At four years old, the only bad things Darcie could imagine were such things as someone taking her toys, or making her go to bed when she was wide awake, or when her mummy made her eat vegetables. The child had no clue as to the trauma of what lay ahead and Shakiya knew she was probably making it worse by trying to warn her. In the end, she had held Darcie close and said, "I will be here when you come back." Darcie had simply stared at her in total ignorance not knowing that the world she thought so utterly terrible was about to dissolve into one ruled by absolute unmitigated evil.

***

When Charn Chai had arrived to collect Darcie, she had, as per his instructions been ready. However, when the child saw him, she became hysterical, clinging to Shakiya's legs and screaming in fear, such was her knowledge of what he now represented, fuelled by the things Shakiya had said were about to befall her. He had been on the point of simply picking her up and bundling her into his car when the whore had spoken up.

"Let me come with you," she had said flatly. "she will listen to me; I can help." He hesitated, this was a change of plan and he did not like changes of plan. However, he did not wish to deliver the child in a state of hysteria – his clients may well decide that a screaming bundle of tears in the dead of night was not worth the trouble and risk.

Charn Chai eyed Shakiya critically, "Very well," he had agreed, "but if she does not behave as I order, there will be severe consequences, for you and for her. The time for play is over, it is time she understood her fate." Shakiya had then taken Darcie by the hand and without demonstrating any emotion or kindness, she had simply said, "Come."

***

Ethan got to the boat a full half hour earlier than the agreed time. He was therefore somewhat disconcerted to see Ronnie waiting for him smoking a cigarette. "Evening Ethan," he said pleasantly, "I like a man with enthusiasm for a job." Ethan had swallowed every ounce of his apprehension and responded accordingly, "I told you Ronnie, I'm as reliable as they come." Ronnie nodded, "We'll see," was all he said. They waited in silence; what was there to say?

At exactly midnight a black Mercedes SUV pulled up silently by the water's edge of the small bay where Ethan was moored. "Ah, here we go," said Ronnie cheerfully as if they were waiting for a social event to begin. A bald headed man stepped out first. He went to the back door and opened it, glancing around cautiously as he did so. Ethan found he was holding his breath. From the back seat of the SUV came a woman; Ethan had not expected that. The woman turned around and seemed to be coaxing someone in the back seat. The man hissed at the woman, who reached into the vehicle with a word, and brought out a child. But this was not just any child. Ethan's breath escaped from his body in a rush of adrenaline as he recognised the terrified face of the missing Darcie Taylor. His blood raced through his veins so fast, it felt like champagne fizzing through him. He realised in that micro second, the enormity of the implications of his simply being here. If anything were to go wrong now ... A lifetime in a Bangkok prison suddenly stared him in the face. From what seemed like a long way off he heard a voice. It was Ronnie, "Ethan, Ethan," he was saying. Ethan felt like he was emerging from a fog. He could not take his eyes off the child. His legs failed him, and he found he could not speak or move. A sharp stab in his lower back jolted him back to reality. Ronnie was prodding him hard, "Ethan," he said aggressively now, "get it together man, hurry up and get this thing moving."

Complying, Ethan started *The Lady Elizabeth*, as the three of them got on board. Ethan felt as if he was on automatic pilot, steering the course he had been given by Ronnie. He prayed that the listening device was working, and recording anything said on the boat. However, to his horror, the woman hoisted the child up and sat her right in front of where he knew the device to be. He tried to intervene, "Err, I shouldn't sit her there," he started, it's not all that safe, she'd be better off down in the cabin if you like." The woman regarded him as if he were something she had scraped off her shoe. She turned her back pointedly and ignored him, leaving the child where she was, blocking the device completely. He cursed silently, but kept steering. Not five minutes into the trip, Ronnie stepped up to him and said lightly, "Oh by the way Ethan, small change of plan. Here's your new co-ordinates," and with that he handed Ethan a totally different destination to the one he'd originally been given. His head reeled with shock, and he struggled to keep it from showing in his face.

"Problem Ethan?" asked Ronnie pleasantly.

Ethan managed to shrug, "Makes no difference to me Ronnie," he replied in a bored voice, "I'm getting paid wherever I drop her off, right?" Ronnie grinned, and in the darkness his teeth looked almost vampirish.

"Right my friend," he laughed, "right on."

Ethan continued to the new drop off point desperately wondering how this could have gone so wrong so easily and swiftly. He thought of Diane back in the flat waiting, he thought of Nicholas and his group of whatever they were, waiting to rescue a child who was no longer coming. *Think,* he commanded his befuddled brain, *think!*

In the darkness several miles away with an inbuilt sense, born from experience, Nicholas Bishop knew something was wrong. He spoke to the men in low tones, "They're not coming," he said bitterly, "something's gone wrong, they should have been here half an hour ago." He had suspected that there were problems when they failed to pick up anything from the listening device.

A bull faced man in a black hat and a camouflaged face had reported to him, "Nothing sir, I'm getting nothing," when he'd asked if they were picking anything up. Nicholas swore under his breath, frustrated beyond belief that once again these men should manage to elude capture. He should have known, and now all he could do was hope that Ethan came out of it unscathed. If they were to suspect for one minute that he was not what he seemed to be, well, Nicholas did not want to think about the consequences. He was under no illusions as to the ruthless nature of the men he was dealing with. They took no prisoners. He gave the signal to the men, and like ghosts, they melted away into the shadows, while Nicholas went back to his car, which was parked in a well-hidden location and waited. There was nothing left to do other than wait and hope.

***

Ethan steered the boat neatly into the tiny bay, which was really no more than an inlet. In the shadows he could see two figures. The bald headed man jumped off the boat and indicated to the woman that she should pass him the child. Ethan swallowed hard to prevent himself from vomiting right there and then. He felt ashamed to his core. Never mind that he had gone along with this to try and help this child, he *hadn't* helped, and now, he was about to hand her over to a pair of animals to do God knows what to her for their perverted entertainment. He felt his fists clenching and unclenching, and his jaw ached from grinding his teeth. He stepped forwards, knowing it was insanity, but knowing he'd never live with himself if he simply stood by and did nothing.

A quiet metallic snick and the touch of cold steel at the base of his neck however persuaded him otherwise. "Don't be a hero my friend," whispered Ronnie. Ethan forced himself to relax. His sense of reality returned to him slowly. He knew that he was of no use to Darcie or Nicholas if he lost it now. He HAD to keep the charade going, he had the co-ordinates, he would be able to find this cove again, despite its small size. There may be evidence here, but it would have to wait. He turned his head ever so slightly and with as much menace as he could muster warned Ronnie, "Take that gun out of my neck or you're going over the side."

Ronnie laughed without mirth and put his gun away. "Never doubted you for a minute," he said and slapped Ethan on the back.

Ethan watched helplessly as Darcie was lifted over the side of the boat. He heard her whimper, heard the woman say something to her, but what he could not catch. And then she was gone, handed over to her fate, like some sacrificial offering to a sadistic God, and Ethan knew that he would never be the same again.

He turned quickly back to the helm and asked roughly "Come on then, is that it? We need to push off before someone sees us." Ronnie grinned in the darkness as the woman got back on board; the bald headed man was staying to guard his valuable package. He was not about to simply hand her over to two unknown farang. He would accompany them to a privately rented house and remain close.

The Old Man did not trust farangs, and this was a package of too high a value to risk losing. “Good man Ethan,” said Ronnie as he cast off, “you just earned yourself a small fortune. There’ll be more when she’s collected later.”

Alone in the darkness where no one could bear witness, bitter tears of guilt and shame, coursed unchecked down Ethan’s face.

Chapter 35

When Alan Slater had met Morris at the airport, both men had shaken hands and delighted in the success of their plan so far. Returning to the low budget hotel just outside Pattaya where they were sharing a room, Alan had assured Morris that no one would bother them here. For Morris, it was the adventure of a lifetime; never having left the shores of the UK in his life, he felt like a celebrity. Alan had explained the plan, in that they were to go to their rendezvous at 00:15 to await delivery of their package. To Morris Powell this was no more than a game and he hugged himself in delight. He knew full well that "the package" was in reality little Darcie Taylor who had been so cruelly abducted. Yet, even with this knowledge the only emotion Morris felt was a brutal anticipation. He loved the idea of code words and secret rendezvous. It made him feel important, like he was in a James Bond movie. He had never felt more aroused in his life and he was already making plans to move to Thailand permanently – after what Alan had told him about the opportunities here, he'd be crazy not to. For now, however, he concentrated on tonight. He and Alan were paying £1000 for the privilege of having this child for a few hours. The pity was, that it could not be longer. *Never mind,* thought Morris; that was more than enough time to enjoy himself. It had taken a lot of persuading to get his mother Gladys to lend him the cash. He knew that she had it stashed up, she had plenty left from his dad's life insurance. The old woman had grumbled as usual, but given it to him all the same. Morris knew, as did Gladys, that she would never get it back.

Morris sat back on the faded chair in the run down room, rubbed his belly and smiled.

***

For Darcie, the nightmare began when she had to leave Shakiya. The bald headed man who smelled of flowers had become angry with her when she had clung to the only person who she had any affinity with. Shakiya had reassured her and reminded her to recall what she had told her. Darcie tried hard to remember all the words Shakiya had said, but all she could think of was, *I am Darcie Taylor, I have a family who love me and who are looking for me*. It was like a mantra going around and around in her head. Everything else Shakiya had said was no more than a blur, a fuzzy mix up of grown up words, tears, hugs and confusion.

When she had been left with the men on the beach, Darcie's anguish had known no bounds. Not even Shakiya's promise that she would see her soon could comfort her. She had watched as Shakiya had sailed away in the boat, which brought her here. The Man who smelled of flowers had stayed with her, but this brought no comfort. Gone was his kind demeanour, he had first showed her when he took her away from the woman who shouted and smacked. Now, he seemed cross and uncaring. Darcie shivered, and not with cold. None of the men said anything to her, but put her roughly in a car. She could not see the new men's faces as they had dark hats pulled right down and scarves pulled right up, meaning that all she could see were their eyes. She did not dare speak, but once again closed her eyes and awaited her fate as the car took her away.

Darcie had been taken to a house; she did not know where. The men left her and went into another room. While they were gone, the bald headed Man had spoken to her in a menacing whisper. "It is time little one," he had said, "time to begin your new life and to earn your living. We have taken great risks in acquiring you, so do not let us down." The man had then disappeared into another room leaving Darcie to await her fate with her breath coming in frightened ragged gulps. Darcie had not understood a word the bald man had said, but her terror had taken on new meaning as the two new men had reappeared wearing clown masks. If there was one thing, which terrified Darcie more than anything it was clowns. She had once been given one as a Christmas present and her mother had to give it away as she had cried and refused to touch it. Her dread at seeing the two men in clown masks was overwhelming.

One man's mask had red curly hair and the other had orange hair. Darcie screamed, and the man in the red hair mask had shushed her loudly. The other man, wearing the orange hair mask laughed at her fear. She was given a glass of fizzy pop which tasted funny. She felt sleepy and when the orange hair man told her to lay on the bed, she had done so willingly, thinking that she was to be allowed to sleep.

Nothing could have prepared her for the terrible, depraved cruelty, which she was to endure for what seemed like an eternity, but what in reality was three long hours. She was bone tired, but this did nothing to prevent the men from carrying out their assault on her fragile and helpless body. Her pitiful screams meant nothing and fell on deaf ears. The men subjected her to such heinous abuse that eventually, she felt herself rise up out of her own body to escape it. She found herself looking down on her own tiny frame, watching with detached interest as first one man, then the other took turns to explore her every orifice. Occasionally, she was aware of that the bald headed Man appeared and was looking at her. He had done nothing to help her but had only grunted and spoken to the two men. "Do not ruin her," he had said one time, which had made the orange hair clown man speak loudly about having paid good money for this and he would do as he pleased. This then made the bald Man cross and there had been angry words. It did nothing to stop Darcie's nightmare though, as after the exchange, the two men had carried on.

When it was over, the men gave her another fizzy drink and a bag of crisps. She had vomited it back over the red haired clown who had exclaimed in disgust as orange hair laughed some more. Darcie could not cry, she could not think or move; she felt sore inside her tummy and though she did not understand it, she was bleeding from the sheer ferocity of the assault on what had previously been virgin territory. After a while, she felt nothing at all and she knew that really she must be dead.

***

Ethan moored his boat back in the same place he had left from less than half an hour ago. He marvelled at how his world could have changed so completely in such a short space of time. He had managed to keep up the charade, but worried that Ronnie or the woman had seen through him. When he switched off the boat however, Ronnie had handed him an envelope, which he guessed contained his payment. *Blood money* thought Ethan bitterly. He had forced a grin and commented, "Nice Ronnie nice," and had been told that there was more where that came from. The woman had ignored him all night.

Ronnie had left him with instructions for the return trip, which would be in a mere three hours. He was to pick Darcie up from where he had left her. Ethan managed a joke, "You sure Ronnie? He said with a humour he did not feel, "No changes of co-ordinates this time then?"

Ronnie's face remained impassive, "No change Ethan, you're in it now up to your neck. I think we can trust you. If not, well, you know what will happen," and with that Ronnie made a slicing action across his own neck, then laughed aloud at his own joke. "Later then Ethan," he said as he disembarked, "I'd get a few hours shut eye if I were you."

"Yeah later," replied Ethan knowing that sleep would be an impossibility. He wondered if he would ever sleep in peace again knowing what he had been a part of here tonight. The woman had already gone. *I didn't even get their names* thought Ethan distractedly, *but one thing's for sure, I won't ever forget their faces.*

***

Once back at home Shakiya sank onto the settee where she had spent so much time with Darcie and sat for a while in total silence as the shame and revulsion of what she was a part of seeped into her hardened heart. Unable to weep for herself for so many years, Shakiya now let go of her emotions and wept without restraint for the child she had so callously delivered into the hands of men who she knew would abuse her without conscience. Shakiya was also acutely aware that she had provided only a temporary refuge for the child. Charn Chai was bound to move her after tonight. She had little time left to act. When her tears finally dried up, Shakiya went to observe herself in her gold framed mirror. Reaching out and touching her own face, she spoke softly but with conviction.

I tell you this, she promised her reflection, *you will snap out of this pit of misery you've lived in all your life. You will get off your lazy whore's ass and you will DO something for this one. You will stop making all the excuses you've made before. Oh yes, you're afraid of the Old Man,* she paused to laugh, *so tell me, what more can he do to you? You are NOT going to sit back and let another child, this child, slip through the net into oblivion and a living hell. You Shakiya Wattana are going to be her goddamned salvation.*

In spite of her deep misery, Shakiya felt something lift within her. *Yes,* she thought, *yes. Enough is enough. It's time for action, and the best of it is, that old bastard won't see it coming.*

***

With Ronnie off the boat, Ethan wasted no time in making a phone call to Nicholas on the phone he had provided for him. A phone, which could not be traced. Nicholas had answered almost before it had rung.

Ethan quickly outlined what had happened on the boat, how Darcie had been brought aboard with an unknown woman and a bald headed Man, along with Ronnie. He described how he had been given new co-ordinates and how the woman sat Darcie in front of the listening device. Nicholas nodded in understanding on hearing this; *that explains it* he thought. Ethan finished his story, telling them how he had dropped Darcie and the bald headed Man off at a tiny cove. His voice cracked as he told him how he had intended to make a move to intervene, but had a gun pressed into his neck by Ronnie. Nicholas' face was a passive mask of anger as he realised how close they had come to rescuing this helpless child. Cursing their misfortune, Nicholas put his feelings aside and focused on the here and now.

"Right," he said decisively, "so, you have to be back at that cove in three hours now, correct?" he did not wait for Ethan to confirm this fact. "Make sure you're there Ethan; this time, we WILL be ready for them." Nicholas hung up and immediately dialled another number. He exchanged terse sentences with someone at the other end. "We're back on," he said giving them the co-ordinates Ethan had for the cove. Yes, three hours to the rendezvous; you had better leave now to make sure you're in position, we cannot fail her again." He hung up; *right* he said to himself, *this time, we'll be ready, and we will end this nightmare once and for all.*

***

Shakiya knew that the man they called Ethan was due to return for Darcie in three hours. While Charn Chai had not instructed her to be present, she was determined to carry out her plan to try and liberate Darcie. To do this, she knew that she HAD to be there and get Darcie back into her care. Once she got her back to her house, she would make good her escape, taking the child with her. As she thought about it, she realised that Ethan was not aware that she had not been instructed to return. Dare she turn up at his boat and simply trust that he would let her on board, assuming she was there for the child? She had nothing to lose by trying. Picking up her phone, she called for a taxi, one she knew would ask no questions, and not report to The Old Man. *You are not the only one with useful contacts*, she thought to herself as she waited.

Now then, there is one last thing I must do.

With one eye on the clock, Shakiya found a pen and paper and began to write. Her labours covered two sides of an A4 piece of paper. She read through what she had written, nodded in satisfaction, and went through to her bedroom. Pulling out her dressing table drawer, she pinned the note to the back of the drawer and replaced it. *Let's see how good you are at your job boys,* she thought to herself wryly. Grabbing her coat, she headed out of the door and towards whatever awaited her.

Chapter 36

Darcie had finally fallen into an exhausted sleep after what seemed like a lifetime of pain and anguish. She awoke again with a jolt to find that one of the men was asleep in the chair snoring softly, his trousers still undone, his hairy paunch hanging out; both testaments to his depravity and evil behaviour. He had taken off his terrifying clown mask and Darcie could see his face. He was a fat man with two chins and a stubbly beard, like daddy got when he didn't shave for a few days and mummy complained that he was scratchy. The other man was elsewhere; Darcie could hear him moving about but could not see him, which only served to heighten her anxiety. She shivered in fear of his return and curled herself up in a foetal position, making herself as small as she could. Darcie felt as if she was in a dream, an almost trance-like state had come over her. She felt pain; pain she had never known before in her short life. It invaded her whole body inside and out. She could not begin to comprehend what these man had done to her. They had terrorised her mind, body and soul and rendered her mute.

The snoring man, the one who had worn the orange hair clown mask began to stir, making Darcie curl tighter in her ball. She heard him yawn loudly and scratch himself. He belched and said, "Pardon me," which given his recent actions was the least of things he needed to be pardoned for. Darcie's eyes were scrunched closed as tight as she could make them. With the heart-breaking innocence of a child's magic thinking, she thought that if she kept her eyes shut, they might not see her, or forget she was there.

Her optimism was short lived as the other man reappeared in his red haired clown mask. He was cross straight away and shouted at the other man, "Idiot, get your mask on, she's right there you fool, she can see your face."

The man quickly reached onto the table and donned the hideous grinning orange haired mask, "She's asleep," he argued belligerently, "she's not seen me." Darcie then heard the red haired mask man say "I think we have time for one more game don't you?" and her nightmare began all over again.

Eventually, it was over; Darcie knew this as The Man who smelled of flowers came in and snapped an order at the other two men. "Enough," he had said, "you have had your money's worth, it is time for us to leave." He hesitated before remarking disdainfully, "You both look ridiculous. Do you really think those childish masks were necessary? The girl will not talk, and if she did, who is she going to tell? Her destiny is set; she will remain within our Organisation until we decide otherwise." The two men had grumbled but did not argue with him. The Man spoke softly to Darcie as he approached her, "Well done my little kitten," he had said, his words sounding confusingly kind. "You have done good work tonight and will be rewarded." Darcie did not understand this, but wondered if this meant she could now go back to her mummy and daddy, maybe this was her reward for doing what the men had wanted. She thought about asking The Man if this was the case, but fear held her prisoner and she kept silent. The Man extended his hand to her, "Come" he said, "let us go now and you can rest."

As Darcie stood up, the Man noticed that she was bleeding, and severely so. "You imbeciles," he snapped at the men, as the blood snaked down her legs, a testament to their cruelty. "I specifically warned you not to ruin her. Have you no common sense? She is but four years old; your rough handling has caused damage and will put her out of action, leading to a loss of revenue for us. The deficit will have to be made up; you will now pay double the agreed price for your uncontrolled and brutal handling of her."

Alan and Morris exchanged horrified glances from under their disguises, "Now look here," began Alan, but his words died on his lips as Charn Chai produced a hand gun. "Maybe you did not understand me," menaced Charn Chai, as he brandished the weapon, "you gentlemen are a long way from home, and farangs are robbed and killed all the time here with little interest from our local police. I suggest that you have the money by this time tomorrow or suffer the consequences?" He paused to allow the threat to hit home, and then added, "And do not assume you can simply leave the country; you will be watched. Wait one hour until you leave this house tonight. Meet me back here tomorrow at midnight with the additional cash and do not be late." In light of the gun, the two men had no choice, but to simply swallow their anger and nod their agreement, their red and orange hair bobbing comically as they did so.

Charn Chai then pulled out his phone and dialled; speaking tersely when it connected, "Yes, Dr Lo? I need your services immediately. Thank you I will send her straight over." As soon as he had finished the call, Charn Chai made another, and within ten minutes, a poker faced Thai woman arrived and took Darcie away to the waiting doctor. It was the first time Darcie would require emergency medical treatment; it would not be the last.

***

Nicholas and the men supporting him were in place at the cove, hidden by darkness and the surrounding scrub, with all their senses on high alert. They had their instructions and like bloodhounds on the scent, they were keen to get on with the operation. Hardened as they were, there was not a man among them who was not sickened to their stomach by Nicholas' account of the missing child and her plight. They were more than ready and waited in the darkness, with fire in their eyes.

***

As he made his way back to the boat, The Man could hear the waves and smell the salty tang of the ocean. He cursed the stupidity of the farang who did not know how to handle such a valuable package. Suddenly, he stopped walking and listened acutely. His senses on hyper alert, The Man swore in his native tongue.

Precisely 10 seconds later, all hell broke loose.

Chapter 37

Ethan had met Ronnie again and had not been particularly surprised to see the woman waiting by his boat as well. He assumed, as she had hoped he would, that she was part of the deal. As they sailed back towards the tiny cove, Ethan had a knot in his stomach the size of a basketball. What if they changed the coordinates again? What if having served his purpose, he was disposable? He ground his teeth as he sailed towards the destination, eyes scanning his surroundings for any sign of trouble. He moored his boat in the cove and made as if to get off. A restraining hand on his shoulder prevented him. "No need to get off," came Ronnie's soft voice, "we'll just wait here as instructed, he won't be long now."

The woman glared contemptuously at Ronnie, and gathering all her courage spoke up. "I am required to go to the child," she said and simply hopped off the boat before Ronnie could disagree. He shrugged; it was of no consequence to him what the whore did. His only concern was Ethan and the boat. The Man had paid him well for this arrangement, and so far, all had gone to plan. He was certain, there would be more work, and he would gladly accept. After all, the money was astonishing.

As Ronnie contemplated his future riches, his peace was interrupted by a shout; a flash of light and the unmistakeable sound of conflict.

"Finally," muttered Ethan as he turned and with great relish punched Ronnie square in the face.

***

Once off the boat, Shakiya had made her way swiftly along the beach; her path lit by the flashlight in her shaking hand. Sweating with fear, she saw the shadowy figure of a familiar shape approaching her. It was Charn Chai but he was alone. Confused, Shakiya was about to shout to him and ask where the child was; however, before she could speak, the scrubland around her came alive and without any warning, she was in the midst of chaos as a group of burly armed men materialised as if from nowhere. "STOP," commanded an authoritarian voice, "stop now or we will open fire."

Charn Chai shouted in annoyance and immediately began to run for the boat. Shakiya followed, screaming at him, "Where is the child," she shouted above the noise, "let me take her to safety," she pleaded. Charn Chai hesitated, which was all it took for one of the men to bear down on him and hit him squarely in the small of his back with the butt of his automatic weapon. He fell heavily, and went sprawling onto the soft sand. Turning swiftly with the agility of a cat, Charn Chai lashed out with feet and fists, catching his attacker off guard and momentarily gaining the advantage. Using the time to draw his weapon, he shot in the direction the man had fallen and was satisfied to hear a grunt of pain. *Got him* he thought grimly as he leapt to his feet and began to run. No one else had time to get a clear shot at Charn Chai who evaporated into the shadows.

"Get down, stay down," shouted the soldier in vain hope of arresting Charn Chai's flight. The light on his helmet threw distorted shadows across the beach as he searched in vain for the child. *Where was she?*

At this point, Ethan entered the melee and in the confusion and darkness careered headlong into Shakiya. The pair fell onto the sand in a tangle of arms and legs. Shakiya realised who it was and began to beat Ethan with her fists, "Son of a pig," she shouted in unabated fury, "deliverer of children unto evil," she continued blinded by rage and terror. Ethan grabbed the spitting hissing woman by the wrists and bore her to the ground.

"I'm here to help," was all he managed before a crack to the side of his temple stunned him into blackness and oblivion.

Shakiya twisted sideways, avoiding the next blow from the butt of the soldier's gun; she leapt to her feet and with a violence she never knew she possessed, shoved the man hard in the chest, taking him off guard and sending him sprawling.

Fuelled by adrenaline and terror, Shakiya raced down the beach. She managed another ten yards before a bullet took her cleanly in the back of the neck, severing her vertebrae and extinguishing her life in the blink of an eye.

All her hopes for liberating Darcie died with her.

The soldier who made the shot, did so from 100 yards away using his night scope, which rendered the hiding place of darkness irrelevant. As he ran towards her inert body, he saw the man come out of the tree line, zig zagged as he ran, demonstrating a fighter's knowledge and preventing a clear shot. Cursing, the soldier gave chase, but the Man clearly knew the terrain better than he did and had once again disappeared into the surrounding bushes.

Using his radio headset to call for back up, the man continued his search, his powerful torch beam illuminating his path, along with his night scope, with which he scanned every inch of the area in his sights. Nothing. He heard the sound of the other men running to his aid; "Spread out," he shouted, the need for silence now pointless, "he can't have gone far."

With the cunning of a cat, Charn Chai had immediately doubled back and was now only yards from the boat. He knew it was a matter of minutes before the soldiers realised this and gave chase. He reached the boat, and leapt in, gunning the engines into life. Ronnie was still on the floor, unconscious, not from Ethan's right hook, but from hitting his head on the deck as he went down. Charn Chai kicked him savagely and growled at him to wake up as he opened the throttle and blasted the boat out into the bay, heading for one of his safe havens. The exertion of the past few minutes had not so much as caused him to raise a sweat. He remained calm and clear headed, knowing that his life depended on his ability to focus in times of crisis and chaos such as this.

Ronnie groaned and began to come round. Charn Chai spoke to him in disgust, "You proved to be of no value to me whatsoever." He knew that Ronnie would have to be retired and made a mental note to ring his usual contact in this regard. Ronnie sported a bruise to his left jaw, and he fingered it tenderly. "That bastard Ethan took me off guard," he complained, "wait till I see him, he'll get what's coming to him," he threatened.

Charn Chai pulled a face in the darkness. "You whine like a woman, and undoubtedly, Ethan was apprehended, but no matter, I will make some phone calls tomorrow to ensure his everlasting silence."

Ronnie grinned, "Good," he said, "no more than he deserves." What Ronnie did not hear was Charn Chai adding softly, "And your silence too my useless friend, yours too."

***

Nicholas sat on the beach in the dark, illuminated only by the flashlight in his hand. His sense of failure and emptiness was crushing. Ethan sat beside him holding his aching head in his hands, his identity now verified by Nicholas as one of the good guys. Ethan did not feel like a good guy, he felt like a complete bastard. It was he who delivered Darcie to this beach, and because of him, she was once again missing.

"We were so damn close," whispered Nicholas, "how did we miss her? I mean, where the hell was she?" Ethan did not answer; he was too far down in a pit of his own misery.

One of the men approached Nicholas, bringing more light with him and making Ethan squint and shield his eyes. "The dead woman hasn't been identified sir," he reported, "the coastguard has been alerted to search for the boat, and local guys are on their way." Nicholas nodded; he knew the local police would have to become involved in the event of a death. He had cleared tonight's operation at the highest level and was not looking forward to reporting on their abject failure. Though there was still a team of men searching the area, and road blocks were in the process of being set up, Nicholas had no confidence that Darcie would be found. He knew that whoever had her would now spirit her away, possibly forever. She was too hot to handle now and Nicholas had a deep feeling of unease, that he might had just sealed the child's fate.

With a deep sigh, he got wearily to his feet and extended a hand to Ethan. "Come on," he said, "let's go back, Diane must be worried."

***

Morris and Alan had pulled off their masks and waited for the hour, as instructed by the bald-headed man whose name they realised they did not know. Watching the clock as the minutes ticked by, they paced the room impatiently, not daring to leave for fear they were indeed being watched as the man had warned.

Morris was the first to speak, "What are we going to do?" he whined, "I can't get caught, not here, not with my record; they'll thrown me in that prison of theirs and throw away the key."

Alan looked at him with contempt, "You knew the risks," he said shortly, "you chose to come with me, no one forced you." Morris looked like a petulant child, "I never knew it would be so dangerous," he moaned. Alan turned on him angrily, "What DID you think then Morris? What DID you imagine it would be like? Maybe you thought we'd be treated like royalty and have a harem of young girls waiting on us. Have you ANY idea how long I've waited for an opportunity like this? Let me tell you, access to a child such as Darcie Taylor is a once in a lifetime opportunity my depraved friend. You PAY for the risk, you PAY for the danger, it's part of the deal. I suggest in future that you stick to touching up your nieces when you babysit, that seems more suited to your talents."

Morris was taken aback; he had not expected Alan to react as he did. He retaliated, "Well, Mr Big Shot," he said sarcastically, "I'm sure you think you know it all and I'm just Nobody from the Deacon Hill Estate, but you're not the only one with ambitions and I can go far here if I play my cards right. I blame you for this mess, meeting up in the middle of nowhere. I said we should have just gone downtown to one of the main places, but no you have to take risks and here we are, stuck with it."

Alan took a deep breath, "Look Morris," he said more reasonably, "fighting amongst ourselves will get us nowhere, what we need to do is think of a plan to get back to England and fast. Never mind trying to stay here, not now; we can always come back next year and try again."

Morris felt only slightly appeased. A spoiled and selfish man, he was used to having his own way. However, he had to admit that staying in Thailand was now too big a risk to take. Reluctantly, he nodded, "Okay," he said, ever the follower "what shall we do then?"

Alan continued, "Well I don't know about you, but I've no intention of paying the extra money this guy wants, so as far as I'm concerned, we need to get out of here and quickly. I know he said we're being watched, but if we wait a bit, maybe we can sneak out."

Morris looked unconvinced, "Sneak out? How? Where to? If he's watching us, there's nowhere to hide."

Alan pulled a face, "Well, perhaps we can create a diversion," he suggested.

"Such as?" asked Morris warming to the idea.

"I don't know," replied Alan exasperated, "why do I have to think of everything? Why don't YOU do some thinking for a change?"

Morris sat down and began to apply himself to the problem. Rubbing his belly, he eventually spoke slowly and deliberately, "How about this?" he said thoughtfully.

As Morris outlined his plan; Alan's face lit up, "Morris Old Man," he said with a grin, "you might just have something there, well done."

Chapter 38

Ethan had arrived back at the flat at around 8 o'clock the following morning, and was met by a white faced Diane who was beside herself with worry after a totally sleepless night. "Did you get her?" she blurted out as soon as she had opened the door to him. She could tell by the look on his face that their mission of salvation had not gone according to plan. "What happened? She asked again urgently, "Tell me you got her, for the love of God Ethan tell me you have her safe."

However, Diane knew something terrible had happened; Ethan's eyes were wild and staring and there was a haunted look she had never seen before. "Ethan," she began, but he waved her away, "I can't talk about it Diane," he said, his voice a choked whisper. "What have I done? What the hell were we thinking getting mixed up in this?" he questioned. Ethan put his head in his hands and inhaled slowly and deeply. "I don't know how I will ever find peace again after what I've been a part of."

Diane looked at Ethan, and a cold hand gripped her heart. All she could think was that she had somehow lost him.

***

Nicholas sat heavily on the bed back in his hotel; his feelings were those of despair and he felt quite ill with fatigue. He had just come from a most uncomfortable morning meeting with his superiors in Thailand. He had not had any sleep before going to explain the story of the bungled rescue attempt of Darcie Taylor. His version of events had finally been accepted, though he had to do some detailed explaining as to how it had all gone so wrong. His superiors had eventually given Nicholas permission to continue his involvement in looking for Darcie. They had also agreed to him liaising with the Berlioz family who, he was informed, had requested a meeting with him. Nicholas had built up a network of so many contacts over his years in the country, that there was really no one else better suited to such a task. Nicholas however, had never felt less than qualified. He felt like a complete failure, despite the coordinates of Ethan's first drop point being changed and despite the fact that Darcie was not even present at the second rendezvous. Nicholas had always had an overdeveloped sense of responsibility, and this was no different. Before he had left the meeting, his superiors had shared some new information with him which had made him sit up and take notice. There was potentially a lead to the Old Man; it was a thin and tenuous possibility, but nevertheless, it was better than nothing. He would have to see how it panned out. He had followed so many leads over the years, most of which had ended in disappointment. He dares not get his hopes up too high. Sighing deeply, and in a state of total exhaustion, he finally allowed sleep to overtake him; plagued as always with the nightmares of old.

***

The blaze at the house had attracted the attention of a vehicle passing on the road half a mile away, the driver of which had called the emergency services. With flames leaping high into the air, it had been a spectacular ruse. Alan had found it hard to believe that for once, Morris had come up with a half decent plan. If they were being watched, the watchers would be forced to leave once the fire brigade turned up.

Hearing the welcome sound of sirens, Alan patted Morris on the back, "Got to hand it to you my friend, this was a brilliant idea, we'll be out of here in no time."

Morris revelled in Alan's praise, "Thanks Alan, I got the idea from a murder mystery I once watched on CBS." It had been easy to set the fire, some crumpled paper and cigarette lighter and bingo; the flames snatched greedily at the paper, engulfing it and looking for more fuel, which they found in the curtains and soft furnishings and before long, the house was ablaze. The men had tossed their clown masks into the furnace before leaving, satisfied that the potentially incriminating accessories were now obliterated. It would have been hard to explain why they were in possession of such things so far out here in the middle of nowhere.

Alan and Morris watched the fire engines pull up, and were pleased to see that they were accompanied by an ambulance. Adopting the injured air of victims of a freak accident, Alan took the lead and explained that they had been trying to cook with the antiquated Calor gas cooker and there had been an explosion. The ambulance had insisted on taking them to the hospital in Pattaya, where they were checked out and released an hour later. During the drive, the assistant occupying the passenger seat had made an unobtrusive, but well-placed phone call. Listening to the instructions given, he had spoken only to confirm he had understood. Hanging up, the man knew that he would be rewarded for his loyalty.

Congratulating themselves on their escape, the two men left the hospital and headed for their hotel in a taxi, intent on collecting their belongings and then travelling to the airport in the hope of catching the first flight out. Unaware that their cunning plan had only delayed the inevitable, the men continued with their intentions, in blissful ignorance. The Old Man's web of contacts were numerous and reliable and had not failed him tonight.

***

Nicholas, Diane and Ethan met again in his hotel room later that day. Still feeling tired, despite grabbing two-hour sleep earlier, Nicholas refocused his mind. "So what now?" asked Diane anxiously. Nicholas frowned as he looked at Ethan, it was clear that the incident on the beach had taken a grave toll on him.

"Ethan," he began, "I know exactly how you are feeling, but sinking into a pit is not going to help this child. I am acutely aware that Darcie Taylor is not the only missing child in Thailand right now. As well as dozens of missing local children, there is of course, the abduction of Angelique Berlioz, a French National, to deal with. Like Darcie, she was taken from a crowd at a time when her parents' attention was diverted. I am told by the local police that the only lead we have is that her older brother claims that she was led away by a nurse. If you still wish to be of assistance to me Ethan, you are going to have to pull it together and be strong. If you no longer wish to help I will understand. This is not for everyone and you have no qualifications for the task other than having been singled out by one of the biggest child trafficking Organisations in the country. They are exploiters of children and little more than slave traders. The Organisation I am involved with has been following their trail for years. We've managed to catch some of them of course, but the main man has always managed to elude us and the loyalty of his operatives is unquestioned. They know what will happen to themselves and their families if they dare to speak out. We do know that he is careful, very careful; trusting no one, and covering his tracks with great skill, our only hope is that he has over stretched himself in taking two European children in one week. I have my own suspicions that somehow, the man who was involved in my own daughter's disappearance all those years ago, is still involved today. When we find that Old Man in the wheelchair, I firmly believe we will have found the brains of the operation."

Ethan was a little taken aback at Nicholas' speech. He had not expected tea and sympathy, but he had expected a bit more in the way of understanding and perhaps some discussion of events. His feelings of self-loathing were immense and he now had some appreciation of what Diane had to deal with on a daily basis as a social worker. The horrifying image of Darcie being carried off into the night, played on a loop in his mind, like a bad movie. It would haunt him forever, and no amount of justification that he was "Trying to help" could erase it.

Diane's voice broke his thoughts, "Ethan, Nicholas is right, we have to focus, for the sake of these children." Even in his depressed state, Ethan realised that this was the first time Diane had shown any strength since the tragedy of Daniel Thompson. He had got used to her tears and sense of hopelessness every time there was a sad event. She wept over events she read about in the newspaper, she even cried over the dozens of abandoned dogs in the street. He could see however, that these missing children had motivated her and that she was beginning to behave like the old Diane. The committed and dedicated social worker Diane that he had fallen in love with.

He looked at her with new respect, "You've had to do this for years," he said, his voice heavy with emotion. Diane squeezed his hand and smiled, "We have to help Ethan; I don't know about you, but I can't think about diving while there is such abject misery all around us."

Ethan remained quiet for many minutes, contemplating his position, before Nicholas broke the silence. "Listen Ethan, maybe this will help you to decide; I can't remain here indefinitely; as you both know I have an important job to do back home and I've already extended my stay by several days. My superiors at home are supportive of me lending my expertise here, but as I say, I can't stay much longer. I need to return to the UK, but I can continue to work from there. I have spoken to the powers that be, here in Thailand and explained the whole story of how you two came to be entangled in all this. I also made it clear as to the risks you exposed yourself to Ethan, in attempting to help Darcie Taylor. They have agreed that if you are willing, you can both remain here and assist in whatever way you can. I repeat, ONLY if you are willing, you know only too well that we are dealing with ruthless individuals. You would operate in the capacity of consultants, answerable to the few men here who I can really trust. I will return as soon as I am able. Before I leave I am to meet with the Berlioz family who are suffering the loss of their five-year-old daughter Angelique. There is little I can offer them in the way of hope. Sad to say they may never see their child again, but my main objective will be to see what details they can recall from the night their child was abducted. You never know, one day we might get lucky, God knows we need it. I appreciate Ethan that your involvement in this conspiracy has left you questioning your own conscience. You are clearly in some distress and shock as to the outcome of our efforts to liberate Darcie. However, I still feel that you have a lot to offer in the way of helping us apprehend these men, but I need to know how you feel about it."

Diane and Ethan sat quietly as they ingested all that Nicholas had said. Diane spoke first. "You know I'm officially off work sick," she said looking at the floor with some embarrassment.

Nicholas inclined his head, "And we know why Diane, you suffered a great tragedy and we all know you were not to blame for it." Diane swallowed hard, "Thank you," she said, "that means a lot; anyway, I'm determined to do all I can to get back to work as soon as I possibly can. I loved my job, social work is what I know I am called to do and I can't stay on holiday or in hiding forever. I know I have to get back in there, face the press again if necessary and get on with what I do best. However, it would seem that, at the moment, I can be of more use here, and so I am more than willing to do whatever I can to bring these men to justice. Ethan?" she said turning to her partner, "How about you?"

Ethan raised his hands in a gesture of hopelessness. "Listen," he said, "I'm a musician, I'm a dive instructor, I'm an easy going guy, I like a laid back life. God knows how I got mixed up in all this. I'm way, way, out of my comfort zone right now and that's a feeling I do not like. But, here's the truth now, when I was on that boat, with that little girl within my reach, I have never felt more helpless in my life. Like most people, I stick my head in the sand when it comes to stuff like child abuse. I don't like to think about it, let alone talk about it. Of course I know it goes on, hell I'm shacked up with a woman who deals with it for a living. I'd rather not know about it all thank you very much, but now I AM involved and I can't ignore it, I can't simply go on with my nice easy life and pretend this never happened. I TOOK that child to her abusers, ME, Ethan Montana, I did that and I have to live with it. Now you're telling me I have an opportunity to maybe put it right and get these guys behind bars where they belong? ... Mr Bishop, I'm in."

Chapter 39

Angelique sat in unusual silence watching Suzy as she applied herself to tidying the meagre rooms they occupied. "Stop staring," snapped Suzy unkindly, "I don't like being stared at."

Angelique shrugged her small shoulders in a perfect copy of her father. Eventually, she spoke up, "When can I go home?" she asked for the hundredth time. Suzy had never met a child like her. She was completely single minded and determined. Her never ending questions were like a dripping tap. Suzy was totally fed up of caring for this incorrigible child and wanted out. Usually, her charges were whining crying little brats who she could silence with a slap and a hiss of words, but this one ... Sheesh, this one drove her nuts. Ignoring Angelique, she carried on with her half-hearted tidying up, one never knew if The Mover might call. She'd been here for two whole days now and not a word from anyone. She was running low on supplies and if someone didn't come soon, she wasn't quite sure what she would do. The house was so remote, that even if she dared to nip out to the shops, there were no shops to go to. Suzy knew that like Darcie Taylor, this child was of high value. She also knew that her compatriot Ruby Wong had overstepped herself in caring for the Taylor girl and her sister had paid a high price for her stupidity. There would be no mistakes from Suzy. She knew her place and had no intention of getting it wrong. "When can I go home?" demanded Angelique for the second time in a few seconds.

Suzy slammed her hand down on the table, "WILL you shut UP," she shouted, "once and for all you are NOT going home and the sooner you accept that the better."

Angelique stuck out her chin defiantly, "I am too going home, you'll see, you just wait and see, I am going home and you will be in big trouble for keeping me here."

Suzy opened her mouth to shout again, but froze at the sound of her phone ringing. "Be quiet now," she ordered, "this is important."

"Is it mummy?" asked Angelique hopefully, "Shhh no," replied Suzy as she answered. Suzy said very little during the 30 second call. When she hung up,

Angelique was afire with questions, "Who was it? Was it about me? When can I go home?"

Wearily, Suzy turned her attention to the hyperactive child, "Right," she said, "big day tomorrow, you're moving house and going somewhere else. We have to get up early, so you need to go to bed soon and sleep, you have a long day ahead of you."

Angelique smiled happily, "Am I going home?" she asked one more time. Suzy just sighed and left the room.

***

Nicholas felt like his life was one long round of meetings and phone calls. Once Diane and Ethan had left, he had rung Melanie to say he would be home in two days, but for now, he was once again in the foyer of his hotel; this time waiting for the Berlioz family to arrive. Nicholas had almost run out of platitude and sympathies, knowing they did no good anyway. However, when the harried and exhausted family arrived, he managed to find more expressions of sorrow as he led them through into the private room he had booked. With a strong feeling of déjà vu from his meeting with the Taylors, he once again set out on an information gathering exercise. He was immediately struck by the difference in the families. Whereas in the Taylor family, it had been Mrs Taylor who seemed to be suffering the most; in this family, the father was clearly the one taking the brunt of the guilt and grief. The mother was as determined a character he had ever met and he warmed to her courage in the face of such tragedy.

It was clear that Claude Berlioz was the parent who felt most responsible for his daughter's disappearance. Like Verity Taylor, he had been right there watching Angelique when the explosion happened, and if he had not responded to try and assist a victim of the explosion, maybe she would still be with them. It was a vicious circle of condemnation and self-destructive guilt, Nicholas knew only too well, he too had suffered in the same way. Nicholas spoke gently to Fabien, knowing that the young boy was as traumatised as any of them, having been a witness to his sister's abduction, and having been helpless to prevent it.

"Fabien," he began, "tell me everything you can remember, take your time it's okay." With great bravery, Fabien told Nicholas about the woman he had seen who was dressed in a nurse's uniform. She had approached Angelique, leaned down and spoken to her and then led her away by the hand. "So the lady didn't drag your sister away Fabien, she just led her away?" asked Nicholas.

Fabien nodded, "Yes sir," he said with his usual reserve, "my sister clearly trusted her and went willingly. I was too far away, I could not get to her," he said, his voice cracking with emotion at the memory. Robyn reached out to her son and held his hand, bright tears in her eyes.

"It's okay Fabien," she soothed, "it was not your fault son."

Nicholas then asked the family the same question he had asked the Taylors; *had any of them seen an Old Man in a wheelchair anywhere at the scene*. One by one, the family all shook their heads and Nicholas felt the disappointment deep within him.

He was about to move on when Robyn suddenly put her hand up, "Wait," she said, "just wait … that morning, Claude, you remember, we had been to the beach. As we were leaving, something Angelique said," she frowned as she tried to recall her daughter's words, "Yes, that was it, she asked me why the man was sitting in a chair with wheels on it, that's what she said. I didn't see him, but Angelique did. What does he have to do with the situation Mr Bishop? Angelique saw this man miles away on the beach at Cha-Am, and yet she was abducted from Bangkok. How can this be the same person?"

Once again, Nicholas found himself taking a family into his confidence and outlining his suspicions that a man in a wheelchair, who would now be a very Old Man, was somehow involved. Whoever he was, he had been seen at too many locations where children were known to have been abducted and yet, no one had been able to track him down. The fact that he had been seen close to where both Darcie AND Angelique had been, was highly suspicious. It would have taken very little effort for him to have the family followed back to Bangkok, where he would have then had them watched.

Claude's face registered the first real emotion since Nicholas had entered the room. "We were followed?" he said with mounting rage. "This man actually stalked my child?"

Nicholas nodded sadly, "I would not put it past him," he said, "he has a wealth of people working for him. At the end of the day, this is simply an organised crime syndicate we are dealing with, and I am only too sorry that you have been caught up in it."

With the usual promises that he and the government would do everything within their power, Nicholas bid the family goodbye. They planned to stay in the area for as long as they possibly could, searching for Angelique. "I know she's out there Mr Bishop," said Robyn as they stood up to leave, "you probably think I'm crazy having so much hope, but I feel it here," she said putting her hand on her heart.

Nicholas put his hand on her shoulder in a gesture of solidarity. "Sometimes Mrs Berlioz, hope is all we have left to hang on to," he said sadly.

Chapter 40

Verity Taylor sat at the kitchen table of the house they were now renting in Bangkok. It had been arranged through the efforts of their family liaison officer Elspeth with the support of the British Embassy. Verity's eyes were vacant and unseeing. Jack pulled at her jumper in a vain effort to gain her attention. Verity was lost in a silent world of unimaginable grief, with a heartache so deep it caused her actual physical pain. Though she tried not to think about where her little girl was, and worse still, what she was going through, images of Darcie haunted her every waking moment and gave her nightmares each time she managed to drift into a fitful sleep; sleep induced by the medication she had been prescribed. She had lost over a stone in weight in less than the two weeks Darcie had been missing. She simply could not think about food and barely touched the offerings, which David and Elspeth put in front of her three or four times a day. She would simply push the food away and weep.

David was in his own private hell. Blaming himself a million times over for not being around when his precious daughter was so cruelly taken from them, he was at a loss as to what to do. Typically for a man, David wanted action and he wanted Darcie found. The wheels of justice were turning too slowly for his liking and no one seemed to be doing anything useful. Nicholas Bishop had told them, with great difficulty, of the bungled attempt to save Darcie, and his stomach cramped into a fist when he thought about the man who had steered the boat, watching as Darcie was led away to God knows what. Why had he not intervened? Why had he just stood by and let her go? David's anger was a living burning thing, fed by the bitter fuel of his passion. More than anything, David wanted his daughter back, but if he could not have that, then his number one priority was revenge.

Darcie's abduction was taking a heavy toll on Verity and David's relationship. It was just another casualty of the tragedy. Hardly able to speak to each other through the wall of guilt and unspoken blame, David and Verity existed in the same space and both knew that the disappearance of their precious child had changed their lives forever. They could not remain in Thailand for much longer, and the knowledge of having to leave the country where their little girl was still missing was tearing them both apart.

Jack was also suffering as the world he had known, slowly dwindled away. Another victim of his sister's kidnapping, Jack was a prime example of the collateral damage of personal tragedy. Having grown up in a stable and loving home, Jack was now feeling the cold winds of uncertainty and abandonment blow around him. Though his basic needs were met, neither parent was emotionally available to him. On the rare occasion, that his mother did respond, she was clingy and cried all the time. His father was distant and angry. Jack did not understand what he had done to cause this, but as all children must, he blamed himself. He knew enough to understand that his sister had been taken away by bad people, and that it had happened when his mummy had been with him after he fell. Maybe if he hadn't fallen down, Darcie would still be here. Maybe the bad men who took her would come back for him. He suffered tummy pains and began to wet the bed again, crying out in his sleep in unspoken terror of bogie men and all things evil, which as every child knows lurk in dark places.

Three people, three kinds of separate hell with no connecting road back to each other, and all for the want of an Old Man's lust and greed.

Chapter 41

Charn Chai arrived to collect Angelique early in the morning as arranged. As instructed, Suzy had her ready, and the child was bouncing off the walls with pent up energy and emotion. However, the presence of the stranger in the room silenced her momentarily. Charn Chai considered her as a farmer might contemplate a new goat or a milk cow. He whistled softy under his breath, *Now THAT is an acquisition*, he thought to himself, *white blonde, with elfin beauty, yes, this was a good choice Old Man. She will command the highest possible price.*

Angelique found her voice, "Have you come to take me home?" she asked directly without fear. Charn Chai felt no emotion at this question, he had heard it from hundreds of children, and it made no difference to his response. "No little one, not home. I have come to take you to your new life, where, if you are wise, you will learn obedience and a sense of duty. If you do not learn these things, you will find life hard and unrewarding. However, if you prove yourself to be of value, this will bring its own rewards." Angelique understood not one word that the bald headed man said. All she heard was that he had not come to take her home. Her disappointment was crushing. She followed the man and Suzy to a big black vehicle, which was outside. Angelique had not been allowed outside in three days, and the fresh air and sunshine made her squint. Lifting her hand to shield her eyes from the sun, she looked around; she saw nothing but fields and trees, no people and no other houses. She may as well have been on the moon. There was no one to help her, she had no choice but to go with these people and hope that they changed their mind.

The journey was long and Angelique could not help but doze off every hour or so. She was exhausted with the sheer effort of surviving. When awake, she bombarded the man and Suzy with questions, "Where are we going? Are we nearly there? Can I see my mummy?"

Eventually the man hissed at Suzy, "If you do not silence her I will put a gag over her mouth."

Suzy knew he was not joking and turned around to Angelique, "Be quiet," she ordered, "stop asking questions or you will be severely punished." This served to quiet Angelique for all of two minutes before she piped up again, "What will you do to punish me? Mummy used to make me sit on the naughty step, but you don't have a naughty step in the car, so what will you do?"

The Man spoke up, "I will tell you what I will do," he said with menacing emphasis on the word "I." "I will stop this car and I will beat you until you understand how to obey instructions. Now BE QUIET." Angelique's bottom lip began to tremble, no one shouted at her, and certainly no one had ever smacked her, never mind beaten her. However, at five years old and oblivious to the real danger she was in and what awaited her, she did not truly appreciate that the Man was indeed deadly serious.

"I will tell my daddy if you beat me," she said defiantly, "and he will tell you off."

Charn Chai clenched his teeth. He knew that he was becoming stressed and strove to overcome this feeling. Though he was loathe to admit it, the attempt by agents to rescue Darcie Taylor had shocked him.

Clearly there was a leak in the Organisation and he had yet to identify who it was. One of their best operatives was dead, though he had to admit, it was her own fault. He had not asked the whore to turn up, so she had got what she deserved for not following orders. However, it would mean awkward questions from the top level of the Organisation. The Old Man had already expressed his intense displeasure at the death of Shakiya – who had, for some reason, been a favourite of his. Charn Chai knew that there would be some sort of consequence and he did not like waiting to find out what it might be. While The Old Man was undoubtedly the brains of the operation, he too had to answer to those in higher power, which reached all the way to the top levels of government. Darcie Taylor was big news, headline news, and a cause of huge embarrassment for the Thai government. Reports of her failed rescue had thankfully not made it to the hungry ears of the media, but the appeals for information regarding her whereabouts were a daily occurrence. The British government had now offered a substantial reward for information leading to her recovery, and Charn Chai had been required to work extremely hard to make sure that she was never found. He trusted no one; everyone had a price and he could not risk someone getting greedy. Following her unforeseen but necessary medical treatment, Charn Chai had moved Darcie to a place where no one would ever find her, and for now, that was where she would have to remain, maybe for many months. She was, in effect, useless to him for now, though he would make sure she made up for it in the future.

Charn Chai needed to think, but the child's incessant chattering in the back seat was distracting and annoying him. He would indeed teach her a lesson if she did not be quiet.

Angelique waited a few minutes but no one answered her. Emboldened by this, she pressed on, "Anyway, my daddy says…" she began, but got no further. Her words were abruptly cut off as Charn Chai's usually calm exterior snapped. He slammed on the brakes of the

SUV, causing Suzy Meesang to bang her head on the dashboard, despite wearing a seatbelt. Losing all sense of propriety and reason, Charn Chai leapt out, his intent was to be true to his word and beat Angelique into an obedient silence. If she did not learn now …

What Charn Chai had failed to appreciate however, was the monstrous 5 axle, 18-wheel tanker, which was bearing down on him from the opposite direction. On the fairly narrow roads on which they were travelling, space was at a premium. At the precise moment that Charn Chai flung open his door and leapt out, the planets aligned, the Gods released the full force of their vengeance and justice, and the truck connected perfectly with both the door and Charn Chai.

Charn Chai's surprise was surpassed only by his disbelief. He felt no immediate pain as was flung over 200 yards into the air by the force of the impact. He did however have one lucid moment of thought, before he hit the tree which would extinguish his corrupt and useless life. With a brief sense of irony, Charn Chai realised that this child, this irritating and troublesome child, had in fact killed him. He almost laughed, but time ran out and instead, his body was smashed to a pulp by the unimaginable violence of the collision.

Suzy Meesang was screaming, a high pitched keening sound, which pierced the air and shattered the eerie silence of the scene. After the initial impact, which had torn the door clean away from the SUV, taking the unfortunate Charn Chai with it, the concussion of the crash rocked the SUV to its core and despite its sturdy construction had succeeded in turning it over onto its roof. The 18-wheel tanker, which was the cause of the carnage had already begun to veer hard right when the driver saw with disbelieving eyes that the door of the SUV on the road ahead was opening. His action had undoubtedly saved Suzy and Angelique from further injury or even death. However, the truck had continued on its path, an out of control 75-foot missile weighing in at 35 tons, the driver had no chance whatsoever of recovering it from its deadly trajectory.

With the trailer wheels skidding in response to the hard braking the driver had been forced to apply, the tanker body was now moving faster than the cab and overtaking it. A jack-knife was inevitable. Closing his eyes, the driver prayed aloud to his Gods, the same Gods that had wreaked their retribution on Charn Chai. The driver could not appreciate that he was their chosen weapon of destruction, and a worthy sacrifice in the overall plan. All he knew was, that death was approaching him at high speed and he was helpless to avoid it. Hitting a tree on the opposite side of the road to where the broken body of Charn Chai hung lifelessly in his own tree, the driver's exit from this world was instant. He would never know the blessing of this, as had the tree not killed him, he would have been engulfed in the furious fire, which ensued as the tanker exploded, and he would have burned to death.

Chapter 42

Alan and Morris had hastily packed their belongings and were about to leave their hotel and head for the airport. Cautious and ever fearful of being followed, Alan went to the window and peered around the grubby net curtains which hung limply there. He felt a sense of unease as he noticed a black Mercedes with tinted windows in the carpark. Not the sort of vehicle he expected to see in a downbeat hotel like this. This was not Alan's first visit to Thailand; he had made the trip several times over the past few years, using different aliases and always travelling alone. He wished he had not invited the fat fool Morris Powell, who despite his good idea about the fire, was proving to be a liability. Alan was growing tired of Morris's whining and complaining. He would be better on his own, it was getting too risky to travel together and Alan Slater had no intention of being caught, not now, and certainly not in the company of Morris Powell. He paced the room as his mind raced to think of a plan.

Down in reception, a forgettable figure spoke quietly but persuasively to the desk clerk. After he left, the man on the desk pocketed the baht he had been given for his cooperation. Glancing at his watch, he knew that the farang would be checking out soon. He made a note of the phone number he had been given; it was of no account to him what happened to the stupid farang. He had no doubt as to where his loyalties lay.

***

Alan glanced out of the window again. The Mercedes had gone, but he had a distinct feeling of unease, which he could not shake. He had survived a long time in this game without detection; this was due in part to his ability to recognise danger when he saw it. Though the Mercedes was no longer in the car park, Alan had no doubt that they were still being watched. He needed some time to think of an exit strategy; rushing headlong into a decision would not be wise at such a potentially delicate time in the visit. No, he must plan carefully if he wanted to get out of this situation in one piece. On past visits, Alan had made some useful and well placed connections. Men who were mere shadows, whose real names he never knew and whose faces were always forgettable. Alan's instincts told him that it might be time to make contact with one of these men, and see if he could extricate himself from the mess he was in. It would cost him of course, but the sight of the Mercedes had unnerved him. He did not want to leave the hotel and find himself in more trouble than he was already in. If anyone managed to connect him to the missing English girl, Alan knew that he was looking at serious jail time.

After a lot of thought, Alan decided that it would be prudent to remain in the hotel for another night. This would give him further time to think and maybe, just maybe throw the opposition into some confusion. They were expected to check out today; staying another night might buy them some time. He picked up the phone and dialled reception; once connected, he told the clerk that they would be staying one more night, and hung up before he could protest. The clerk immediately rung the number he had been given, "They are stalling," he said anxiously, "they are here for one more night." Listening to the instructions, he nodded without speaking and hung up. The farang were not out of the woods, not by a long way.

***

Suzy realised that by some miracle, she was actually alive. She had no idea that Chan Chai had been so violently killed; all she knew was, that she had to get out of the car. Despite being hundreds of feet away, Suzy could feel the intense heat from the blazing tanker. Spurred on by fear, Suzy managed to undo her seat belt, and dropped hard onto the roof of the car, which was now the floor. Her sense of survival drove her to get out of the car as quickly as possible, but her sense of compassion forced her to turn and consider the child in the back seat. Angelique was, for once, completely silent, a thick stream of blood ran from her scalp and into her much valued hair, which in her suspended state hung down below her like a silver curtain. "Angelique" shouted Suzy desperately, "wake up little one, we must get out." There was no response and the sense of panic Suzy felt, threatened to overwhelm her. Wriggling through the space between the seats, she fought to undo Angelique's seat belt, but it was stuck fast.

"Oh come *on,*" she said in a voice that shook with emotion, "come on damn you; open." Suzy continued to struggle with the belt and Angelique began to stir. Suzy laughed in relief, "Oh thank God, are you okay my little chatter box?" Angelique's eyes were hazy and unfocused, she was clearly suffering from concussion, if not more serious injuries. In the midst of the chaos and confusion, Suzy Meesang's life seemed to pass in front of her eyes, and in the seconds that followed, she made a life-changing decision. While she wanted to help the child, she knew that this might be her one and only opportunity to escape. She had no idea where she was, but she knew they were many miles now from Bangkok and the immediate clutches and reach of the Old Man. Fearing that Charn Chai would appear at any moment, Suzy put her hand on Angelique's cheek, "I'm sorry baby," she said with genuine regret, "I'm sure someone will find you soon, but I have to go." With that, Suzy Meesang slipped out of the opening where the driver's door used to be and into oblivion, never to be seen or heard from again.

***

Angelique's head was pounding, not only from the deep gash in her temple, but also from her impossible position where she had hung for over ten minutes now. She was completely terrified and alone. The heat from the inferno, which used to be the tanker, was intense, even from a distance and her heart was hammering in fear. With the blood rushing in her ears, Angelique's hearing was impaired. However, as she listened, she could not fail to hear the urgent sound of sirens, which even at five years old, she knew meant that someone was coming to help. Within minutes, she felt strong hands reaching into the car, voices talking to her soothingly in a language she did not understand. "Where's my mummy?" asked Angelique in a haze of pain and confusion.

The man tending to her changed to English, and suddenly, she could understand what he was saying to her. "Okay baby, we'll find mummy, don't worry, we'll soon have you out of here. Can you tell me where you hurt?" Angelique's hope soared on hearing the man say he would find her mummy.

Struggling to break free of her restraints, Angelique began to shout, "Get my mummy, and my daddy, quickly before the bad man comes back." The man tending to her, knew that she had a head injury, and in her concussed state was not making sense. "Shhh baby doll," he soothed, "There's no bad man, you're safe now and we're here to help you. Can you tell me where you hurt?" he asked again. Angelique started to cry, "My head hurts," she whimpered "And there IS a bad man, he was right here in the car until the lorry hit him and the lady left me on my own, and I want my mummy." The man frowned as he cut the seat belt, which had been holding Angelique prisoner for so long. Cradling and supporting her as she was released, he gently laid her down to allow her to re-orientate herself. Angelique felt faint as the blood began to drain from her head and the world was righted before her. The man wrapped a blanket around her. Angelique closed her eyes at the comfort of his touch, and before she could help herself, she turned her head and vomited.

"Come on people," said the man calmly but with meaning, "let's get the baby out of here, quickly now." He waited until Angelique had finished being sick, wiping her mouth with a clean cloth.

"I'm not a baby," Angelique managed indignantly, "I am five years old." The man smiled at her, "And what is your name Miss five year's old?" he asked kindly, "My Name is Angelique Berlioz," she announced, not knowing the furore this would create, "and will someone *please* find my mummy?"

The man who had been so calm went white. He gave a shout in the language Angelique did not understand, and then there was a great commotion.

She was passed out of the car like a neat parcel and handed to a kind faced woman who put her on a stretcher and stroked her face. "Poor baby," she heard her whisper, "now, be brave, you will feel a sting." Angelique cried out as the needle went into her arm, and the woman set up a drip.

"Ouch" she cried, "you hurt me."

The woman carried on with her ministrations, "Sorry little doll," she apologised, "soon be done." Angelique was lifted with exaggerated care into the waiting ambulance, leaving the emergency services at the scene to sift through the destruction and try and piece together what had happened.

One of the fire officers scratched his head when he found what was left of Charn Chai in the tree. "What the hell?" he exclaimed, "how'd you get up there buddy?" he asked out loud as he called for ladders to retrieve his body.

Robyn Berlioz was going through the motions of making lunch when she got the call. Claude looked at her in alarm as her entire body froze and every bit of colour drained from her face.

Fearing the worst, he leapt to her side, "What?" he demanded, "Tell me quickly."

Later, Robyn would not recall dropping the phone, she would not recall screaming and falling into her husband's arms, all she would recall were the words,

Robyn ... we have her; she's safe.

Robyn, Claude and Fabien raced to the hospital in record time. Bursting through the main doors, they were met by Nicholas Bishop who had also been advised of Angelique's recovery and the circumstances of the accident. "Where is she?" demanded Claude tightly, "Where is my baby?"

Nicholas could not help it, he grabbed Claude Berlioz in a bear hug and slapped him on the back, "Through here Claude, she's just in here and driving us all mad with her demands." Robyn had tears coursing down her cheeks, and on hearing Nicholas' words, she laughed, "sounds like my girl," she said hurrying to the door of Angelique's room. Fabien looked shell shocked; it was so much for a boy of 12 to take in, but he was carried along in the tidal wave of joy and into his sister's room.

Angelique was sat up in bed eating ice cream when her parents and brother walked in to the room. She was sporting a bandage to her head, under which was hiding a neatly stitched wound in her left temple. "Maman," she cried in utter delight, "Papa, Fabien, I knew you would find me," and with that, she began to thrown back the covers of her bed, but Robyn beat her to it and enveloped her in her arms, smothering her with tears and kisses. Claude went one better and managed to embrace them both, closing his eyes and offering a silent prayer of thanks as he did so. After many minutes of weeping and hugging, both parents remembered Fabien and drew the boy into the close circle. Abandoning his usual reserve, Fabien broke down as he held his little sister in his arms, "I have missed you," he said sincerely, as he too broke down.

Once the family had had time to reunite, Nicholas came through to speak to them. He was still smiling, "This is excellent," he beamed, "truly excellent. However, there are many questions to be answered, and some close friends of mine in the police would like to talk to Angelique if she feels up to it. You may stay of course," he said to Claude and Robyn, "but it might be better if Fabien comes with me." Claude shook his head, "No," he said firmly, "no more separations, I will stay with Fabien, and Robyn can stay with Angelique."

Robyn nodded in agreement, "Yes, that is the way it will be," she said, "now Mr Bishop, let's get some answers."

***

When Verity heard the news of Angelique's recovery, she had of course wept tears of joy for the family. She had also felt a bitter stab of jealousy that it was not her own child who had been found. She immediately felt guilty for such an emotion, but could not help it. Why could Darcie not be found as well? David clearly felt the same way as he too questioned how Angelique had been saved and not their own child. "I can't see what they're doing," he said angrily over his newspaper, which carried the story of Angelique's miraculous recovery. "Once Nicholas Bishop leaves Thailand; I don't know who else we can trust." He looked at his wife, and thought with deep regret that she seemed more and more like a stranger to him now. He sighed deeply, "Verity," he said as kindly as he could, "we're going to have to go back to England pretty soon. We can't just stay here hoping and praying. I need to get back to work and Jack should go back to nursery and get into a routine again. I'm sure the authorities here will keep us informed, but honestly there's little more we can do here and we're going to run out of funds soon."

Verity's eyes flashed at him, the first sign of positive emotion he'd seen since Darcie had disappeared, "Leave?" she spat at him, "leave while there is a chance that our daughter might still be here? Are you out of your mind? I will never, and I mean NEVER leave here David, not while there is breath in my body. If I have to move to this God damned country to keep on looking, then I will, but don't ever, EVER ask me to leave. You go if you must, but I'm staying."

David was startled. Verity had never been a very forceful or demanding woman, which was one of the reasons he had married her. He liked her compliant, easy going nature; they had always complimented each other. He was at a loss for words, but tried to reason with her. "Verity, be reasonable, you can't stay here alone, what about Jack? What about us?"

Verity looked across the table at her husband of ten years. "What about us David?" she said coldly, "This is not about us anymore, it's about our child, who even as we speak is probably being subjected to some unimaginable horror. You think I give a damn about us anymore? I hate to burst your bubble David, but we're not living on Walton's mountain and whatever happiness we might have had is gone forever. All that matters now is Darcie and I will spend the rest of my life looking for her and hoping. Until someone tells me otherwise, SHE is my number one priority, not you David and sadly not Jack."

David nodded slowly, "I see," he said, his voice heavy with emotion, "Well it would seem you have your mind made up. Okay Verity, have it your own way, stay here if you can find a way, but I am not prepared to leave Jack here, on that I am quite clear." Verity's eyes welled with tears and she reached out and took her husband's hand. "I wish it could be different David," she said with regret, "but it can't. This has destroyed us; we both know it, and there is no way back. I want us to remain friends though, we have to for Darcie's sake. I must stay here, and as much as it will wrench my heart out, I agree that Jack must go with you back to England. My sister will help with his care and I'll come back and visit of course, but I need to live here. I have to be close to her David, even if it's only in spirit."

David squeezed Verity's hand in return; he knew she was right. He only wished he had her determination and felt the burden of guilt on his heart as he knew he wanted this nightmare to be over. He wanted to run away and hide. He didn't want to be strong, he felt like he was about to lose his mind. Returning to England was his way of making life normal again, though he knew it never would be. "Okay," he said simply, "okay, let's work out the details. I'm not giving up Verity, but I'm not like you and I cannot stay here and relive what happened every day of the week and neither can Jack."

Chapter 43

Over 250 miles away in her latest prison, unaware of the breakup of her beloved family, Darcie sat once again on a grubby stained mattress. Her physical scars were beginning to heal, but nothing would ever heal her broken heart and shattered soul. The weight of loneliness, which pressed upon her was almost enough to demolish her altogether. Her shoulder throbbed with new pain where she had been forced to submit to a tattoo, though she was too young to understand what it was, or why it was there. She had no tears left to cry, no feelings beyond emptiness and no hope other than words of an old whore, who had died trying to liberate her. Words that played over and over in her tortured mind.

My name is Darcie Taylor, I have a family who love me and they are looking for me.

The words now seemed to be from another time, another dimension. Did she ever have a loving family? Were they really looking for her? Her childhood gone forever, her life beyond repair, Darcie Taylor slipped into oblivion; one of the lost children. However, there would be no Never Never land, no Wendy or Peter Pan to save her.

Darcie Taylor was well and truly lost.

Chapter 44

Angelique's eyes were drooping. A combination of her head injury, emotion and tiredness. She had been talking to the specially trained police officer for over half an hour now and the effort of concentrating had worn her out. "I think that's enough now," said Robyn intervening as she noted her daughter's exhaustion. "She has been through so much; any more questions will have to wait for another day."

The police officer nodded his agreement, "Well done Miss Angelique," he said in genuine kindness, "maybe I will talk to you tomorrow." As he left the room, Angelique held out her hand to Robyn, "Maman," she said softly. Biting back the tears, Robyn caught the little hand in hers and sat quietly by as Angelique fell into a deep, healing sleep.

As her daughter slept, Robyn heard a gentle knock on the door, it was Nicholas. Robyn waved him in with her free hand and he sat on the hard hospital chair to talk to her.

"I've spoken to the police," he said quietly but grimly, "Angelique did extremely well in sharing so much information. She's a bright little spark that one, and I'm convinced her sharp wits and self-confidence went a long way in sustaining her throughout her terrible ordeal. It seems that the woman who was with Angelique, was the one who has been posing as a nurse, though we don't have a name. She was clever enough not to let that slip. All we know is that she was unkind to her and was in the car when it crashed, but left the scene soon after, and is no doubt many miles away by now if she has any sense. It's not much to go on, but it's a start and we do have a description of her from Angelique as well. Then there's the man, the one who was dead at the scene. We strongly suspect that he was The Old Man's right hand man, though we're awaiting finger prints to formally identify him. Who knows, he may give us the lead we've been waiting for, for so many years." Nicholas lowered his voice and spoke in a conspiratorial whisper to Robyn. "I understand from the doctors that Angelique has not been sexually assaulted."

Robyn closed her eyes to prevent more tears from escaping, "Yes," she breathed, "Thank God for small mercies. She was not sexually assaulted."

Nicholas shook his head, "She was one of the lucky ones, there must have been good reason to prevent her being sold to the highest bidder. All I can think of, is they were too taken up with Darcie to fully focus on Angelique. I can tell you though Robyn, it would not have been long, and who knows, she may even have been on her way to a buyer when the accident occurred." Robyn's face hardened, "In that case Nicholas," she said harshly "I have to say I am thankful for the crash, despite it killing an innocent lorry driver. It saved my little girl's life."

Nicholas stood up, "Right," he said, "I'm leaving tomorrow, so thought I'd just drop in to say farewell. I'll be back as soon as I can, but for now I have to get back to England and do some work. I take it that you will all be leaving as soon as possible?"

Robyn nodded, "As soon as Angelique is given the all clear, we will leave this terrible country and never return as long as we live," she said with venom. "This was supposed to be a happy family holiday and it turned into a nightmare. I am only grateful that the outcome was a positive one. We are aware that it could have ended so differently, and we feel deeply for the Taylor's who are still in agony from waiting for news of Darcie."

Nicholas hesitated, "I sincerely hope that they too can recover their daughter," he said solemnly, "but to be honest with you, I have my doubts. The Organisation, which is undoubtedly responsible for the abduction of both girls, will now be on high alert. They have lost Angelique and almost lost Darcie. My view is that if Darcie is still alive, she will have been moved to a distant location, possible even out of Thailand. They will batten down the hatches now and go to ground for a while, that is if they have any sense. Ah well, we must live in hope. Goodbye Robyn, please give my regards to Claude and Fabien," and with that, Nicholas was gone.

Nicholas was wrong about one thing – the Organisation were not exercising good sense at this time. They were in a fury of incandescent rage and were about to make the biggest mistake in their long and sordid history.

***

At the same time that Nicholas was taking his leave of Robyn and Angelique, Ruang Sak Yunram was having the senior equivalent of a temper tantrum. From his wheelchair, he shouted and raged, throwing any item within his reach across the room. "IDIOTS," he screamed as he aimed a valuable glass vase at the head of his youngest son, "I am surrounded by idiots."

The son looked nervously at his five brothers, all of whom had been summoned to see The Old Man. Stooping to pick up the now shattered vase, he tried to calm him. "Father," he began as reverently as he could under the circumstances, "father, your health, remember what your physicians have said, you must not excite yourself so."

Ruang Sak stopped, his hand around the stem of a cut glass wine glass, "My health?" he shrieked, "my health? It is a wonder I have not died of shame and disgrace." He threw the glass at the head of another son before continuing his diatribe. "I am betrayed, I am forsaken by those who should be serving me, even as I speak."

Ruang Sak's oldest son stepped forwards to speak, "Father," he said reasonably keeping an eye open for missiles, "Charn Chai could not help being killed. I doubt it was on his agenda for the day and he could not have foreseen the consequences of his untimely death."

The Old Man's energy was suddenly spent. He wheezed and coughed and spat on the floor. "Your sarcasm is of such value to me," he retorted with equal sarcasm, "even so," he said still with force in his quavering voice, "I have lost an asset of high value and yet another asset has had to be hidden away, like an unused treasure. I will not tolerate it; the rescued girl must be replaced. I insist on it. I will be taken quickly to look for a replacement."

All six of his sons looked taken aback. His second son who had up until now been silent spoke up, "Father, the risks are too high, the police, those not in our pay, are looking for you. Now they have the body of Charn Chai, they may find a link to you. It would be foolish indeed to be seen in public; you risk everything."

It was a brave speech, especially for a second son. Ruang Sak's small eyes narrowed, until they almost disappeared, "Am I so disrespected now that my word is to be challenged?" he demanded. "Is my word not still law in this family?" he said more loudly, his temper rising again. All of his sons began to murmur and mutter to appease him. There was not one of them who would dare to disagree with their irate and domineering father who had ruled them with a rod of iron all their lives. Satisfied, Ruang Sak sank back into his wheelchair, "Then it is decided, I will be taken out to make my selection. And find me another nurse," he snapped, "The consequences for the one who has dared to disappear will be severe when she is found, and she WILL be found. No one crosses me, no one leaves this Organisation other than through death itself. Charn Chai was indeed unfortunate, but Suzy Meesang will find herself more so, once she is found. She will rue the day she thought to betray me."

The sons bowed their heads in mutual acquiescence. "Father, if I may," said the youngest son again, "I am sure that this would have been your plan, but may I boldly suggest that we take you to make your selection at a location far from here?" The Old Man thought for a few seconds before answering, "Of course that would have been my suggestion," he said haughtily, "I was about to make the instruction before you so rudely spoke out of turn." The sons breathed a small sigh of relief, at least they could remove him from the immediate area, where he was being so keenly sought. One by one, they bowed and left the room, each of them lost in his own thoughts, and wondering if he would be the one to succeed the Old Man once he had left them. All of them were of the same thought, *it surely could not be long now?*

***

Ethan and Diane were sat in their apartment considering what might happen next when they got the call from Nicholas to say that Angelique had been found alive and apart from a cut on her head, she was well. They hugged each other and Diane wept with joy. "If only Darcie could know the same freedom," she remarked as she dried her eyes. "Nicholas is on his way round, he wants to talk to us about his plan," she said.

Ethan nodded, "Okay, why don't we have something to eat before he gets here and then we can talk without interruption." They were finishing their pizza half an hour later when Nicholas arrived.

After celebratory hugs, they got down to business. "I'm going back to England," he announced without preamble. "My job there will suffer if I don't go back soon, and while there is much to do here, I can't delay any longer. All I can do is ask you both to be available should anything develop. The police are trying to identify the dead man in the tree at the scene of Angelique's accident. Clearly he was involved in her abduction, but until we know who he is, we can't hope to trace any potential associates. Angelique told us about a woman who was in the car, but who fled the scene leaving her alone. It would appear that this is our mystery nurse, the one who leads the children away. She could tell us so much, but I seriously doubt we will ever find her. If the Organisation doesn't get to her first, chances are, she's gone to ground and wisely so. Our other mystery lady, who sadly died on the beach last week is yet to be identified."

"What about Ronnie?" Ethan asked quietly. He had been worrying about Ronnie and his fellow criminals since the night of Darcie's disappearance. He was convinced that they would come looking for him and did not want to think about the possible consequences of such a visit.

Nicholas sighed, "We don't know, is the short answer. No one has seen or heard from him or his associates; they are simply not on our radar. We're hoping that given the high profile nature of Darcie's case, he too will have seen sense and made himself scarce. Don't forget Ethan, as far as Ronnie is concerned, YOU were arrested that night, which will worry him more than anything as he knows you can identify him. I don't think you need worry about Ronnie returning anytime soon."

"When do you leave?" Asked Diane feeling suddenly alone; she had come to like and respect her Director far more than she did when working in the UK when she hardly knew him at all.

"Tomorrow morning," replied Nicholas, I have a flight booked for 9am. I'll keep in touch though, and you have my number and email address should you need to contact me."

Diane thought for a moment before replying, "Tell Glenda I'll be back soon," she said firmly, "I've been away too long and I'm ready to get back to work, once we've finished here that is."

Nicholas looked serious for a moment, "Diane," he began, "There is something I'd like you to consider, but not now. When you feel ready, we will talk, so bear that in mind before you jump back into anything will you?" Diane's eyes widened in mock surprise, "I'm intrigued," she said, "but I promise I'll bear it in mind."

"Right then, there's nothing left to say. I'll be off, and if anything should come up regarding Darcie, don't hesitate to let me know, day or night, it doesn't matter, contact me immediately. I'll try and get back out soon, but I can't say when."

The three of them shook hands and Nicholas left in his usual haste. Diane and Ethan regarded each other, "That's that then," said Ethan, "we're on our own. I wonder what the old rogue has in store for you."

Diane shrugged, "I've no idea, but it's sure to be interesting whatever it is."

***

Less than half an hour away in the Bay of Bangkok, Ronnie Lewis's body lay with a large rock tied firmly around his neck. Small shoals of fish nibbled at his rotting corpse. His eyes were already gone and it would not be too long before any trace of Ronnie Lewis was obliterated altogether. Nicholas was right, Ronnie would not be returning; not now, not ever.

Chapter 45

Once Nicholas had left, Ethan and Diane reviewed their position. Angelique was thankfully safe and relatively unharmed. She would hopefully recover quickly from her physical injuries, though her psychological wounds would take much longer to heal. Her family planned to leave Thailand as soon as they possibly could, which was perfectly understandable. Darcie Taylor was still missing, with no news, apart from the sad tidings that the heavy burden of the traumatic experience had caused the Taylor's to separate. Diane had been to visit Verity, who had understandably asked for some space and time to adjust to her new life, which she intended to make in Thailand. She repeated her vow to Diane, never to leave and never to give up searching and hoping. David had left the country and was trying to make a new life for himself and little Jack, but was finding it almost impossible.

Ethan and Diane agreed that given the circumstances, they could afford to take a day or two off. "We could use a break," Diane agreed, "and we won't be gone long, then we can come back and decide what's next."

Ethan smiled for the first time in days, "Okay then, where shall we go? How about visiting one of the beaches on the West of the Gulf? Hey, what about Hua Hin? What do you say Di? We'd have to leave really early, but it'd be well worth the effort. We can drive down and just chill out on the beach like tourists."

Diane hugged herself, "Really? Can we?"

Ethan nodded enthusiastically, "Why not?" He said with equal enthusiasm.

Diane beamed, "Then what are you waiting for Mr Montana, let's get going."

They both laughed, never imagining the consequences that their simple decision would have.

***

The Old Man had chosen his second son as his escort for the outing, which had worryingly, been planned with less care than usual, such was his haste to identify another victim. All of Ruang Sak's sons had discussed the matter privately among themselves and all had expressed their reservations, agreeing that their father seemed to be getting careless. Usually, he would make meticulous plans before he ventured out. This even extended to when he went out to eat, or made any appearance in public. He was so careful; years of experience had taught him that there was no substitute for careful planning, but lately he seemed to be acting with reckless abandon. They knew that Charn Chai's death had hit him harder than he cared to admit. Added to this was the real fear that the uncorrupted among the police, might make a connection, which tied their father to the dead man. The bottom line however, was, that their father was not used to disappointment. He always got his own way, and the anger he felt at losing the French girl was indescribable and leading him down a careless path.

After their discussions, it was agreed that nothing could be done to dissuade The Old Man. He had spoken and so must be obeyed. The fourth son had found another pliant young woman to act as his father's nurse. She was the youngest daughter from a family who were already in the debt of The Old Man, a family whose older daughter was working in one of their Bangkok brothels to pay that same debt. The family dare not refuse and the ingratiating manner in which they sacrificed yet another innocent on the Old Man's altar of depravity was almost embarrassing. The girl had been given clear instructions as to her role, along with the usual threats as to what would happen should she fail them.

"Are you ready father," asked the second son politely as he arrived at his father's home in Bangkok with the anxious looking replacement nurse in tow. "We have a long journey ahead of us. I have food and drink for the journey, so you can be assured of comfort along the way," he added respectfully.

"Do you have a flask of my favourite soup?" quavered the Old Man.

The second son nodded in accord, "Naturally," he replied, "it is in a flask heated to your taste."

The Old Man grunted; Tom Yam Goong soup, was one of his few remaining pleasures. "Then why do we tarry?" he asked petulantly, "let us be off." The second son took a deep breath, this would be a long trip and one he was not anticipating with any pleasure.

***

Nicholas arrived home exhausted after a flight of almost 12-hours duration. After waiting for a taxi to bring him home, and with the time difference, it was almost six o'clock in the morning when Nicholas finally opened his front door. He was startled to find Melanie waiting for him. She usually went to bed when she knew he was going to be so late home. "Darling?" he said in faint surprise, "I didn't expect to find you up. How are you?" Melanie seemed to be struggling for words, and her eyes were filled with tears. "Melanie what is it?" asked Nicholas immediately alarmed at this uncharacteristic display of emotion. "Are you unwell?" Melanie's mouth opened and closed, but she could not find the words. Nicholas moved closer to her and held her by the shoulders, scrutinising her face as if for clues. "Melanie, really, come now, what is the matter?" As he stood close to his wife, Nicholas was aware of an unfamiliar smell. "Melanie," he said in disbelief, "have you been drinking?" His question was more of an accusation, and was all Melanie needed to completely dissolve. Like most men faced with raw emotion, Nicholas was uncomfortable. He was tired, wrung out and the last thing he needed right now was to come home to a crying wife. However, he steeled himself, took Melanie firmly by the arm and steered her to the kitchen. "Come on my dear," he said resigning himself, "let's hear all about it." Parking Melanie on one of the kitchen chairs, he put the kettle on and prepared himself to listen.

***

Ethan and Diane shared an unspoken agreement that neither of them would mention Darcie Taylor, child abductions, paedophile rings or anything negative while on their mini excursion. Carefully avoiding anything, which even remotely related to the taboo subjects, they chatted about the weather, the need for a new washer for the tap in their flat, their next dive, anything, which kept them off subject. As Ethan drove closer to their destination, Diane looked out over the sensational vista of the Gulf of Thailand and began to feel as if she was coming back to herself. She felt as if she had been away on a long trip, but now was returning. Things started to feel more familiar and comfortable. She was aware that she had not cried in several days, other than the tears of joy on hearing that Angelique had been found safe and well. She felt stronger, and despite the awful circumstances they were embroiled in, she felt as if she was on familiar territory. Her dedication as a social worker meant that she was absolutely committed to the wellbeing of children, whether she was in the UK or Thailand. She felt a huge sense of relief to know that she was approaching the end of a long tunnel and she could indeed see the light.

"How much longer?" she asked Ethan who was as deep in thought as she had been.

He glanced at her and smiled his impossibly roguish smile, "Lean over here and kiss me and I might tell you," he invited.

Diane raised her eyebrows, "You're driving," She said in mock disapproval, "but I accept the challenge," and they both laughed, glad to be free, even for a day, from the tragedies of the past two weeks.

"Not long now," Ethan said after Diane had managed to lean across and kiss him on the cheek, with a dire warning to keep his eyes on the road as she did so. "We'll get parked up somewhere, and then maybe grab a bite to eat shall we?"

Diane felt happier than she had done in many months. "I'd love to look around, maybe buy a souvenir or two while we're here. I'd like a fridge magnet from here. I bet no one in Deacon Hill will have a Hua Hin magnet," she said laughing.

Less than an hour later, with the 4x4 parked close to the sea front, they strolled hand in hand along the beach. "It's busier than I expected," Ethan remarked as they sidestepped a game of volleyball being played out on the snow white sands.

"Mmmm," mused Diane, "I don't care, it's just nice to be here. Don't forget, its holiday time; half term in many countries, so it will be busy."

Realisation dawned on Ethan's face, "Of course it is," he said, "I forget these things, with not having kids."

Diane smiled, "I never forget these things, being a social worker," she laughed, "our lives often revolve around school term dates, and when we can and can't have meetings because it's school holidays."

"Fancy a drink?" asked Ethan as they passed by one of the many little bars.

"Go on then," replied Diane, "but no alcohol, not yet, it's too early."

Ethan shook his head, "No, I just meant a fruit juice or something, we can enjoy a glass of wine or two later on." Five minutes later, with tall glasses of sweet fruit juices, crammed with fresh fruit, they sat at a table under the shade of an enormous umbrella, which saved them from the full ferocity of the sun. Despite the beach being thronged with holiday makers, many of whom were engaged in noisy water sports or beach games, Ethan and Diane felt the peace of the place wash over them. “Goodness, I feel quite sleepy,” Diane remarked as she stifled a yawn. “I don’t know about shopping for souvenirs Ethan, I think I could just snooze the day away.”

“Well there’s no reason we can’t do that,” he replied, “We’re on our own schedule here, no clients, no bosses, and no one to tell us where to be or what to do. It’s up to us darlin, and if you want to sleep, then you sleep. Do you want to hire a couple of sun beds?”

Diane contemplated the question for a minute before deciding, “Yes, let’s stay here,” she said impulsively, “I like the busyness of it all, I feel I want to be a part of something normal like this for a while.” Ethan signalled to the boy who was in charge of the hiring of beds. Paying a few baht for the pleasure they soon had two comfortable sun beds complete with shade.

“I wish I’d brought my book now,” said Diane frowning.

“I thought you wanted to sleep,” Ethan replied rolling his eyes. “Honestly you women.”

Diane stuck out her tongue and laid back on the cushioned bed and within five minutes, despite the hubbub all around her, she was fast asleep. Ethan grinned, and shifted the umbrella slightly so it covered her completely. *You burn like a baby* he thought to himself as he sat watching the various scenarios play out before him on the beach. He would not sleep, not while Diane was sleeping. Someone had to keep an eye on their stuff, and given his recent experiences, he trusted no one. As he lay on his sunbed, Ethan tried not to dwell on the past two weeks, but it was impossible not to. He had no idea what their next move might be. Maybe nothing, given that Angelique was now safe and Darcie was probably hundreds of miles away, that is, if the poor child were even still alive. He wanted to help, he really did. Ethan felt a deep sense of guilt still about Darcie and his role in her loss. He knew he would spend the rest of his life trying to make amends. Sighing deeply, he forced himself to focus on the antics of a stray dog chasing a tourist on a horse further up the beach.

Ethan Montana had no idea that within a few short hours he would get to make some of those amends, which were so important to him.

***

"Hurry," demanded The Old Man, "the sun will be gone and we will lose valuable time." The second son knew that this was a complete exaggeration, the sun had not yet reached its zenith, and there was more than enough time to find a suitably concealed spot for his father to watch from. Still nervous about coming out so soon after the two European girls had been taken, the second son was extra cautious, checking this way and that for any tell-tale signs of police, or undercover operatives. Not that he would always be able to recognise them as such, but they tended to have a certain "look" about them. With his father's disabled parking badge, the son had managed to find a space close to the beach, where parking was normally limited. Satisfied that the coast was clear, and at his father's continued insistence, he pushed the wheelchair to the edge of the bleached white sands under a palm tree, and set the brake. He made sure his father had his straw sun hat, and, despite the heat, a blanket over his reed thin legs. Giving instruction to the new woman who would act as his nurse, he then disappeared to a safe distance to wait in case there was any action. He would need to move as swiftly and as invisibly as possible should his father spot a potential target. As well as their own car, there was a van waiting, as always. Inside the van, was Ruang Sak's fourth son, who was as alert as his brother, but more nervous. The new nurse would join him in the van with any child his father managed to identify. It was always a highly anxious time, fraught with potential problems, not least of which was the ever present danger of being caught. However, the second son was confident that every possible outcome had been considered.

He could not have been more wrong.

Chapter 46

Nicholas gave Melanie her tea, and with his own cup of strong coffee in hand, he sat in front of her in the warmth of their kitchen and simply said, "Let's have it."

Melanie managed to look Nicholas in the eye with a level gaze before she began. "I need you to listen to me Nicholas, and to listen carefully," she said, her voice faltering a little. "Please let me say everything I need to say without interrupting me. I am not proud of what I am about to tell you Nicholas, and I know that you are going to be extremely angry. However, I need to speak honestly and openly with you and then hear what you have to say." Nicholas shifted uncomfortably in his chair, his mind whirling with the possibilities of what his wife was about to divulge. Melanie hesitated only a moment longer before launching emotionally into a long impassioned speech about how she had been in his study, and looked on his laptop. She described the file marked Thailand and the information contained therein. As she spoke, Nicholas's face grew darker; his jaw tightened and several times he closed his eyes in disbelief at what he was hearing. While he had agreed not to interrupt, it was impossible, and twice he spoke up, uttering only one word each time,

"WHAT?" and then managing to control himself as Melanie held up one hand and continued talking.

Eventually, she finished, petering out slowly, her earlier resolve now evaporating in the presence of her husband's silent brooding fury. She looked down at her hands and bit her lip. Nicholas did not speak for a full three minutes, though to Melanie, it felt like three hours. His eyes seemed to be boring right into her soul, and she could not bear to meet his terrible gaze. When he finally broke his silence, nothing could have prepared her for his response.

Nicholas's time in Thailand had given him a lot of food for thought. Never completely comfortable at keeping his young wife in the dark as regarded his status and fabricated lifestyle, his razor sharp mind had been in overdrive as he listened to her. Horrified that she had mistrusted him and been into his most private sanctuary, his sense of wounded pride and indignation gave way to one of understanding. He HAD kept her in the dark, he HAD been living a lie. Her actions, though reprehensible, were completely understandable. He felt a level of guilt when he thought about how he had shared his most closely guarded secrets with people in Thailand who were, in effect, total strangers, and yet, he had never told Melanie. She had stood by him patiently and lovingly, and he knew in that moment, that he had treated her poorly and without any real trust or respect.

"Well Melanie," he began slowly and deliberately, "This is a fine welcome home. To say I am disappointed in you is an understatement of epic proportion, but what is done is done. I really don't know where to begin, but in light of recent events in Thailand, which are not yet concluded, I feel I owe you some sort of explanation. Believe me when I tell you though my dear, it will not be what you were expecting to hear."

***

Diane woke up with a start. She had slept for an hour, and felt an inordinate sense of security to wake and see Ethan sat beside her, quietly watching over her. "Hello sleepy head," he said. "Ready for something to eat now?"

Diane stretched lazily like a cat, revelling in the warmth of the sun and in the sheer decadence of their day out together. "Can we get food to eat here?" she asked hopefully, "I feel quite settled and don't want to move and lose our spot."

Ethan adopted a pained expression, "You mean you want me to wait on you madam? Is that it?" Diane fixed him with a regal stare, "Why of course," she replied, "what is the point of having you here if not to wait on me, now be gone, before I have you horse whipped."

Ethan laughed out loud, it had been too long since he had heard Diane make any attempt at a joke, or have anything resembling fun. He bowed to her, feigning his reverence, "At once milady," he said solemnly and then added cheekily, "so, what'll it be, your majesty; burger and chips?"

Diane looked around for something to throw at him, but finding nothing suitable, she simply laughed back at him and said, "That would be perfect, nothing like a bit of local cuisine."

With Ethan gone in search of food, Diane sat up on the sun bed, with her legs hugged up to her chin and drank in the beauty of the landscape around her. Forcing down the anxiety, which told her that her new found feelings of happiness would not last, she breathed deeply and evenly, forcing herself to remain relaxed. The minutes ticked by and Diane grew restless and hungry. Where was Ethan? Looking around, Diane realised with a pang of guilt that the food stands were a good few hundred yards from where they had settled with their sun beds. Ethan was no doubt stuck in a queue of equally hungry tourists, all of whom now wanted to eat. As she looked around the crowded beach, Diane's eyes were suddenly drawn to a lone figure sitting under a palm tree. Situated almost out of sight of the crowds on the beach, Diane studied the figure more closely. As she did so, every fibre in her body came alive.

Adrenaline began coursing through her veins, her breathing increased and she began to sweat. Diane's heart pounded in her own ears as her eyes refused to believe what she was seeing.

At that exact moment, Ethan returned bearing 2 paper plates of junk food. "Ta da," he said in triumph as he plonked himself down on his sun bed, "It took me half an hour to queue up and get this, so I hope you appreciate it your highness." Ethan attacked his food with relish and grabbed a chip, "Don't let it go cold Di," he said, but then he stopped, the chip mid-way to his mouth as he realised that Diane's face had blanched to the colour of milk. She was staring across towards the back of the beach, completely frozen in some sort of horror.

Ethan spun around and stared in the same direction. At first, he saw nothing but people, children, dogs and palm trees. However, as he focused his attention along the horizon of the beach, he tensed in alarm. "Oh holy crap," he said irreverently, all thought of food forgotten, "it's him."

***

Melanie Blake had been listening to her husband talk for over an hour. She felt as if she was in a bad TV drama, one in which she had been allocated the part of the stupid, naïve, dumbstruck wife. As Nicholas talked, all Melanie could think was, *he's making this up*, so fantastic was his story. A previous life, not to mention a previous wife and all the lies to his parents. He had shocked her to the core when he had confessed the whole truth to her about Lily Rose and their daughter who had been kidnapped; a child, who had never been found, and whose disappearance caused his wife to kill herself. According to Nicholas, an elusive Old Man in a wheelchair was the mastermind behind the whole Operation. Added to this was the gut wrenching impact of hearing that he had been working undercover for a government Organisation for God knows how many years. *It's a lie,* she thought dumbly to herself, *all of it's been a lie. My whole life is nothing more than a charade.* Nicholas ended by telling her about events in Thailand, and his suspicions that The Old Man in a wheelchair may still be alive and responsible for the abduction of more children.

She continued to listen but was no longer really hearing him. How in God's name had she got into such a sham of a marriage? As Nicholas finally finished talking, Melanie's first words to him were sarcastic and cutting, "So, you're asking me to believe that you're a spy? Is that it Nicholas? You are actually a spy, not the Director of Social Services, no, that's just a front, in real life, you're a spy."

Nicholas sighed, he had feared she would not understand. "Melanie," he began, "this is precisely the reason you were not told. I knew you would find it all too incredible, and besides which, it is highly confidential. My work falls under the legislation of The Official Secrets Act. I shouldn't be telling you or anyone else for that matter, but you have forced my hand."

Melanie stared at him open mouthed, "So this is MY fault?" she demanded, her voice rising in anger, "you have kept me in the dark all our married life and you are going to blame ME? I don't think so Nicholas. You may or may not be working for the government, and if you are, then maybe you couldn't talk about that, but you damn well should have told me you'd been married before and had a child. Don't get me wrong, I am sorry about your child, but I had a right to know that she existed. Is our marriage even valid? You're supposed to declare if you've been married before and you didn't. Oh God, we're probably not even legally married. I can't take this in, I really can't. I need to go and think. No, don't say another word Nicholas, I can't even look at you right now."

Nicholas was left alone with his thoughts as his wife stalked out of the room, slamming the door behind her. Nicholas groaned, both in fatigue and frustration. *I need to sleep,* he told himself. *It'll all look better in the morning and Melanie will understand eventually.* As he stood up to make his way wearily to bed, his phone rang. Sighing resentfully, he answered, "Nicholas Bishop," he said, wondering who could be calling him at this hour. "Ethan? Yes, I've been back a couple of hours. Slow down man, slow down, it's a bad line; you think you've seen *who* on the beach?" Two minutes later, Nicholas Bishop was in a maelstrom of indecision. With the situation with Melanie, he knew he needed to be here with her, but the information Ethan had just given him, could mean only one thing.

He had to return to Thailand and quickly, but first, he had a few eminently important and well placed phone calls to make.

Chapter 47

Steve Blake was shaving when his phone rang. It was not the unexpected noise, which made him jump and nick himself, but the ring tone. The phone in question was a burn phone, which never left his side, though it hardly ever rang. The unexpected strains of Elvis Presley's Mystery Train at this hour of the morning had his immediate and full attention. Grabbing a towel to remove the last traces of shaving gel, he snatched up the phone. "Yes?" he said tersely, "Blake here." The voice at the other end wasted no time in explaining the purpose of the call. Steve Blake nodded to himself before asking, "Usual place?" and after waiting for the confirmation, hung up.

Emerging from the shower room with his hair still slightly damp, Steve kissed his wife Fiona on the top of her head and stole the piece of toast she was buttering from under her nose. "Mr Blake," she declared in mock indignation, "get your own toast." With a grin, Steve retreated, munching on the toast with a twinkle in his eye. Fiona shook her head and put two more slices in the toaster. It was still early, and none of their three daughters were yet out of bed. Steve and Fiona cherished the short time they had to themselves each morning before the school routine began; they would sit, drink coffee and just be together, content in each other's company. Neither of them ever mentioned the horrific episode, which had befallen them when they lived on the outskirts of the notorious Deacon Hill Estate. Their 10-year-old daughter Daisy had been victimised in what should have been the safe haven of their church, by sex offender Morris Powell. Shortly thereafter, Powell, had been badly beaten in the street, and hospitalised. Fiona had her own ideas as to who was responsible for the attack, but kept silent on the matter. They had moved away from the area to begin life afresh; Daisy was thriving and both parents could see her returning to the happy little girl she had always been before the assault, though Morris Powell had stolen something from her that day, which could never be recovered.

"I'm nipping out for a while," Steve said casually as he brushed the last few crumbs from his t shirt, "shan't be too long. I'll take Max with me and give him a walk while I'm out." Max was the family's newest addition. A fun loving golden Labrador; Steve and Fiona had agreed to get him to help Daisy in recovering from her ordeal. It had worked. A perfect distraction, Max had quickly become the love of the girls' lives, and they fought fiercely for his affections. Fiona nodded in silent understanding at Steve's announcement. As an ex Special Forces veteran, who had seen much action, Fiona was aware that there was a side to Steve, which she knew little about. She accepted this, asking no questions, and making no judgements.

There were times when Steve had to go on trips, often overseas; he never talked about these trips and Fiona knew better than to ask about them. "Be careful," she called after him as he picked up his jacket and left the house.

He turned and gave her a boyish grin, "You know me," he said, "born careful; come on Max, let's go." Max offered no argument, and followed Steve, tongue lolling, tail wagging, happy to be going out with his master.

***

"Don't stare," Ethan hissed at Diane after he had made the call to Nicholas. "What did he say," she asked, still shaken at the sight of the Old Man in the wheelchair but forcing herself to look away. "I mean should we even have rung him? What if it's not him Ethan, it could just be what it appears to be, an Old Man in a wheelchair."

Ethan shook his head, "Don't you think that's a bit of a coincidence?" he asked, "How many old men in wheelchairs have you ever seen on the beach here? Under the circumstances, I think we can be fairly confident he's our man. He's alone Di, no one with him. That's suspicious don't you agree?"

Diane nodded, hardly daring to look in The Old Man's direction again. "Is he still there?" she whispered.

Ethan glanced across the beach and nodded. "He is; Nicholas said to keep an eye on him, and watch him like a hawk. He can only be here for one purpose and that is to stake out another innocent victim. He must be really angry that Angelique got away. I bet he's looking to replace her."

"Shouldn't we tell the police?" Diane asked anxiously. "I mean, if this guy is the mastermind here, then surely we have a duty and an obligation to alert the proper authorities."

"No," said Ethan firmly, "Nicholas wants us to watch him, and if we can, to follow him. We have to have more evidence that it IS him, and try and discover where he lives. Nicholas is going to fly out and hopefully get back here in a day or two. Until then, he's asked us to stick to this old guy like glue. You up for that darlin?"

Diane's resolve returned to strengthen her. "Hell yes I'm up for it," she answered with fire in her eyes. "He'll not be abducting any children on MY watch," she said with determination.

Despite the seriousness of their situation, Ethan grinned, "That's my girl," he said, "that's my girl."

***

Steve Blake arrived at the given rendezvous exactly on time. It was an hour's drive from his home, far enough away where no one would recognise him if he was seen. He would not be making face to face contact with anyone; that was far too great a risk. Instead, he strolled casually through the woods on the edge of the small village in question, just a man out walking his dog. When he got to the wooden bridge over the stream, he stopped and made a show of looking down into the water below. A few minutes ticked by and apart from the sound of a woodpecker hammering his way into a tree trunk, all around was silence. Steve unobtrusively checked his surroundings, and when satisfied that no one else was in the woods, he reached under the bridge at the fourth upright post. There it was, his dead drop, concealed in a simple three-inch long metal tube, which had been taped under the bridge. Steve took no more than 10 seconds to make the pickup. He placed the tube in his pocket and strolled on. He would examine the contents later when he got home. As he made his way back to his car, he thought about the possibilities of a new mission. He had not been called upon for several months now, and he wondered what or who required his attention now.

Steve had carried out over two dozen special missions; some while he was serving overseas, and some while on leave. While many of his missions were no more than information gathering exercises, some had a more sinister theme and required more physical action. Steve had contacts in most of the major European countries, but his reputation extended further afield into the Middle and Far East, where he had been called upon to undertake several successful missions. Always covert, and always going solo, Steve had to admit a certain sense of anticipation when he received new orders. A soldier through and through, he had an inbuilt sense of loyalty; fighting injustices and protecting the weak. Arriving back at the car, he opened the back allowing Max to jump in. "So," he said to a contented tail wagging Max, "what's in store for me this time I wonder?" Max answered him with a sloppy lick to the back of his hand.

Chapter 48

The body of Shakiya Wattana lay unidentified in a Bangkok morgue, peaceful in death as she had never been in life. Her lifeless body had been subject to almost as much probing and examination as when she had still occupied it. Shakiya might even have smiled at the irony. The white coated doctor who had performed the autopsy confirmed that this particular Jane Doe, had died from the single bullet wound, which had effectively severed her windpipe, along with her spine, making death instantaneous. Having taken all the samples, he required for the toxicology screen and a barrage of other tests, which would include DNA as she had still not been formally identified, the man respectfully covered her body and finished writing his report.

Not least among his findings was a note of a small tattoo on her left shoulder. The tattoo depicted a tiny pair of handcuffs, which the doctor had seen too many times in his long and often distressing career. Realising the significance of the insignia, he folded his lips into a line, as if to prevent himself from speaking. However, as he left the room, he bent and whispered to the deaf blind corpse, “Rest in peace, now my dear, they can’t hurt you anymore.”

Chapter 49

Ethan and Diane adopted their new responsibility as observers of The Old Man in the wheelchair with serious intent. They watched as unobtrusively as possible as The Old Man sat, hour after hour almost without movement, until at last, the beach began to empty of its day tourists, and make way for the party goers of the night. The families with children drifted off to their hotels for showers and a meal, and were replaced by a younger set, whose main goal was to drink as much alcohol as possible in as short a time as possible. There were no children among these revellers, this was a strictly adults only crowd.

"He's moving," said Diane, immediately alert; they watched as a younger man appeared and began to make preparations to move The Old Man from the beach. Also at his side was a young woman, who was of keen interest to the pair.

"She's in a nurse's uniform," gasped Ethan in disbelief, "My God Di, it IS him and THAT'S the woman who takes the children." Despite the ongoing heat of the sun, a cold chill ran down Diane's back as she realised that it was true.

"He's given up then, he's failed; it must have been too busy for him to single any one child out. Thank God for that," said Diane in heartfelt relief. We have to follow him," she said urgently, "quickly, get back to the car and try and pick up his trail."

Ethan frowned, "We need to know what he's driving first darlin, come on, and follow my lead." He leapt to his feet, grabbed their small rucksacks and began to walk casually, but determinedly in the direction of the Old Man. Rucksacks on his back, he held Diane's hand and chatted to her as they walked. "Now listen," he said sounding business-like, "I'm going to be talking to you, but you need to be looking at HIM. I don't want him to get suspicious, so don't stare, but see if you can see what vehicle he gets in and better still a registration number." They drew almost level with the small group as the second son was opening the door of a black Mercedes with tinted windows. Diane did no more than glance in their direction as she continued to look for all the world as if she was hanging onto Ethan's every word. She played her part to perfection taking in the vital information they needed, while Ethan never once looked in their direction.

"Got it," muttered Diane as they passed by, "let's go, quickly."

As they picked up the pace and began to stride to their 4x4, which was parked only a few hundred yards away, Diane repeated the registration number of the Mercedes over and over again like a mantra. Once at their own vehicle, she jumped in, rooted a pen from her rucksack and wrote it down on the back of her hand. "It won't be easy to miss a vehicle like that," Ethan remarked sardonically as he fired up his engine. "The Old Guy doesn't exactly hide his status does he?" Swinging the Mitsubishi around, Ethan drove right past The Old Man's Mercedes and pulled in again a good way up the street, where they could observe the direction it took. The second son and the nurse had taken some time in getting The Old Man from his wheelchair into the comfort of the car and were oblivious to the 4x4. They then had to fold the wheelchair and place it in the boot, before the car eventually set off slowly in Diane and Ethan's direction. "Look the other way," he ordered quickly, and both did so, pretending to stare out over the sea. Ethan allowed the Mercedes to get ahead of him by several hundred yards, before he began his covert pursuit. "He's going north," he commented once they got to the main roads. Ethan allowed several cars to drive between them and the Mercedes to avoid being suspected of tailing it. Diane's senses were all on high alert as they slowly followed the sinister looking vehicle all the way back to Bangkok. "Well, surprise, surprise," said Ethan as they arrived in one of the high class neighbourhoods of the city. "The old devil lives right here under everyone's nose."

"Not quite," Diane contradicted him as the Mercedes began winding its way through smaller and smaller side streets. "He's hardly centre stage here Ethan, more like backstage." Ethan nodded, it was going dark, and as the streets got smaller, there was less traffic.

As the Mercedes turned into yet another street, Ethan hesitated. The roads were getting too small, and the risk of detection was great. "I need to pull back," he said, "they'll see us; we're the only car in the road with them now, and we can't risk it."

As he said it, Diane took a sharp intake of breath, "They're stopping," she said quickly, "His brakes lights are on, yes they're stopping outside that big house at the end." With that Ethan continued past the road end and turned off up the next street. Diane was bewildered, "Ethan, what are you doing?"

Don't worry, "I'm not going to lose him," he said grimly, "come on." With that, Ethan hastily parked the Mitsubishi and got out. Diane followed his lead and once again Ethan grabbed her hand. "He drives like my granny," he remarked, "and you saw how long it took them to get him in the car, it'll be the same getting him out." Ethan was right; by the time the second son and the nurse had got The Old Man out of the car, Ethan and Diane were stood unseen in the shadows at the end of the street, watching as he was wheeled up the ramp to his home. "Got you now, you old bastard," growled Ethan.

They waited until the entourage had disappeared, but only minutes later, the second son reappeared, and drove the Mercedes into the large detached garage, which stood to the left of the house. Diane and Ethan held their breath as the automatic door of the garage came slowly down, concealing any evidence of the black car. The son emerged from a small side door and once again disappeared inside the house. Once satisfied that all activity was over, Diane and Ethan risked a stroll past the considerable property. The house was set back off the street, with high fencing all around it. The ramp to allow wheelchair access, led to a high gate, which Ethan could now see was accessed by digital code. Its LED control panel glowed softly in the dark, guarding its secrets well.

"Hidden in plain sight." said Diane as they wandered back to their own car, "all this time, he's right here in suburbia. I don't know why but I expected him to live in the middle of nowhere," she said in mild surprise.

"Don't forget," Ethan interjected, "he's been doing this for decades now, he and his family have no doubt lived here unmolested for all that time. Why should he move? He's arrogant and has no fear of retribution from the local police. Hell, according to Nicholas, most of them are in his pay. He probably throws parties for them all the time." They climbed back into their 4x4 and set off for their own, less palatial flat.

"Well, at least now we know where to find him," said Diane with great satisfaction.

"Too right," Ethan agreed, "and tomorrow, we'll be back to tail him again. We need to know where he goes, where he eats, who he sees and much more. We need to keep him firmly in our sights. We can't allow him to abduct another child."

Diane nodded, "Like I said before," she confirmed, "not on my watch."

Chapter 50

"I'm back," called Steve to Fiona as he came through the door. "Max, hang on, you've got wet paws." Steve stopped to towel dry Max's paws, before letting him lose to race around the kitchen where Fiona was in the process of making lunch.

"You were a long time," she said as she went to kiss him. "Naah," replied Steve, "just a quick walk for Max and a bit of exercise for me." Fiona said no more about Steve's outing. "Food is about ready," She continued brightly. "Want some?"

Steve shook his head, "Not just yet, give me ten minutes to clean up and I will." With that, he disappeared into the bedroom and retrieved the metal tube from his pocket. He knew that Fiona would not disturb him, he knew that she knew he was in here considering the outcome of his long morning's outing. Steve opened the tube and read the message therein. As his eyes scanned over the page, his body stiffened in anger as he recognised one of the names on the paper. However, as he read further, he realised that this person was not his intended target, but part of a bigger picture, and whose details, along with those of other parties, had been included for information purposes only.

He committed the words to memory and like every good undercover operative, he shredded the piece of paper over the toilet, letting the confetti sized pieces flush away. As he left the bedroom, to go and eat, he spoke softly to himself, “So, you’re in Thailand eh Morris? Well, well, this WILL be interesting.”

Chapter 51

Nicholas allowed himself a few hours sleep, knowing he would be of no use to anyone without it. Melanie had unsurprisingly slept in the spare room, and he made his way there with a certain amount of trepidation. Knocking softly, he was surprised when she opened it almost immediately. "Melanie," his voice was apologetic; he knew he had not been fair to her. Melanie looked drained and had obviously been crying. "Melanie, I know we need to talk some more, but I'm sorry, I really am going to have to return to Thailand as soon as I possibly can, maybe as early as tomorrow if I can get a flight."

Melanie stared at him almost disinterestedly, "Oh I'm sure you have lots to do Nicholas," she said bitterly, "none of which concerns me of course. You go, do what you have to do, but don't expect me to be here when you get back." Nicholas was stunned, never in a million years had he expected this response. He reached out to her, but she flinched and drew back, "No," she said harshly this time, "no Nicholas, you've made a complete fool of me. I realise now that I'm little more than an accessory to you, the good and obedient wife who stays home and cooks the dinner. I gave up a promising teaching career for you, and for what? For a lie, that's what. I'm devastated Nicholas, and I really do not wish to be around you right now. I've spoken to Livvy and I'm going to fly to Spain and stay with her until I decide what to do."

"Melanie," he began with genuine compassion, "I completely understand your being so upset, the things I've told you are unprecedented, and I can only apologise for being the cause of your hurt and pain. Please don't leave now, not like this. Can you wait until I get back from Thailand? Then we can talk some more." Melanie regarded him intently, "You don't get it do you Nicholas?" she asked, "you ask ME not to leave, and yet, in the same breath, you announce that you're jetting off back to Thailand. Our problems can't be THAT important to you if you're prepared to put that trip first. How about this Nicholas, how about YOU stay and I'LL consider whether or not we have more to discuss." It was a challenge he could not meet and he sighed in defeat. "I can't," he said simply, "I have had word that the man who may well be the master mind of the child trafficking Organisation has been located. I have people watching him as we speak, and it is imperative that our Organisation works swiftly and decisively to apprehend him before he takes another child. Melanie, this may well be the same Man who took my only child all those years ago. Please appreciate my commitment to this, along with all the years I have already invested. I'm sorry, but I simply HAVE to go."

***

With a huge amount of care and stealth, Diane and Ethan managed to follow The Old Man the next day. They had got up ridiculously early and parked close enough to his house to monitor his comings and goings, but not close enough to arouse suspicion. Their patience had been rewarded, as just before lunchtime, The Old Man emerged, accompanied by his second son. As soon as Ethan saw the doors of the house opening, he had driven slowly away waiting in a side street, where he could observe the Mercedes passing by. The Old Man had been taken to a well-known restaurant just off the Khao San Road in Bangkok. His son had helped him from the car and taken him inside, but had returned minutes later alone. He then drove away, leaving Diane and Ethan watching the restaurant. "What now?" Asked Diane. Ethan thought a minute before deciding, "I think we should park up and sit somewhere at one of these tables," he said indicating the street cafes along the road. "We can then see when he comes out, but with a bit of luck, this might just be a regular haunt for him. I can't imagine he spreads himself too thinly, it's too risky."

The Old Man remained in the restaurant for precisely an hour and a half, before another of his numerous sons came back to collect him. Ethan and Diane tailed him slowly back to his house, and, satisfied that he was not planning to make any further trips to the beach that day, they went back to their flat to ring Nicholas. "No answer," said Ethan pulling a face, "he may not have landed yet, or maybe he's not even got a flight. I'm not risking leaving a message, so I guess we just wait."

Ethan was right. Nicholas was, at that moment in the air on his return flight to Thailand. He felt a deep sense of sadness at leaving Melanie in the way he had done, and hoped that she would not go to Spain to stay with Olivia, but would be there when he got home, so they could try and work this out. On landing, Nicholas noticed a missed call from Ethan, and he wasted no time in returning it. Ethan answered immediately and Nicholas listened carefully and with some satisfaction when he learned that they now knew where The Old Man lived, or at least the house he was currently staying in. Also the couple seemed to have identified a restaurant where The Old Man ate lunch. This was all good information, and Nicholas promised to drop by their flat as soon as he had checked in with his superiors and shared this latest Intel.

***

In the luxury surroundings of the exclusive villa, Melanie Bishop was once again pouring her heart out to Olivia De Santiago. Livvy had been quick to offer her friend a bolt hole when she had explained that she needed time away from Nicholas. However, Olivia had been ignorant of the discussions, which had taken place between Melanie and Nicholas. She listened with ever widening eyes at Melanie's dramatic disclosures. "I know I can trust you," Melanie said between bouts of tears, "I've no one else I can turn to Livvy." Olivia waited until she had heard everything Melanie had to tell her before giving her opinion. Usually reliable as a lover of gossip and scandal, Olivia surprised Melanie by adopting a serious and introspective look. When Melanie had first told her about her suspicions that Nicholas might be involved in something as heinous as the trafficking and abuse of children, Olivia had found it incomprehensible. She had challenged Melanie to report her concerns to the proper authorities, but in her heart, Olivia, had not believed it to be true. Listening to her friend explain the reality of Nicholas's situation, she felt justified in her original belief, and to her own surprise, she felt supportive of Nicholas.

"Carino," she began and the tone of her voice made Melanie sit up, "Carino, I know you are mad with him, I would be mad too, but for different reasons."

Melanie leaned forwards, "What do you mean?" she asked hearing the petulant edge in her own voice.

Olivia shrugged, "The man should have told you about his wife and child, that much I agree with, but my dear friend, an undercover operative for a high level government Organisation and you expect that he should have shared this with you? I cannot agree carino. You know that my husband has many business interests, some of which are perhaps more legitimate than others, who knows? I would not expect to know all about his business and his private dealings. No, this is the world of men. I am not so old fashioned as to believe that women have not the right to be informed and share in the lives of their husbands, but carino, please. A government agent and you are sulking because he kept this to himself? Pah, I think you are like a child if you truly believe that he had the freedom to tell you of this."

Melanie sat back in her chair, too stunned to speak. However, Oliva was not done. “I tell you this as a friend, your closest and most trusted friend. If you had not gone into his study, then this man of yours would not have had to tell you this; you and he would have continued in your lives, and who knows, maybe gone along for many more years in blissful ignorance. But you DID go into his study, and now you DO know about his double life, which has given you choices. Either you choose to stay and offer your support, like the supportive wife you have always been, or you behave as you are doing, by leaving him alone with it and taking offence that he obeyed the tenants of his job and did not share it with you. So, carino, what will you choose?”

***

It was a tired and subdued Nicholas who sat heavily on the sofa in Diane and Ethan’s tiny flat late in the evening. The three of them shared a drink and discussed possible plans well into the early hours of the morning. At no point did Nicholas mention the problems he had left behind in the UK. He had put those issues firmly on hold to be dealt with when he had concluded his business here. “My Organisation at home and here in Thailand are liaising closely with one another, and looking with great interest at the information you two have so brilliantly managed to gather. We have waited many years for an opportunity such as this, and it is not one to be wasted or missed. We have our very best men on it, and I am confident that action will be taken and quickly. I have been told that the dead man at the scene of Angelique’s accident has been identified as Charn Chai Boonjan, a 35-year-old Thai National, with links to Turkey, and one whom the police have good reason to believe was working for an Organisation known to traffic children. Information on the Organisation is scarce; they have been incredibly careful over the years, but their influence seems to be far reaching. They undoubtedly have many people in their pocket, from police officers and judges right up to government officials. From information gathered at his home, we have managed to link Charn Chai Boonjan to a brothel in Pattaya, one, which we suspect is offering children as young as 11 years of age to clients. We have special agents on their way to this establishment as we speak, where they will undertake a raid and hopefully liberate these children. We do not anticipate that Darcie Taylor will be among them; she is undoubtedly very well hidden by now. The other thing I have been told is that Charn Chai was most definitely involved in Darcie's kidnap and movement, and there is evidence to suggest that he is indirectly responsible for the deaths of William and Rose Bailey."

On hearing the two names, Diane gasped, "That was that Scottish couple," she interrupted, "Ethan, you remember, I read it out to you, but I thought they were killed by robbers."

Nicholas shook his head, "Almost certainly not," he said gravely, "It transpires that they are the parents of Nathan Bailey, the man I previously told you about who is in prison in Bangkok for the abuse of young children. It would appear that the Bailey's were in the country to try and offer support to their errant son. It is our belief that the Organisation got to them, and in some way blackmailed them into caring for the children they moved across the country. We suspect that Darcie may have been with them for a time, and that their deaths are linked to this, though we don't yet know how." Nicholas frowned as he searched his mind for any additional information. "Ah," he said as he recalled something else, "The other thing I meant to mention was that I had a call from the coroner when I landed, he wants me to meet with him today at around 2 o'clock, not sure what it's all about, but I think they've managed to identify the dead woman from the crime scene on the beach.

Ethan whistled under his breath, "Boy, there's a lot to take in," he commented, "so what now?"

Nicholas met him with a level gaze, "We have never been so close to them," he said solemnly, "we absolutely have to close in on The Old Man and any associates we can identify who surround him. He holds the key to so many unanswered questions, not least my own daughter's disappearance over thirty years ago. However, my biggest hope is that he can lead us to Darcie. I am sad to say though, that in order to secure Darcie's freedom, the government may be forced to do a deal with him." Nicholas held his hands up on seeing Diane's horrified expression. "He won't get off Scot free Diane, but he would be offered a reduced sentence for information leading to Darcie's safe recovery. However, given his advanced age, it is highly likely that he would still die in prison."

Diane nodded in satisfaction, "And so he should," she said vehemently, "so he damn well should."

"I agree," said Nicholas with some force, "I've made several phone calls, which I am hoping with bring us some positive results and good news for a change."

What Nicholas Bishop was not aware of, was that one of the phone calls he had made had been the catalyst for a chain reaction of activity that was already in motion.

***

Once Nicholas had left, Diane and Ethan stayed up another hour thrashing out the possible scenarios to the drama that continued to unfold around them. "Don't worry Di they'll get him," said Ethan by way of encouragement.

Diane nodded briefly, "I know they will," she agreed, "but the trouble is, there are too many people waiting to step into his shoes Ethan. Even if they DO get The Old Man, what then? No doubt he'll have sons to take over, or other well placed individuals. It never ends Ethan, I'm afraid, it never ends."

Ethan took her hand, "Come on darlin, time for bed. We can only do what we can do, and in our own small way try and help. Don't get too discouraged, at least we've been able to be a part of this. Isn't that worth a smile?" Diane managed a thin smile and allowed Ethan to lead her off to bed, where they fell into an immediate and exhausted sleep.

***

After a few hours' sleep, Nicholas showered and changed and made his way to the coroner's office in Bangkok. The coroner had the air of a man who had spent his life living among sadness and death. Despondency hung on him like a cloak and he spoke in quiet mournful tones. "Mr Bishop," he began, "I have already spoken to the police and advised them of my findings. I have asked to see you on your own to share the information I have, which I know will be of enormous significance to you."

Nicholas was puzzled, if the police, the trusted ones, already had the information they required, he did not see why his presence was required here. Usually, the police would pass on any relevant information to him anyway.

In the end, it took less than five minutes for Nicholas to understand the reasons for his invitation to meet with the coroner.

Nothing could have prepared him for the information he had been given, and he stumbled like a blind man back to his hotel. Fumbling in the mini bar he selected a small bottle of whisky, which he downed in one gulp. With his mind reeling in disbelief, Nicholas Bishop sat down on his bed and for the first time in over thirty years, he wept.

Chapter 52

After a sleepless night in their dreary hotel room, Alan was gathering his thoughts. While Morris had snored the night away, Alan had been alert and vigilant, checking out of the window every few minutes. He had been unnerved at 3am to see the black Mercedes driving past, and he knew it was time for action. It was a matter of time before the occupants of the vehicle paid them a personal visit, and Alan had no intention of playing host to them.

Turning to Morris who was emerging from the bathroom wearing one of his hideous tourist's shirts, he spoke up, "Morris old friend," he said with what he hoped was genuine warmth, "I just need to nip down to reception and pay the bill, then we'll be ready to roll. This one's on me, no don't worry about giving me any more cash, I know that this trip has been a costly one. I'll get this and we'll call it quits for your bright idea which got us away from the safe house."

Morris beamed, no one had ever been so generous to him or included him in their plans the way Alan did. He was a really great guy. "Okay then mate," he said in an overfamiliar tone, which set Alan's teeth on edge, "shall I wait here?"

Alan nodded, "I think it's best; you wait here so we're not seen together in reception. Tell you what, I'll call a taxi from down there and once I'm inside, I'll give you a quick call and you can nip down as quickly as you can and jump in. Then, we'll be on our way. How does that sound?"

Morris would have agreed to anything Alan said, knowing he was far more experienced in such matters. "That's a plan Alan" he agreed, I'll sit tight here and wait for you to call. How long will it be, five minutes or so?"

Alan made a show of consulting his watch and pursing his lips, "No more than ten," he concurred, "see you in a bit then," and he left the room with a cheery wave of his hand. Once in the lobby, Alan Slater moved fast. Ignoring the receptionist, he went into a quiet corner and dialled one of his old contacts. Breathing a sigh of relief when the call connected he spoke quietly, but quickly. The voice on the other end was equally as keen, especially when Alan named the price of his gratitude. Less than five minutes later, Alan Slater walked through the hotel kitchens, out of the back door and into the waiting car. Settling hastily into the back seat and sinking low down out of sight, he knew full well that he had just bought himself a reprieve. "Thanks Manny," he said to the driver, "I owe you." Manny Dershowitz smiled knowingly. A man of many talents; his family were among some of the original Jewish immigrants to populate the City back in the 70's when they had fled from persecution in Iran. With his finger in too many pies to count, Manny had many useful and often lucrative connections. Manny gave Alan a knowing grin, "Always a pleasure Mr Slater," he said as he sped away, "always a pleasure."

In room 283 Morris Powell consulted his watch, *not be long now,* he thought to himself, *then we'll be on our way and out of this Godforsaken country.* Morris looked forward to being back in the comfort of his own home, where he would replay the happy hours he had spent with the

Taylor girl in his perverted mind. Every time he saw a fresh appeal for news of Darcie, Morris felt a thrill of excitement that he had been involved in something so huge. Checking his watch again, he waited for Alan's call.

In the car park of the hotel, the black Mercedes had returned and was silently watching … Waiting.

Chapter 53

Steve Blake made his way through the throngs of people in the centre of Bangkok. The sheer volume of noise, colour and vibrancy of the place was wasted on him as he focused on the task in hand. Steve had arrived in the early hours of the morning, landing at a private airstrip a few miles out of the city. He was due to leave later today by the same means. His visit had but one purpose, and if all went according to plan, it would not take long. Steve had no reason to question or doubt the Intel he had received on his target. The source was a reliable one, and Steve was satisfied that he could be trusted. Situating himself at a small intersection on the Khao San Road, Steve ordered iced tea and pretended to read a newspaper. He paid particular attention to the restaurant directly across the street. After five minutes, a black Mercedes with tinted windows pulled up outside. A young man got out, and assisted his passenger into a waiting wheelchair and pushed him inside.

Steve waited a few minutes, finished his tea and quietly made his way to the back of the restaurant, which was situated just off the Khao San Road. There was a young man of around 20, standing idly outside smoking a cigarette. In dirty overalls, he paid no attention to Steve, but applied himself to his cigarette. With no hesitation, Steve walked in through the back doors, which gave him access to the kitchens.

Once inside, Steve's right hand went instinctively to his pocket to check he still had the small vial he had been given when he landed at the secure airstrip. With a baseball hat pulled down low over his face, he was in and out of the kitchen in less than a minute, the vial now empty.

Steve exited the same way he had entered. The cigarette smoking young man had gone, leaving Steve to blend into the back packers, tourists and locals without being observed. *Mission accomplished* he thought with satisfaction, *now for a little unofficial business.*

***

Ruang Sak had more on his mind than ordering his favourite Tom Yam Goong soup. Following the unfortunate demise of Charn Chai, he needed to apply himself to appointing a successor. While he had held Charn Chai in contempt most of the time, he could not deny that the man did an outstanding job and would be nigh on impossible to replace. Trustworthy, highly intelligent and completely loyal, he had proved his worth many times over. His death was highly inconvenient and identifying a successor would be annoyingly time consuming. He awaited the arrival of his oldest son with great impatience. He was late by five minutes, and was delaying his lunch. Ruang Sak had reluctantly agreed to meet with his son to discuss the issue of a replacement. Knowing that his son fully expected to BE that replacement was going to be awkward. Ruang Sak knew that his eldest son was weak and unstable, a trait he had inherited from his mother of course. Now in his late 40's, his son had a string of unsuccessful relationships and a serious opium habit. No, he was not suitable at all, and Ruang Sak fully intended to break this news to him over lunch, if he ever arrived. Harder still for his first son, would be hearing the news that he intended to make his second son his successor.

Eventually, his son came through the door offering apologies as he approached. “Sit,” ordered Ruang Sak sharply, “you dishonour me with your lack of punctuality.”

The son bowed in response and sat. “My apologies revered father,” he said, “the taxi was slow.”

The Old Man pulled a face in disgust. “A poor excuse,” he said, “more likely you were taking your pleasure with some whore. Well, you are here now, so you had better order quickly, I am not in the habit of delaying my lunch.” The son ordered quickly and without much interest in the menu. His father had been right, he had indeed been with a whore, and an expensive one at that. She was a new addition to the brothel, which his father allowed him to run, and naturally, he had to make sure she was capable of providing pleasure and worth the money he was asking for sharing her company.

Bringing his mind back to the present he forced a smile and asked pleasantly, “So father, what did you order today?” Ruang Sak was in no mood for small talk but the proprieties had to be observed, “The Tom Yam Goong soup, is the best available,” he answered shortly, “I order nothing else, you should eat some.”

The son avoided pulling a face but answered politely, “Fish soup is not to my taste father, but I am grateful for the suggestion.”

Son and father waited in awkward silence for the food to arrive. To even contemplate discussing business before they had eaten was unthinkable. While they sat, the son could think of nothing else but his hatred for The Old Man before him. Denied a real place in the lucrative Organisation, the son was bitter, and jealous of his younger brothers who were afforded far more prestigious positions and given more trust. His anger sat like bile in his stomach. *One-day Old Man* he thought, *one day. You can't last forever.* Eventually the food arrived and the Old Man applied himself with relish to his soup. “It is the best,” he crowed, his mood improved by eating. He opened his mouth to speak further, displaying his blackened teeth and a half chewed prawn. However, the words never reached his lips. Instead, he made a gasping sound and began to claw at his throat with his gnarled fingers. His eyes bulged and took on a wild and desperate look.

His son stood up, "Father?" he said in fascinated concern, "father what is it?" The Old Man's eyes were terrible now, almost popping out of his head in his frantic search for air.

"Get help," the son shouted to the restaurant owner, "quickly fool, call an ambulance," but it was too late. Ruang Sak fell face forward in his favourite soup, quite dead. The son stood displaying no outward emotion whatsoever, while inside he was rejoicing. The ambulance arrived and removed The Old Man's shrivelled corpse. He looked no better in death than he had in life. As they took his father away, the son bowed, as if in sorrow and respect.

Well father, he thought as he watched the ambulance drive away, *that was sooner than I had anticipated, but is most welcome all the same.*

He left the restaurant smiling. He had always hated fish soup.

Chapter 54

With the anxious Alan Slater delivered to his destination, and with a healthy roll of cash added to his pockets, Manny Dershowitz pulled over to the side of the road and made a call. "It's me," he said to the voice at the other end, "yes, he contacted me as we hoped he would. I just dropped him at the airport. The other guy is still at the hotel; yes, that's the one, best of luck," and with that, Manny Dershowitz simply hung up and disappeared back into the shadows of his mysterious and covert life.

***

Steve Blake strode away from the restaurant and melted into the teeming streets of the city. He was deep in thought as to his next mission, one which was strictly off the books when his phone rang. Ducking into a doorway occupied only by a drunk and his dog who were sharing a well-worn blanket, he answered. "Blake," was all he said. Listening avidly to the message, Steve nodded in understanding, and hung up.

***

Morris was puzzled. It had been twenty minutes since Alan left him to go down and pay the bill and get a taxi. Morris wondered what was taking him so long. He dare not go down, in case Alan was still in reception. He had said they should not be seen together and Morris was anxious to stick to Alan's plan. *Maybe there's a queue*, he said aloud to himself. *Yes, that's it, there must be a queue.* He sat back down on the unmade bed and tried not to worry. The minutes ticked by and Morris spent the time fantasising about Darcie Taylor, revelling in the adventure he had enjoyed and knowing that it was unlikely he would ever have a better experience. His daydreams were abruptly interrupted by a soft knock on the door. *Must be Alan*, he thought as he went to answer it, *must be a change of plan.*

Morris could not have anticipated just how drastically his plans were about to change. As he opened the door, his mind refused to accept what his eyes were seeing, "YOU," he stuttered in total disbelief and tried in vain to close the door. His assailant was more than a match for him, and Morris hardly felt the tiny needle which drove into the soft flesh of his fat neck, but he felt the effects almost immediately. As he drifted quietly away, Morris Powell heard the last words he would ever hear, "Don't say I didn't warn you."

Chapter 55

Sally Palmer double checked the screen in front of her. No, there was no doubt about it. Standing up so abruptly, that her office chair fell over backwards, she once again hurried into Jim Cooper's office with no more than a brief knock on his door. He looked up startled, "Sally?" he asked in query to her dramatic entry, "It's Slater sir, Alan Slater, and he's on the move."

A look of consternation flitted across Jim Cooper's face, "What the hell?" he said in alarm. "Where's he off to Sally?" he demanded, his mind beginning to focus.

"He left Thailand less than two hours ago, destination Manchester England, ETA about eight hours' time sir," she said efficiently.

Jim stroked his hand absentmindedly over two days of facial hair. "What are you up to Alan?" he said softly to himself, "what's gone wrong? And more importantly where's your buddy Morris? Okay Sally, leave it with me, I'll make some calls and we'll have him picked up at Manchester, though right now, without any evidence of a crime being committed, we can't detain him for long, only some routine questions. Damn the man, he has the luck of Lucifer himself." Jim spent a frustrating hour on the phone to his well-placed contacts in Thailand, but no one could give him any information on Alan Slater. No one knew where he had been, or who he had been with during his few days in the country. It would almost appear that he had not been there at all. He had used no credit cards, and had left no trail as to his whereabouts.

Jim Cooper was right, they had not been able to hold him for long. Alan Slater had been duly detained on arrival back in the UK, and had been questioned by officers from a team dedicated to the prevention of child abuse and trafficking. The good pastor had provided a perfectly innocent explanation for his trip to Thailand, telling them that he had been there to look into the possibility of starting a church in one of the outlying villages. No, he had not spoken to many people, no he did not recall the names of the small hostels he had stayed in. He was sorry he could not be of more help. Morris Powell? No, he had certainly NOT met up with him, and he was shocked to hear that a man who was a regular member of his congregation was a sex offender. He would be sure to take action in that regard when he returned to his church. The members of the team had reported back to a frustrated Jim Cooper who had in turn sworn and kicked the desk in anger. "We'll get you yet Slater," he had said as his foot connected with the hard wood. "We'll get you yet you bastard."

***

Diane was having a dream; in the dream, she had found Darcie, but the child was behind a glass door. The door was locked and though Diane could see Darcie, she could not get in to rescue her. Darcie was pleading with her, crying and holding out her arms, but Diane was powerless to help her. The sound of the phone ringing brought her fully awake, though the remnants of the dream still floated around in her mind, disturbing and unsettling her. She picked up the phone while Ethan mumbled and turned over, still clinging to the vestiges of sleep.

It was Nicholas. Diane checked the clock and saw it was only 6am, "Nicholas, hi," she said, her voice croaking in that morning way. She cleared her throat and tried again, "Sorry Nicholas, what's up?" Diane listened in complete disbelief as Nicholas relayed the news to her, news he had himself only just received from his most reliable sources. "Oh my God," she said in a loud enough voice to wake Ethan, "This is incredible Nicholas," she went on, gripping the phone so tightly, it actually creaked in her hands.

Ethan sat up in bed, his hair all awry. "What is it?" he whispered.

Diane shook her head and held up her hand to silence him. "Yes okay Nicholas, we'll see you later on, yes that's fine, come around nine and we can have breakfast." Hanging up the phone with a wide eyed Ethan looking questioningly at her, Diane sustained an air of the dramatic by getting out of bed and announcing, "Hang on, I need the loo," leaving Ethan in suspense.

She returned in minutes, hastily finishing drying her hands on her pyjama trousers. Plonking herself on the bed and curling her knees up under her chin, she announced, "You are never going to believe what has happened."

Ethan stared at her in mock boredom, "I'm not playing 20 questions Di, so just tell me," he said, still wishing he was asleep.

"You're no fun," she replied, but was too desperate to share the news to argue. Hesitating only a few seconds more, she took a deep breath and said "The Old Man is dead."

Ethan was suddenly wide awake and all ears, "What?" he asked incredulously, "he's DEAD? How?"

"No one knows," she replied, satisfied that she had his full attention, "Nicholas has only just been told. Apparently, he died yesterday; he was having lunch at that restaurant where we saw him the other day. Just keeled over and died. Obviously, they will do an autopsy, but given his age, it may be a heart attack. Either way, he's dead. The only trouble is, no one can now ask him about Darcie, though the police are busy rounding up all his known associates as well as his sons. He had six sons you know, six, imagine that. In fact, he probably died while Nicholas was here talking to us about him and what we might do next. Nicholas is coming over around nine to have breakfast with us and tell us what he knows. I suppose we had better get up and showered and ready.

Ethan grinned, and Diane responded immediately, “Oh no you don’t Ethan Montana, I know that grin, but we have things to do, so get up.”

Ethan got Diane by the hand before she had time to move. “Now think about it darlin,” he reasoned as he kissed her hand, “The Old Man is dead; nothing we can do about that. Nicholas won’t be here for three hours yet and here we are both wide awake. I say we use put our time to good use.” With that, he pulled her close and planted a kiss on her mouth. Diane struggled feebly, but her heart wasn’t really in it, and she tumbled back into bed with Ethan, revelling in his warmth and strength. “Okay,” she mumbled between kisses, “but *then* we have to get up.”

***

By the time Nicholas arrived, Diane and Ethan were frying bacon and looking smug. Nicholas sat down, waving aside offers of a bacon sandwich, but agreeing to coffee. Diane noticed absentmindedly that he looked extremely tired and his eyes looked sore. “Well,” he began, “all hell has broken loose. The Old Man was dead on arrival at the hospital, and his sons seem to have evaporated into thin air. If anything, we’re further away from any chance of locating Darcie than ever. I’ve also been told that Alan Slater is now back in the UK, minus his travelling companion Morris Powell. No one knows what has happened to Powell, but Slater was detained and questioned. Sad to say, they had to let him go as there was absolutely no proof that any crime had been committed. It’s a huge setback for the NCA who had been monitoring him so closely, and will of course continue to do so. Nathan Bailey is back in the picture, and proved to have an interesting story to tell when pressed. The police paid him a visit and apparently, the prospect of another twenty years or more in Bang Kwang prison was less than appealing to him. He cut a deal and shared information on Charn Chai Boonjan, who had indeed been to see him in prison; he had basically tricked him into giving him all his contacts in the underworld here. Bailey agreed to give it all up to the police. In exchange, he gets extradited to the UK and will serve out his sentence there."

Diane huffed angrily, "How unfair," she exclaimed, "no doubt he will only serve a few years and then be out again in no time, doing the same thing."

Nicholas agreed with her, "I know Diane, I know it's very frustrating, but you have to consider that the information he shared with the police is worth ten years of undercover surveillance and hard slog. The police consider it a fair exchange. He will still be brought to justice for his crimes against those two little girls, make no mistake about that."

"What did the coroner want," asked Ethan, "did they identify that dead woman on the beach?" Diane noticed a shadow cross Nicholas' face and he grimaced as if in pain when Ethan asked the question.

"Are you okay Nicholas?" she asked in concern.

Nicholas recovered his composure and went on, "Yes, yes," he said with an edge of impatience, "I'm fine, the woman was apparently a well-known prostitute. The coroner told me that she had a small tattoo on her shoulder – a small pair of handcuffs. Apparently, this is the well-known insignia of one of the most feared Organised crime families in Thailand, which we suspect is, or certainly was, headed by The Old Man and others. She was known only as Shakiya, and it would appear at first glance that she was involved with Darcie's abduction and possible sale to the highest bidder. However, once they had identified her, the police located her flat and searched it thoroughly. They found a 2-page letter hidden at the back of a drawer, a letter which will just about blow the lid off the whole syndicate. In it, she explains that she was on her way to try and liberate Darcie. Darcie had definitely been in her care and Shakiya was on that beach with one intention – to try and save Darcie." Nicholas almost choked on his words and he seemed to be having great difficulty in relaying the story.

"Wow, she was brave," said Diane, "Especially given her situation, I mean she must have known that the consequences for her actions would mean almost certain death for her, and yet she went ahead and tried anyway. I feel for her, I really do. What must have gone through her mind? She must have had some sort of premonition that she wouldn't make it or she wouldn't have written the letter."

Nicholas had once again regained his composure. "Indeed," he said abruptly, "it would seem that she had serious doubts as to her ability to save Darcie, and left the letter as a sort of insurance, to make sure the people responsible were brought to justice, should she fail. Sadly, in some ways, it was too little too late. Darcie was not on the beach, and so this woman never had her opportunity, and as we all know, she was tragically shot and killed. However, at least we know that she died trying to put things right, rather than being there as part of the problem. In other ways though, her letter will be of enormous value; she names many highly placed individuals, who she claims are involved in a highly organised child trafficking ring. She named Charn Chai Boonjan, and The Old Man, who we now know is called Ruang Sak Yunram. She names all six of his sons, and a host of corrupt police officers and government officials, many of whom were apparently regular clients of hers. The information she has left behind is priceless. It is a great and terrible pity that she died so unnecessarily. She would have had much to live for," Nicholas sighed deeply before continuing. "What remains is for the police and most trusted government officials to collate the information and then act on it in the way they feel is best. They raided the brothel in Pattaya and have managed to liberate many young girls aged between 11 and 16 years. Most of them were from poor families in the country. It will be a long hard road for them, as sadly, many of the families will not accept them back into the communities due to the shame of the work they have been forced to do."

Diane was horrified, "What?" she exclaimed, "they won't have them back, despite the fact that it was their families who sold them into certain slavery and prostitution? How can THAT be right?" she cried.

"It's not right, it's very wrong," agreed Nicholas, "but you must understand Diane that many of the families sent them off in good faith. They thought they were sending them to a better life, to receive an education and work at a job. They too have to live with the shame of their own actions, and often it is simply too much for them to bear. To accept a daughter back in such circumstances, would be to be faced with their own actions and resulting tragedy every day of the week. No, the girls will be rehabilitated into a government run programme, where they can firstly tell their terrible stories, and then begin healing and receive proper care and counselling."

"So that's it then?" said Ethan, voicing Diane's own thoughts, "is there nothing left for us to do here?" Nicholas smiled a wry smile, "There will always be work to do here Ethan, but for the moment, I don't think that there is any more you two can do to assist. You have both been hugely helpful, and resourceful. However, with The Old Man dead, along with at least one of his associates, it will take the Organisation time to regroup and make another move. This will have hurt them, and now we have the information from Shakiya, we are in a position to place many suspects under surveillance. Darcie is the main casualty in all this, and I hate to admit defeat, but we really have no leads as to her whereabouts. The deaths of the main players have made sure that most people who knew of her whereabouts have now been silenced for good. Naturally, someone knows where she is, but she will be a hot commodity, and they will keep her out of sight for many months, if not longer. I know that her mother has set up a home here in Thailand, which is another tragic consequence of it all. She and her husband have separated and their little boy is now without his mother to bring him up. It goes on and on and all we can do is keep chipping away in whatever small way we can to make a difference. At least Angelique was recovered; her family have gone back to France now, and will pick up the pieces of their lives and try and move on."

Diane looked from Ethan to Nicholas, "So that's really it? We can go back to diving, or go back to England, whichever we like?"

Nicholas nodded, "Of course; your decision to help out here was your own choice, of course you are free to do whatever you wish, but before you decide, I have a proposition for you, actually, for both of you." He hesitated before going on, but seeing that he had their full attention, he continued. "As you know, the NCA, or National Crime Agency to give it its full title, has been a big part of our investigations here. They are at the forefront of fighting crime and cyber-crime. There are many opportunities within the Agency for bright young people such as yourselves. I would like you both to consider such an opportunity. Diane, there are openings for social workers to work on the front line in preventing child trafficking and exploitation, and for you Ethan, there are several roles where your natural skills and abilities would be put to good use. All I ask is that you both give it some serious thought. I would be more than happy to provide references for both of you."

Diane and Ethan exchanged looks of surprise, "Wow, I never expected this," said Ethan, "I mean, I'm a musician and a dive instructor, how could I fit in at the NCA?"

Nicholas smiled, "Oh we'd find something for you Ethan, and many of your skills are transferrable, you're an intelligent man, and there is always a way forward for such people. How about you Diane?" he asked, "Will you consider it?" Diane looked thoughtful, "I will consider it Nicholas," she agreed, "But I'm not making any promises. I AM ready to get back to work, but my heart has always been on the front line of child protection in my own community, but I promise I will think about it."

"Right then," said Nicholas with some finality, "I guess that this is it then. I'm flying home in three days, which gives me time to sort out a few lose ends. What do you think your plans will be?"

Ethan and Diane shrugged in unison, and Diane spoke first, "Well, we were going to stay for the summer, but the police still have Ethan's boat impounded after it was found adrift. However, we still have the flat, so I feel a bit uncertain."

Ethan nodded, "I agree with Diane, it's only February, and I should have had the boat until June. I guess it all depends whether or not I get it back anytime soon, but as Diane says, we're committed to keeping the flat, so I guess we'll stay."

Nicholas stood up, "Well, don't leave it too long to come and see us, and make sure you keep in touch. We've been through a lot here in a short time, and it would be good to reflect on it all now and again, and let us never forget, we will always be looking for Darcie. That search will never cease."

Diane's eyes misted over when she thought of the missing child, "Yes," she agreed softly, "We will never forget Darcie."

Chapter 56

Situated on the banks of the Chao Phraya River, The Bangkok Protestant Cemetery accepted very few internments. However, this request had come from on high and had been hurriedly agreed and rubber stamped. The ceremony was simple in the extreme, after all, the woman had been an infamous whore. There was but one person to mourn her passing, one who had requested that the ceremony be utterly private and confidential. When it was over, the protestant priest who had conducted the burial was awkward in his approach to the lone man who stood dry eyed by the side of the grave. Waiting respectfully as the man placed a single stemmed rose and a single lily on the coffin, the priest stepped forwards to offer his condolences.

"You knew her well?" he asked in an attempt to make conversation. The man regarded him for only a moment before he walked away.

The priest barely heard the man's parting words as he strode away, "She was my daughter."

Turning back to the headstone, which was a simple as the ceremony the priest read the inscription there, which read.

Misumi Bishop, beloved only daughter of Nicholas and Lily Rose, home at last and now at peace.

Chapter 57

Nicholas arrived back in England tired and with a great deal of apprehension. He had not been able to get hold of Melanie, and feared that his decision to return to Thailand had probably been the last straw. As he put his key in the lock, he was surprised when the door yielded immediately and opened. "Melanie," he exclaimed, "You're here."

Melanie managed a smile, "Where else would I be, you old fool?" she asked in mock exasperation, "well, don't stand there on the doorstep, you and I have a lot to talk about."

Chapter 58

England; Four Months Later

Elsie and Bernard Summers were making the short journey to the small but popular church in the heart of their village in the far north of Scotland. "I'm looking forward to hearing the new pastor today," said Elsie pleasantly, I hear he's moved all the way up from way down south." Bernard nodded, "Yes," he agreed, "He has; Bill met him last week, and said he's a nice fellow by the name of Douglas McBride." As the couple made their way into the church, the newly appointed Douglas McBride was in his office preparing for his first sermon. He took one last look at his own reflection in the office mirror as he made his way out. *Hello Douglas*, smirked Alan Slater to himself; *don't forget to speak in a Scottish accent,* he reminded his reflection as he walked out in front of the unsuspecting congregation.

***

"I can't believe were back," said Diane as she and Ethan piled their stuff into Diane's flat.

"I know, it feels like no time since we were leaving for Thailand, and now here we are back in good old Blighty," said Ethan as he wrestled with bags, coats and various bits of luggage. Sinking onto the sofa, Diane's mood changed and she became very quiet. Ethan dumped all the baggage and walked over to her, "Are you sure about this?" he asked, "You can change your mind you know."

Diane smiled wistfully, "I know I can honey, but you know how I feel about it. Anyway, you're going to be busy yourself, you have loads of training to do Mr newly appointed NCA person."

Ethan immediately looked worried, "Don't remind me," he said, "I still don't know how I allowed Nicholas to talk me into this. I feel like a complete beginner."

"Well you are a complete beginner," Diane agreed, but you will have lots of support and training and before you know it, you'll be telling me what to do. Let's get the kettle on and have an early night. I've got to get back into my routine again and that means, up at 6am." In bed, Diane had a restless night, tossing and turning and trying to imagine what the future might hold for them both. She eventually managed to fall into a fitful sleep, waking out of habit, before her 6 am alarm.

By 8:30 am that morning, Diane walked into the building she had once known so well. Knocking softly on the familiar door, she pushed it open on hearing a welcoming, "Come in."

Taking a deep breath, she went into the office and immediately felt at home, "Hello Glenda," she said with genuine pleasure on seeing her old boss, "what have you got for me then?"

Diane Foster was back.

Epilogue; Thailand Ten Years Later

Adam Brown was just about to leave his desk and go for his lunch when his intercom buzzed. "What is it Anna?" he asked. From her position at the front desk reception of The British Embassy in Bangkok, Anna Stevenson's crisp reply came back to him, "I'm sorry to trouble you Mr Brown, but I think you had better come down." Intrigued, Adam, left his desk and made his way to the foyer of the Embassy where he had been the British Ambassador for the past four years. It was highly irregular for Ms Stevenson to make such a request, and he knew that she would not do so lightly.

Once downstairs, Adam stopped and took in the scene before him. There was a young woman who he estimated to be around fourteen or fifteen years old stood at the front desk. Her long blonde hair was dirty and bedraggled; she looked thin, pale and on the point of collapse. She wore cut-off jeans and a skimpy tee shirt, which hung off her skinny shoulders exposing a tattoo of a tiny pair of handcuffs, though Adam failed to recognise the significance of such a seemingly insignificant detail. Stepping smartly forwards, he offered his arm to the girl and signalled for his aide to bring a chair and some water. The girl almost fell backwards onto the chair and her mouth was opening and closing as she tried to form words. Close up, Adam could see a plum coloured bruise under her left eye and another fading on her left cheek. Assuming authority, he spoke gently but firmly, "You're safe now, can you tell us who you are?"

The girl's blue eyes focussed and she came upright in the chair. She pushed her hair out of her eyes in a heartbreakingly defiant gesture and spoke in a voice, which resonated clear across the hall.

"My name is Darcie Taylor, I have a family who love me and they are looking for me," and with that, she fell into the arms of a very startled Adam Brown.

Somewhere in her confused and exhausted mind, Darcie fancied that she could hear the voice of a woman she had once known; a woman whose name was lost in the long and terrible passage of time, but who was the reason that she remembered her own name.

Well done little one, you remembered. Well done.

***

Precisely one hour later, in the small Bangkok apartment, which she had called home for the past ten years, Verity Taylor's phone began to ring.

"Mrs Taylor? ... My name is Adam Brown."

THE END

Useful Links and Organisations

This is not by any means an exhaustive list. It is a small selection of support groups, useful information, reports and crime fighting organisations. All were correct at time of printing.

If you suspect that a child or adult is being exploited in any way, please report the matter immediately to the appropriate authorities.

https://www.gov.uk/government/publications/support-for-victims-of-human-trafficking

http://www.nationalcrimeagency.gov.uk/

http://www.nationalcrimeagency.gov.uk/about-us/what-we-do/child-exploitation-online-protection-ceop

http://www.state.gov/documents/organization/245365.pdf

https://en.wikipedia.org/wiki/List_of_organizations_that_combat_human_trafficking

https://www.notforsalecampaign.org/

http://www.ecpat.net/

http://hopeforjustice.org/#

http://www.stopthetraffik.org/uk/

https://www.crin.org

http://www.icmec.org/

http://www.missingkids.org/GMCN

http://www.findthekids.com/europe.html

http://www.findthekids.org/ngo.html

About the Author

Freya Barrington is the pen name of the author *Known to Social Services,* the #1 UK Bestseller in the Social Work Category in early 2015 and again in mid-2016. Known to Social Services won its section in the 2015 London Book Festival and won an honourable mention in the 2016 Paris Book Festival.

The book titled *Gozo: Is the Grass Greener?* was Freya's second work, and earned an honourable mention in the 2015 London Book Festival and won its section in the 2016 Paris Book Festival.

Caught in Traffick is Freya's third book to date and is the sequel to *Known to Social Services.*

Freya grew up in Lancashire, England with an overriding passion for animals, specifically horses. After attending a girls grammar school where English was her strongest subject, the only desire Freya held was to work with her beloved horses. To the dismay of her parents, she went to work in a racing yard.

Realising that it was not a passing phase, her parents eventually encouraged Freya in her chosen career and she went on to work with event horses, show jumpers and hunters, gaining several *British Horse Society* qualifications along the way – namely, the BHSAI, BHSII and BHSI (SM). All this enabled Freya to work as a riding instructor and trainer, which she did on a freelance basis. Freya continued working in the equestrian field for many years, eventually running her own yard.

A chance conversation with a friend brought about a change of career for Freya and she moved away from her life with horses, into the unknown world of residential childcare. To her surprise, Freya found that she enjoyed that line of work and progressed to being a full-time foster carer for the local authority. It was at that time Freya first put pen to paper in a creative way, writing poems about the children with whom she came into contact. A short book of poetry was soon published and the proceeds were used to raise money for a local youth group.

During her time as a foster carer, Freya came into contact with social workers. Their dedication and expertise inspired her to also train as a social worker, gaining the Diploma in Social Work in 2001 from the University of Derby, with an award for excellence in practice. Freya also gained the Post-Qualifying Award in 2007. She is a registered member in good standing with the Health and Care Professions Council (HCPC) of the United Kingdom.

Freya's main area of expertise is as a senior child protection social worker. She has been the principal social worker and mentor within a number of teams. Freya has also worked as a foster carer's support social worker, as a court advisor and hospital social worker. Since 2006, Freya has worked exclusively as an agency social worker, with specific focus on working for local authorities that require experienced social workers to offer support in the face of staff shortages. Freya's assessments and reports are in high demand, with managers from several local authority areas making specific requests for her to join their teams.

In 2010, Freya moved with her husband, Steve, to the island of Gozo (Maltese Islands). Meanwhile, she continued working in England as an agency social worker, flying back and forth on a fortnightly basis. This attracted comments from colleagues who said that they would never again complain about their commute to work! It was at that time that the idea for writing her nonfiction books started taking shape, so with the full support of her husband, Freya took a year's sabbatical to write.

Freya lived in Gozo with her husband from 2010 to mid-2015. It is the experiences they went through in this small, beautiful island in the

Mediterranean that are presented in her second book titled *Gozo: Is the Grass Greener?* Freya is presently in Brittany, France, where she is currently writing short stories, before commencing work on another novel.

More about Freya Barrington and her work can be found at:

- ☐ *Amazon* http://www.amazon.co.uk/Freya-Barrington/e/B00U228K5I/ref=ntt_athr_dp_pel_1
- ☐ *Facebook Page* facebook.com/FreyaBarrington
- ☐ *Twitter* @freyabarrington
- ☐ *Google+* plus.google.com/107614255402573788705/posts

Website;

- www.freyabarrington.com

☐ *Blogs;*

- www.freyabarrington.blogspot.com
- www.breakfastinbrittany.blogspot.com
- www.gozoisthegrassgreener.blogspot.com

Other Faraxa Titles

Poems

Young Adults

Non-Fiction

Fiction

17744162R00185

Printed in Great Britain
by Amazon